BELGIUM, LUXEMBOURG, AND THE NETHERLANDS

THE BRITANNICA GUIDE TO COUNTRIES OF THE EUROPEAN UNION

BELGIUM, LUXEMBOURG, AND THE NETHERLANDS

EDITED BY JEFF WALLENFELDT, MANAGER, GEOGRAPHY AND HISTORY

Britannica®
Educational Publishing

IN ASSOCIATION WITH

ROSEN
EDUCATIONAL SERVICES

Published in 2014 by Britannica Educational Publishing
(a trademark of Encyclopædia Britannica, Inc.)
in association with Rosen Educational Services, LLC
29 East 21st Street, New York, NY 10010.

Distributed exclusively by Rosen Educational Services.
For a listing of additional Britannica Educational Publishing titles, call toll free (800) 237-9932.

First Edition

Britannica Educational Publishing
J.E. Luebering, Senior Manager
Adam Augustyn, Assistant Manager
Marilyn L. Barton: Senior Coordinator, Production Control
Steven Bosco: Director, Editorial Technologies
Lisa S. Braucher: Senior Producer and Data Editor
Yvette Charboneau: Senior Copy Editor
Kathy Nakamura: Manager, Media Acquisition
Jeff Wallenfeldt, Manager, Geography and History

Rosen Educational Services
Nicholas Croce: Editor
Nelson Sá: Art Director
Cindy Reiman: Photography Manager
Karen Huang: Photo Researcher
Brian Garvey: Designer, Cover Design
Introduction by Alexandra Hanson-Harding

Library of Congress Cataloging-in-Publication Data

Belgium, Luxembourg, and the Netherlands/edited by Jeff Wallenfeldt. 1st ed.
    p. cm.—(The Britannica guide to countries of the European Union)
"In association with Britannica Educational Publishing, Rosen Educational Services."
Includes bibliographical references and index.
ISBN 978-1-61530-973-3 (library binding)
1. Benelux countries—History. I. Wallenfeldt, Jeff.
DH107.B45 2014
949.2—dc23

                                            2012035289

Manufactured in the United States of America

On the Cover: A composite image of the European Parliament building and a statue that
stands on its grounds in Brussels, Belgium. *Georges Gobet/AFP/Getty Images (Parliament),
Mark Renders/Getty Images (statue)*

Cover, p. iii (map and stars), back cover, multiple interior pages (stars) © iStockphoto.
com/pop_jop; cover, multiple interior pages (background graphic) Mina De La O/Digital
Vision/Getty Images

CONTENTS

3

8

33

78

82

99

185

209

INTRODUCTION

NETHERLANDS

BELGIUM

FRANCE

GERMANY

UXEMBOURG

What might one recall when thinking of Belgium, Luxembourg, and the Netherlands? Rich Belgian chocolate? Windmills and wooden shoes? Colourful tulip fields? That Luxembourg is one of the world's smallest countries? Or that the three countries were the signatories of the Benelux Treaty in 1948, which promoted free movement of goods and workers and was a model for the creation of the European Union (EU)? Readers might know that these modern, prosperous countries have an outsized influence for their small size. This volume explains why.

For much of their histories, the Low Countries— Belgium, Luxembourg and the Netherlands—were controlled by empires. Yet each country developed its own culture long before its independence. Early hints of human life in the Low Countries include burial mounds made of 164-foot (50-metre) stone blocks from the late Neolithic Period (3300-2900 BCE). Starting in the 1st century BCE, the Romans conquered these lands and built an extensive road network for trade. However, in the 400s CE, the Low Countries were invaded by Germanic tribes. Eventually, they became part of the Frankish empire. After the empire's greatest emperor, Charlemagne, died in 814, the Vikings spread destruction in the region until about 900, prompting the fortification of towns and monasteries.

By 925, much of the Low Countries in effect had become provinces that owed allegiance to the Germanic Holy Roman Empire. Although French and English influence grew in the 13th century, increasingly independent principalities arose in

Satellite image of Belgium, Luxembourg, and the Netherlands.. © Universal Image Group/Getty Images

the region. By this time, Flanders, which would become part of Belgium, had become renowned for its tapestries. Markets were set up to help merchants from around Europe to buy these products. Soon, Flanders had the first large export industry in northern Europe and tradespeople established guilds to establish prices, set quality standards, and promote their interests with local governments.

As early as the 1st century CE Lowlanders built the first dikes on the coast and inland to tame the region's flat, marshy, flood-prone land. Because the fragile dikes could be damaged by storms or animals, water authorities were formed in the 13th century to maintain them. This gave local communities the opportunity to practice self-government. This sense of community would eventually help bring the Lowlanders a sense of independence from the larger empires and dynasties that dominated them.

In time, by conquest and marriage, the Low Countries were ruled by Philip III, duke of Burgundy. Philip the Good, as he was known, worked hard to build political consensus while respecting each province's individuality. Burgundians ruled these lands until, eventually, the fanatical Catholic King Philip II of the Spanish Habsburg empire inherited them in 1555. He opposed the new Protestantism that had taken hold in the northern Netherlands. This led to resistance led by William, prince of Orange.

In 1579, the Protestant provinces signed the Union of Utrecht, which effectively established the United Provinces of the Netherlands and indicated that they would fight Spain's power. William wanted the Netherlands under the protection of foreign figureheads, whose rule would be limited. Eventually, however, these rulers became tyrants, and in 1587, the United Provinces gave up trying to get foreign protection and started to form a new, independent government. Although predominantly Catholic Belgium and Luxembourg would remain under Spanish control, the Netherlands took its first real step in becoming a nation.

Today, the Kingdom of the Netherlands is a constitutional monarchy, led by Queen Beatrix. But her power is only ceremonial—the prime minister and parliament do the real work of government. The Netherlands' capital is Amsterdam, but its seat of government is The Hague, which is also home to the United Nation's International Court of Justice. Although the Netherlands is located in northwestern Europe, the kingdom also includes some autonomous states and special municipalities in the Lesser Antilles. In addition to the EU, the Netherlands is a member of Benelux, the North Atlantic Treaty Organization (NATO), and the United Nations.

The Netherlands is known for its tulip bulbs, but its economy is based much more on transportation, trade, banking, and business. Dutch ships handle about two-fifths of the EU's freight transport by water. More important, however, the Dutch have for centuries been great traders. The Amsterdam Stock Exchange, one of the oldest in the world, started in the 1600s.

Despite endless conflicts, such as a war with Spain that only ended with the recognition of the Netherlands' independence in 1648, the determined Dutch managed to carry on trade, dike building, creating export products, and exploring. The years 1609–1713 are considered the Golden Age of the Netherlands, which became an imperial powerhouse through trade and exploration. Through the Dutch East India Company's colonization of Indonesia and other islands in the East Indies, the Netherlands became the West's main supplier of spices and other exotic goods. The Dutch West India Company focused on piracy and the slave trade. Trade allowed Dutch society to become wealthy, and some of that wealth helped to support some of the world's greatest artists, including Rembrandt van Rijn, creator of the group portrait *Night Watch*; Hiëronymus Bosch, whose nightmarish paintings bring the grimness of hell to mind; portrait painter Frans Hals; and the incomparable Johannes Vermeer.

During this time, the Netherlands attracted many members of persecuted minorities, such as French Huguenots and Jews. These groups helped open Dutch society to new ways of thinking. Philosopher Benedict Spinoza, who was of Spanish Jewish descent, and philosopher Rene Descartes, who was French, lived in the Netherlands. Prominent Dutch-born thinkers included scientists Christiaan Huygens, who invented the pendulum clock and helped develop calculus, and

Antonie van Leeuwenhoek, the first microbiologist, who was the first to see single-cell creatures. (He called them animalcules.)

Meanwhile, the Dutch skirmished with Britain, which became the world's pre-eminent naval force. As a result Dutch trade suffered. After running roughshod over much of Europe in the 1790s, French general-cum-emperor Napoleon Bonaparte installed his brother Louis as the Netherlands' king in 1806. After Napoleon's defeat, the northern Netherlands (modern-day Netherlands) and the southern Netherlands (modern-day Belgium) became the Kingdom of the Netherlands under William I of Orange in 1815.

The Dutch stayed neutral through World War I but were pulled into World War II in the spring of 1940, when the Germans attacked and took over the Netherlands in less than a week. The country remained occupied until the end of the war. According to the U.S. Holocaust Museum, the Germans and their Dutch collaborators deported 107,000 Jews to concentration camps, and fewer than 25 percent of Dutch Jews survived the Holocaust. That survival rate was considerably lower than the comparable rates of Jewish survival in Belgium and France (60 percent and 75 percent, respectively), according to the Israeli organization Yad Vashem. German-Jewish refugee Anne Frank's sensitive diary of hiding in a "secret annex" in Amsterdam brought to life the experience of one of those innocent victims.

Devastated during World War II, the Netherlands suffered a severe lack of jobs and housing in the war's aftermath. The government urged its people to emigrate, and 500,000 Dutch did. In the prosperous Netherlands of the early 21st century, birth and death rates are extremely low, an indication of increasing longevity. Currently, most population growth comes from immigration. About one-fifth of the Netherland's residents have at least one parent who was born abroad. Many of these recent arrivals to the country come from former Dutch colonies, including Indonesia (independent since 1960); others are "guest workers" from Turkey and Morocco. Largely as a result of this immigration, 6 percent of the population of the Netherlands in the 21st century was Muslim. Since 2006, immigrants have been tested on Dutch language and culture before they can enter the Netherlands. Notwithstanding this approach, which some have criticised as xenophobic, the Netherlands has maintained a reputation for progressive thinking.

The Kingdom of Belgium is a constitutional monarchy, led by King Albert II, whose duties are mostly formal. As in the Netherlands, the real business of governing is done by elected officials. All citizens are required to vote, though women only received the vote in 1949. Belgium has a unique form of federal government that is a result of the country's two dominant ethnic-linguistic groups. In the north, the Flemish speak Dutch. In the south, the Walloons speak French. National authorities share power with executive and legislative bodies representing the country's major politically defined regions—the Flemish Region (Flanders), the Walloon Region (Wallonia), and the Brussels-Capital Region—and the major language communities of the country (Flemish, French, and German).

After the land that would become Belgium was, like the land that would become the modern-day Netherlands, under Burgundian rule, it came under the dominance of the Spanish and Austrian Habsburg dynasties for the 16th, 17th, and 18th centuries. Belgium was under Austrian control, when it was invaded by Napoleon and incorporated into the French empire. It was the site of Napoleon's downfall in 1814, when he lost the Battle of Waterloo, near Brussels. In 1815 the northern and southern portions of the Netherlands joined together again to form a single country (as they had been until the 16th century). But, unhappy with Dutch dominance, Belgium won its independence in 1831.

It was an exciting, innovative time for Belgium, which was an early industrial leader—the first country on the European continent to have trains. Adolphe Saxe invented the saxophone in 1848. Architect Victor Horta became a leader in the Art Nouveau movement. Today, four of his buildings in Brussels are UNESCO World Heritage sites that visitors can tour. Belgium's contributions to world culture continued into the 20th century. Several Belgians won Nobel Prizes, among them Maurice Maeterlinck for Literature (1911), and in 1919, Jules Bordet for Physiology or Medicine for his discoveries relating to immunity. Later in the century singer

Jacques Brel and jazz guitarist Django Reinhardt were internationally famous, as was the painter Rene Magritte. Belgium is also home to comic writers Hergé (*The Adventures of Tintin*) and Peyo (The Smurfs).

One dark chapter in Belgium's history was its tenure as a colonial power in the Congo. The regime, under King Leopold II's unrestrained personal control, became notorious for its brutal treatment of Congolese workers on rubber plantations. Beatings and lashings were used to force villages to meet their rubber-gathering quotas.

Belgium was dragged into World War I after having been in invaded by Germany in 1914, and it was occupied by Germany again during World War II. In the postwar world the Belgians sought economic and political security through membership in international organizations such as Benelux, NATO, and the EU. Tensions within Belgium between the Flemish and Walloons that had mounted in the last half of the 20th century were addressed by the St. Michael's Agreement of 1992, which established the country's modern federal structure. Nevertheless, Belgium's volatile political mix could lead to significant impasses that gave new meaning to the term *gridlock*, such as the 541 days (a modern world record) when the country was unable to form an official government in 2010–11.

Luxembourg has been a political entity since 963, when Siegfried, Count de Ardennes, traded his lands for a strategically located ancient Roman castle, Lucilinburhuc ("Little Fortress"), which gave Luxembourg its name. One descendent of Siegfried became Holy Roman Emperor Henry VII in 1308. This Luxembourg dynasty continued as Holy Roman emperors. But in 1443, Luxembourg, like the other Low Countries, fell under Burgundian control. Over the centuries, Luxembourg came under Spanish, Austrian, French, and Dutch rule. It gained its independence in 1867.

In 1929 the Luxembourgian government encouraged large corporations to register their holding companies in Luxembourg by offering a lower tax rate than that of many other countries. As a result, Luxembourg became the European headquarters for a number of corporations. After World War II, Luxembourg joined Benelux, the United Nations, NATO, and the EU. Luxembourg City became home to the European Court of Justice and the offices of the European Investment Bank. It is also home to more than 100 banks. Today, Luxembourg has one of the highest standards of living in the world.

Three languages are spoken in Luxembourg: German, French, and Luxembourgish, a German dialect mixed with French. Northern Luxembourg's population is mostly rural, while the urban south contains the country's capital, Luxembourg City. Most citizens are Roman Catholic. Luxembourg has a very low birth rate, and the resulting labour shortage has encouraged immigration. Luxembourg has a higher percentage of immigrants than any other European country.

Politically, Luxembourg is a constitutional monarchy. Grand Duke Henri's power is mostly ceremonial—the real power of governing rests with the prime minister and popularly elected parliament. Every adult (age 18 and over) citizen is required to vote.

Culturally, Luxembourg is known for its National Museum of History and Art and the popular Radiotelevision Luxembourg (RTL). The duchy's architecture spans from ancient Roman villas to medieval castles and modern buildings.

Some countries are important because of their large size or vast resources. The small Low Countries managed to become successful almost because of their complicated histories and relative lack of ability to defend themselves. They adapted by working with the international community in creative ways—from banking to governmental work to trade—while at the same time treasuring their distinct cultures. As cornerstones of the organizations that would evolve into the European Union, they could take special pleasure when, in October 2012, the Norwegian Nobel Committee awarded the European Union its peace prize for the bloc's ongoing commitment to peace and cooperation. Despite their problems, the Low Countries have served as a model for the value of both cooperation and independence for the rest of the world.

CHAPTER 1

PREHISTORY OF THE LOW COUNTRIES

For historical purposes, the name Low Countries is generally understood to include the territory of what is today the Netherlands, Belgium, and Luxembourg, as well as parts of northern France. However, Belgium, although it was not constituted as an independent kingdom until 1831, became a distinct entity after 1585, when the southern provinces were definitively reconquered by Spain and separated from the northern sector. For a brief period, from 1814 to 1830, an attempt was made to unite the Low Countries into one kingdom again, but both regions by this time had developed cultures too different to form a single entity under a central government. Here, therefore, the history of the Low Countries will be surveyed as a whole to the late 16th century. The later individual histories of the Netherlands, Belgium, and Luxembourg are treated in the separate chapters on the histories of those countries.

NEOLITHIC (4000–2900 BCE)

Farmers of the Linear Pottery culture, settling on the loess of Dutch Limburg and Belgium about 6500 BP, were among the first to bring Neolithic lifeways to the region. Large-scale excavations in Sittard, Geleen, Elsloo, and Stein in the Netherlands and at sites including Rosmeer and Darion in Belgium have rendered considerable remains from this early Neolithic group. This northwesternmost branch of the culture met with other communities that left, by contrast,

BP (BEFORE PRESENT)

The designation BP ("before present") appears after a date (e.g., 7000–5000 BP) that was determined through the carbon-14, or radiocarbon, dating process. Developed in the mid-1940s by scientist William F. Libby, carbon-14 dating relies on the measurement of a certain type of radioactive particle, carbon-14, that is present in the atmosphere and that is absorbed by all living plants and taken up by animals when they eat plants. After an organism dies, it no longer absorbs carbon-14; rather, the particles begin to decay at a regular, predictable rate. The regular decay of radiocarbon ultimately allows scientists to calculate about how long ago a given organism died by comparing the amount of carbon-14 remaining in the organism to the amount of carbon-14 in the atmosphere at "present." For ease of calculation, scientists fixed the "present" at 1950 in commemoration of the year in which the results of the first carbon-14 dating experiments were published.

Caution must be taken whenever attempting to convert BP dates to their BCE ("before the common era") or CE ("common era") equivalents. Because the concentration of carbon-14 in the atmosphere has changed somewhat over time, figures need to be calibrated to reflect conditions at the actual time of measurement. Such calibrated dates are indicated cal BP, meaning the number of years before 1950, and they may easily be converted to exact calendar years. Conversion to BCE or CE of uncalibrated BP dates are typically rendered as date ranges.

few relics and are identified only by minimal scatters of their characteristic pottery, called Hoguette and Limburg. These early communities had widespread internal contacts, documented by remains that include adzes made of exotic stone, and external contacts with late Mesolithic communities to the north, especially along the Meuse River.

Other cultures briefly rose up (Blicquy in Belgium and Rössen in Germany) and in their turn were succeeded about 4100 BP by the northwesternmost branch of the Michelsberg culture in Belgium and, somewhat later, the Funnel Beaker culture in the Netherlands. The evolution of these groups represents principally a transformation in the style of material culture of native communities. Among the most significant Michelsberg remains are the extensive fields of deep flint mines at Spiennes in Hainaut and Rijckholt in Dutch Limburg. Contacts by the Michelsberg with late Mesolithic hunter-gatherers north of the loess zone gave rise to semiagricultural communities, as evidenced by relics from about 4000 BCE found in the Netherlands delta at Swifterbant in Flevoland and Hazendonkborn and Bergschenhoekborn in Zuid-Holland.

Illustration of late-Mesolithic or early-Neolithic hunters. © Image Asset Management Ltd./SuperStock

The late Neolithic (3300–2900 BCE) is characterized in the eastern Netherlands, especially in Drenthe, by the Funnel Beaker culture, which is particularly distinguished by megalithic burial monuments (the so-called *hunebedden*), the precise origins of which are still unknown. Composed of large stone blocks left behind by receding glaciers, these monuments mark collective tombs and may extend for up to 160 feet (about 50 metres) in length. In addition to the beakers for which the culture is named, the remains include collared flasks, buckets, and bowls—often decorated with horizontal and vertical grooves—and polished stone and flint tools. Southern Belgium was reached in this period by the northern fringes of the French Seine-Oise-Marne culture. A third cultural entity has been identified in the Netherlands delta as the Vlaardingen group; it comprises fully agrarian as well as semiagrarian settlements.

Transitional between the Neolithic and Bronze ages is the beaker phase (2900–2000 BCE). A distinguishing characteristic of the culture is its change to exclusively individual burial, in which specific grave goods (battle-axes, daggers, beakers) were included; the body, arranged in a flexed posture, was placed in an east-west orientation. This custom is assumed to indirectly reflect essential changes in society, possibly brought about by technological innovations, such as the plow, the wheel, and the cart, which might have caused a restructuring of the agrarian system.

THE BRONZE AGE (2000–700 BCE)

The early Bronze Age in the region was characterized by a continuation of the beaker tradition, the beginnings of bronze imports (from central and northern Europe and the British Isles), and a modest local bronze industry. The origin of cremation and the burial of ashes in urns in the southern Netherlands and Belgium (Hilversum culture) can be related to close contacts with Wessex, in Britain.

Finds from the middle Bronze Age (1500–1100 BCE) reflect the establishment of an essentially more advanced agricultural system: remains of some 80- to 130-foot-long farmhouses, including stable sections, provide evidence of true mixed farming, including manuring, care for winter fodder, and, presumably, the use of straw in stables. Cattle were by far the dominant livestock. This contrasts sharply with the Neolithic cultures, in which agricultural activities are presumed to have been less interrelated. Burial during the period was under barrows, now surrounded by post circles, with human remains either extended in coffins (common to the northern Netherlands) or cremated in urns (as in the south).

While settlement tradition continued, changes in burial custom took place about 1100 BCE, with urn burial now taking place in small, individual barrows surrounded by ditches of various types. A northern sphere connected with Westphalia, a central sphere in Noord-Brabant–Limburg connected with the Rhineland, and a southern Flemish group are distinct examples of this type of burial. Modest native bronze industries have been identified in the north (Hunze-Eems industry) as well as along the Meuse in Limburg, while bronze weapons and implements were imported from Great Britain and various other sources.

THE IRON AGE (c. 700 BCE TO ROMAN TIMES)

The Iron Age in the Low Countries is characterized by Celtic and Germanic influences. In the south, Hallstatt (Celtic) and La Tène traditions can be traced through prestigious warrior chieftain graves at such sites as Court Saint Etienne (Hainaut, Belgium), Eigenbilzen (Belgium), and Oss (Netherlands), which were stocked with chariots and harnesses, bronze weapons, implements, and even wine services. These traditions are also reflected in fortified hilltop settlements, in pottery styles, and in ornaments and other artifacts. On the sands to the north people had to cope with a deteriorating environment, especially impoverishment of the soils, podzolization, and wind erosion. They responded to these conditions with a more diversified agriculture and the more protective system of Celtic fields (small plots with low earthen banks formed around them). Other illustrations of renewed adaptability were demonstrated by the colonization of newly formed salt marshes and the building of artificial dwelling mounds called *terpen* in the north, the new settlement of creek and peat landscapes of the western river estuaries, salt production along the coast, and the breeding of horses elsewhere.

CHAPTER 2

ANCIENT AND EARLY MEDIEVAL TIMES

At the time of the Roman conquest (1st century BCE), the Low Countries were inhabited by a number of Celtic tribes to the south and west of the Rhine and by a number of Germanic tribes to the north. Cultural and ethnic influences in both directions, however, make it difficult to draw the line between Celtic and Germanic peoples. On the coast of northern France and in Flanders lived the Morini; to the north of them, between the Schelde River and the sea, the Menapii, who had been temporarily expelled from their home in the winter of 56–55 BCE by two immigrant German peoples, the Usipetes and Tencteriby; in Artois, the Nervii; between the Schelde and the Rhine, the Eburones and the Aduatuci; and, in what is now Luxembourg, the Treveri, a Belgic people.

North of the Rhine, the Frisii (Frisians) were the principal inhabitants, although the arrival of the Romans brought about a number of movements: the Batavi came to the area of the lower reaches of the Rhine, the Canninefates to the western coastal area of the mouth of the Rhine, the Marsaci to the islands of Zeeland, the Toxandri to the Campine (Kempenland), the Cugerni to the Xanten district, and the Tungri to part of the area originally inhabited by the Eburones.

THE ROMAN PERIOD

The Roman conquest of Gaul, which was completed by Caesar in 59–52 BCE, stopped short at the Rhine. The emperor Augustus' attempt to extend Roman military power over the Elbe failed, and the area occupied by the Frisians, north of the Rhine, was therefore never under Roman rule. In the Rhine delta and to the south and west of the Rhine, the Romans set up the same administrative organizations as those found in other parts of Gaul. The Low Countries formed part of the provinces of Belgica and Germania Inferior (later Belgica Secunda and Germania Secunda), which themselves were subdivided into *civitates*: in Belgica, those of the Morini, Menapii, Treveri, Tungri, and possibly the Toxandri; in Germania Inferior, those of the Batavi, Canninefates, and Cugerni. Because of the later adoption by the church of the division into *civitates*, a number of centres of the *civitates* have become the seats of bishoprics; among these are Thérouanne, Tournai, Tongeren (Tongres), and Trier (Trèves).

From the mid-1st to the mid-3rd century CE, the Gallo-Roman culture penetrated the northern provinces of the empire. The famous road network was constructed, and important garrisons were concentrated along the Rhine and also on the Waal at present-day Nijmegen. This affected a whole region: a more inland city such as Tongres became an important market for grain to be brought to Cologne. Along the great Cologne-Tongres-Bavai-Boulogne axis, relatively rich *villae* were located at regular distances. One of these, the city of Maastricht, profited from the river trade on the Meuse and had baths as early as the 1st century, while graves in the vicinity contained sarcophagi with bas-relief ornamentation, as well as splendid glass and sculptures of Mediterranean origin. The Gallo-Roman elite were concentrated along the main roads and especially on the richest lime soils. Some large industrial settlements producing iron works and clay tiles were located near the Schelde close to crossings of secondary roads to the north.

THE MORINI

The ancient Celtic people known as the Morini lived in the northwestern part of the region between the Seine and the Rhine rivers at the period when Julius Caesar began his conquest of Gaul. Closely allied to two other tribes, the Ambiani and the Atrebates, the Morini were separated from the Atrebates in the Roman division of the province. Up to this time the Celts were organized by tribes, groups related by kinship, that formed a military band at need. They were excellent ironworkers and horsemen, living in small agricultural settlements. The last historical record of the Morini reports that they revolted against Rome in 33 BCE and again in 30 BCE.

City of Maastricht, Netherlands. iStockphoto/Thinkstock

In the mid-3rd century Roman power in the Low Countries began to weaken, and the forts were abandoned. This was the result not only of a resurgence of the Germanic tribes but also probably of the encroachment of the sea, which in all likelihood brought about a drastic change in the area's economy. A temporary recovery began at the end of the 3rd century. In particular, Julian, Caesar of Gaul, waged several wars in the Low Countries between 355 and 360 and was able to put new strength, for a time, into the Rhine border. A great invasion by Germanic tribes in 406–407, however, ended the Roman occupation of the Low Countries. The Romans had already tolerated the Germanic penetration of their territory and had given some tribes the task of protecting the borders of the empire. The Franks, who had settled in Toxandria, in Brabant, were given the job of defending the border areas, which they did until the mid-5th century.

DAGOBERT I

The son of Chlotar II, Dagobert (born 605—died January 19, 639, Saint-Denis, France) became king of Austrasia in 623 and of the entire Frankish realm in 629. Dagobert secured his realm by making a friendship treaty with the Byzantine emperor Heraclius, defeating the Gascons and Bretons, and campaigning against the Slavs on his eastern frontier. In 631 he sent an army to Spain to help the Visigothic usurper Swinthila (Svintila). He moved his capital from Austrasia to Paris, a central location from which the kingdom could be governed more effectively. He then appeased the Austrasians by making his three-year-old son Sigebert their king in 634. Famed for his love of justice, Dagobert was nevertheless greedy and dissolute. He was succeeded by Sigebert III and another son, Clovis II.

The prosperity of Dagobert's reign, and the revival of the arts during this period, can be judged from the rich contents of the tombs of the period and from the goldsmiths' work for the churches. Dagobert revised Frankish law, encouraged learning, patronized the arts, and founded the first great abbey of role of Dagobert I Saint-Denis, to which he made many gifts.

FRANKISH RULE

The Franks were probably influenced considerably by Roman culture, becoming familiar with the Roman world and way of life, although the expansion of their own race and their growing self-confidence were barriers to complete Romanization. About 450 they moved southward, founding a new Frankish kingdom in a region that was centred on the road from Tongres to Boulogne. The Gallo-Roman population had left the less-populated sandy areas in the north and withdrawn south of that road. The first king of the Merovingian Franks, Childeric I (died 481/482), ruled the region around Tournai, while his son Clovis I (ruled 481/482–511) extended the kingdom, eliminating other Frankish leaders and becoming ruler of much of Gaul. During the 6th century, Salian Franks had settled in the region between the Loire River in present-day France and the Coal Forest in the south of present-day Belgium. From the late 6th century, Ripuarian Franks pushed from the Rhineland westward to the Schelde. Their immigration strengthened the Germanic faction in that region, which had been almost completely evacuated by the Gallo-Romans. The Salian Franks, on the other hand, had penetrated a more densely Latinized area where they came under the strong influence of the dominant Roman culture.

The area occupied by the Frisians in the north was completely outside the Frankish sphere of influence, but the Rhine delta and even what is now Noord-Brabant also appear to have retained the virtually independent status they had possessed during the Roman era.

The Frisians were part of a North Sea culture that formed a distinct foil to Frankish power. The Frisians played an important role in trade, which sought routes along the Rhine and the Meuse and across the North Sea. Industrial products were imported from northern France, the Meuse plain, and the Rhineland, where Merovingian power was more firmly established and where centres of commerce (e.g., Dinant, Namur, Huy, and Liège) developed. The more or less independent area on the North Sea coast, however, found itself threatened during the 7th century by the rise of the Frankish nobles. In particular, the family of the Pippins, who came from the centre of Austrasia (the Ardennes and upper Meuse), was able to secure land in Limburg.

Moreover, encouraged by Dagobert, the Frankish church began an offensive that led to the foundation of the bishopric of Thérouanne (the *civitas* of the Morini).

THE LOW COUNTRIES UNDER THE CAROLINGIANS

This collaboration between church and nobles prepared the way for an expansion of political power to the north, which was carried out under the leadership of the Pippins, who as majordomos ("mayors of the palace") in Austrasia had virtually taken over power from the weakened Merovingian kings. Charles Martel, a bastard son of Pippin II, who managed after several years' fighting (714–719) to grasp supreme power over the whole Frankish empire, succeeded in 734 in forcing his way through to the northern centres of the Frisians and gaining a victory near the Boorne River. His victory was later consolidated by Pippin III and his son Charlemagne (ruled 768–814). The whole area of the Low Countries thus effectively formed part of the Frankish empire, which was then ruled by the Pippin, or Carolingian, dynasty.

GOVERNMENT

The administrative organization of the Low Countries during this period was basically the same as that of the rest of the Frankish empire. Supreme authority was held by the king, who, aided by servants of the palace, toured the country incessantly. The Carolingian kings naturally made several visits to the Low Countries, where they had old palaces or built new ones (Herstal, Meerssen, Nijmegen, Aix-la-Chapelle) and where they also possessed extensive crown estates. Their authority (*bannus*) was delegated to counts who had control of counties, or *gauen* (*pagi*), some of which corresponded to Roman *civitates*. Among these counties in the Low Countries were the *pagus* Taruanensis (centred on Thérouanne), *pagus* Mempiscus, *pagus* Flandrensis (around Brugge), *pagus* Turnacensis (around Tournai), *pagus* Gandensis (Ghent), *pagus* Bracbatensis (between the Schelde and the Dijle rivers), *pagus* Toxandrie (modern Noord-Brabant), and, north of the great rivers, Marssum, Lake et Isla, Teisterbant, Circa oras Rheni, Kinnem, Westflinge, Texla, Salon, Hamaland, and Twente. In the north, however, it is frequently not possible to determine with certainty whether the word *gau* in fact denoted a region controlled by a count who exercised the king's authority or indicated simply a region of land without reference to its government. Smaller administrative units were the *centenae*, or hundreds, and districts called *ambachten*. These last were mainly in what are now the provinces of Vlaanderen, Zeeland, and Holland.

RELIGION

The conversion to Christianity of the southern Low Countries, which took place largely during the 7th century, led to the foundation of further bishoprics at Arras, Tournai, and Cambrai, which were part of the ecclesiastical province of Rheims (the former Roman province of Belgica Secunda). Germania Secunda contained the ecclesiastical province of Cologne, in which the *civitas* of Tongres seems to have had an

uninterrupted existence as a bishopric since Roman times; the centre of this bishopric was moved for a time to Maastricht (6th and 7th centuries) until, about 720, Liège became the seat of the bishopric. Christianity was brought to the north of the Low Countries mainly by Anglo-Saxon preachers, by Frisians influenced by them, and by Franks. This Anglo-Saxon Christianity was particularly important in the missionary bishopric of Utrecht, which at first, because of its missionary character, had no precisely defined borders. True, the city of Utrecht had been named as the see of the bishopric, but, as in England, the monasteries played an important part in the missionary work; among these was the monastery of Echternach in Luxembourg and the two important Benedictine abbeys in and near Ghent, founded by St. Amand in the early 7th century. The country between the Meuse and the Waal rivers and the area around Nijmegen belonged to the bishopric of Cologne, while certain districts in the north and east were part of the bishopric of Münster (founded by Charlemagne).

SOCIAL CLASSES

The social structure of the Low Countries in the Frankish era included a number of classes. At the top was an elite that probably already operated on a hereditary system and of which the members were bound to the king as vassals and rewarded by fiefs (*beneficia*). Next were the freemen (*liberi, ingenui*), bound to the king by an oath of allegiance and traditionally under an obligation to serve in the army and in the law courts. A freeman's *Wergeld*—the sum that had to be paid to his family if he was killed—was in principle 200 shillings (*solidi*); but the *ingenui Franci*, or *homines Franci* (found in the region of the great rivers; probably descended from native nobles who had early placed themselves in the service of the Franks in their policy of conquest), had a much higher *Wergeld*. At the bottom of the ladder were the bondsmen, who were closely dependent on a lord (often an important landowner), in whose service they stood, in most cases working on his estates. It may be supposed that the position of the bondsmen was relatively favourable in the coastal areas of Holland and Friesland, where there were no large estates and, moreover, where the struggle against the sea required as much manpower as the community was able to offer.

ECONOMY

Economically, the structure of the Low Countries in the Frankish period was principally agrarian. Particularly in the south and east, it was common practice to exploit the land from a central farmhouse (*villa*, or *curtis*), using the services of dependent subjects (bondsmen), who were duty-bound to work on the domain of the lord and to this end received small farms from him. The nature of the land in the west and north, however, probably to a large extent precluded this classical type of exploitation of the domains; there was scattered, even fragmentary, ownership of land, and the *curtis* was no more than a gathering place to which the bondsmen had to take a part of their produce. In Holland and Friesland, fishing and the raising and selling of cattle were of importance. This Frisian trade, of which Dorestad (near Wijk bij Duurstede, in the river area southeast of Utrecht) was a centre, was greatly stimulated by absorption into the Frankish empire, and it reached its zenith under Charlemagne and Louis I the Pious (ruled 814–840). Moreover, by virtue of its becoming part of the Frankish empire, Friesland obtained an important hinterland in the southern regions of the Meuse and Rhine and was thus in a position to develop export and through trade to Denmark, Norway, and the Baltic countries. The importance of Frisian trade may be seen in the Carolingian coins found in Dorestad, where there was a toll and a royal mint. This trade was supplied by the southern Low Countries. Thus the cloths that were sold as Frisian cloths were produced in the area of the Schelde (later called Flanders). Quentovic (now Étaples), at the mouth of the Canche, was another trading centre; it, too, had a toll and a mint. Smaller trade settlements (*portus,* or *vicus*) emerged at Tournai, Ghent, Brugge, Antwerp, Dinant, Namur, Huy, Liège, and Maastricht—a clear indication of the commercial importance of the Schelde and the Meuse.

DECLINE OF THE FRANKISH EMPIRE

The great Carolingian dynasty passed into a decline as early as the reign of Louis the Pious, and the process was accelerated after his death in 840. Repeated wars broke out under his sons, leading eventually to the partition of the empire. The dissolution of Carolingian power was further helped by Viking, Magyar, and Saracen attacks—the Viking attacks being of greatest import for the Low Countries. The attacks had begun immediately after the death of Charlemagne (814) in the form of plundering raids, the magnitude and danger of which soon increased. (Dorestad, for example, was destroyed four times between 834 and 837.) Churches and monasteries, with their rich treasures, were the principal targets for the Vikings, who soon took to spending the winter in the Low Countries. In order to ward off the danger, attempts were made to throw up walls around towns and monasteries or even to drive off the Vikings by fierce counterattacks—a procedure that enjoyed some success—so that the counts of Flanders, for example, were able to lay a firm foundation for their own power. Another method of defense was to admit the Vikings on the condition that they defend the areas given them against other Vikings. The danger diminished after 900.

CHAPTER 3

THE DEVELOPMENT OF THE TERRITORIAL PRINCIPALITIES AND THE RISE OF THE TOWNS (925–c. 1350)

Politically speaking, the period between 925 and about 1350 is characterized by the emergence, growth, and eventual independence of secular and ecclesiastical territorial principalities. The rulers of these principalities—both secular and spiritual—had a feudal relationship with the German king (the Holy Roman emperor), with the exception of the count of Flanders, who held his land principally as the vassal of the French king, with only the eastern part of his county, Imperial Flanders, being held in fealty to the German king. While the secular principalities came into being as a result of individual initiative on the part of local rulers and of their taking the law into their own hands, to the detriment of the king's authority, the development of the spiritual princes' authority was systematically furthered and supported from above by the king himself. The secular principalities that arose in the Low Countries and whose borders were more or less fixed at the end of the 13th century were the counties of Flanders and Hainaut, the duchies of Brabant and Limburg (after 1288 joined in personal union), the county of Namur, the county of Loon (which was, however, to a large degree dependent on the bishopric of Liège and incorporated in it from 1366), the county of Holland and Zeeland, and the county (after 1339, duchy) of Guelders. The Frisian areas (approximately corresponding to the modern provinces of Friesland and Groningen, but excluding the city of Groningen) had no sovereign authority. The spiritual principalities were Liège, Utrecht, Tournai, and Cambrai. The secular authority of the bishop of Utrecht was exercised over two separate areas: the Nedersticht (now the province of Utrecht) and the Oversticht (now the provinces of Overijssel and Drenthe and the city of Groningen).

Although these principalities eventually displayed common characteristics in their economies, social structures, and cultures, it was the intrusion of the Burgundian dynasty that brought about a certain degree of political unity, which in turn furthered economic, social, and cultural unity and even led to the beginnings of a common national feeling (which was nevertheless too weak to prevent partition in the late 16th century).

THE SECULAR PRINCIPALITIES

The secular princes consolidated their power in a number of ways. The count still exercised the rights that had for centuries been attached to the Carolingian office of count, denoted by the term *comitatus*.

They included the administration of justice, various military powers, and the right to levy fines and tolls. To these rights fiefs were attached, which during the passage of time were expanded by the counts, who eventually owned such large estates that they were by far the greatest landowners in their territories.

Soon the term *comitatus* covered not only the office, or duty, but also the whole area over which that office was exercised; thus it could be said that the count held his county in fief of the king. An important element of the count's authority was supervision over the county's religious foundations, especially the monasteries. In the 10th century, the counts sometimes even assumed the function of abbot (lay abbot); but they later contented themselves with the control of appointments to ecclesiastical offices, through which they often had great influence over the monasteries and profited from the income from monastic land. Thus, monasteries such as

COMITATUS

In ancient Republican Rome, a *comitatus* (Latin: "retinue") was formed in the assembly when one of the leading men announced that he needed followers to accompany him on a foray into enemy territory. Those who were attracted by the proposal, usually the more well-to-do warriors, would volunteer their services. At that time the relationship between leader and followers, who were called *comites* ("companions"), was a temporary one, lasting only for the duration of the raid. Later, the arrangement became permanent; the leader fed the comitatus and kept the company about him in peace as well as in war. He supplied the members with their weapons and horses and shared with them the spoils of war. A military force was thus established over which the other warriors had little or no control. Members of the comitatus were willing to fight to the death for their leader; it was a disgrace for them to survive him.

St. Vaast (near Arras), St. Amand (on the Scarpe), St. Bertin (near St. Omer), and St. Bavon and St. Peter (in Ghent) became centres of the power and authority of the counts of Flanders; Nivelles and Gembloux, of the dukes of Brabant; and Egmond and Rijnsburg, of the counts of Holland.

At the end of the 9th and in the 10th century, during the Viking attacks and while connections with the empire were loosening, the local counts built up their power by joining a number of *pagi* together and building forts to ensure their safety. The counts of Flanders amalgamated the *pagi* Flandrensis, Rodanensis, Gandensis, Curtracensis, Iserae, and Mempiscus, the whole being thenceforth called Flanders; they fortified this area of their power with new or surviving Roman citadels. In the northern coastal regions, the Viking Gerulf was granted in about 885 the rights over a number of counties between the Meuse and the Vlie (Masalant, Kinnem, Texla, Westflinge, and a district known as Circa oras Rheni, which was, as the name implies, on both sides of the Rhine); his descendants consolidated their power there as counts of west Frisia and, after 1100, took the title of counts of Holland. In Brabant and Guelders, the amalgamation of fragmentary and dispersed estates took place later than in Flanders and Holland.

During the 10th and 11th centuries, the German kings of the Saxon and Salian dynasties attempted to impose their authority on the increasingly powerful secular principalities by the appointment of dukes. In Lorraine, during the reign of Otto I (936–973), the king appointed his brother, Bruno, the archbishop of Cologne, to the position of duke. Bruno soon split Lorraine into two dukedoms—Upper and Lower Lorraine. In Lower Lorraine, the title of duke was given to the counts of Leuven and the counts of Limburg—the former at first called themselves dukes of Lorraine but soon assumed the title of dukes of Brabant; the latter were known as the dukes of Limburg.

THE SPIRITUAL PRINCIPALITIES

That the German kings failed to integrate Lorraine into the Holy Roman Empire as a duchy ruled by a viceroy may be attributed to the fact that the kings soon developed another way to strengthen their power, not only in Lorraine but throughout the empire, by systematically investing bishops and abbots with secular powers and making them pillars of authority.

This procedure, developed by Otto I and reaching its summit under Henry III, was carried out in phases and led eventually to the establishment of the imperial church (*Reichskirche*), in which the spiritual and secular principalities played an important part. The most important ecclesiastical principalities in the Low Countries were the bishoprics of Liège, Utrecht, and, to a lesser degree, Cambrai, which, though within the Holy Roman Empire, belonged to the French church province of Rheims. The secular powers enjoyed by

HOLY ROMAN EMPIRE

Traditionally believed to have been established by Charlemagne, who was crowned emperor by Pope Leo III in 800, the Holy Roman Empire lasted until the renunciation of the imperial title by Francis II in 1806. The reign of the German Otto I (962–973), who revived the imperial title after Carolingian decline, is also sometimes regarded as the beginning of the empire. The name Holy Roman Empire (not adopted until the reign of Frederick I Barbarossa) reflected Charlemagne's claim that his empire was the successor to the Roman Empire and that this temporal power was augmented by his status as God's principal vicar in the temporal realm (parallel to the pope's in the spiritual realm). The empire's core consisted of Germany, Austria, Bohemia, and Moravia. Switzerland, the Netherlands, and northern Italy sometimes formed part of it; France, Poland, Hungary, and Denmark were initially included, and Britain and Spain were nominal components. From the mid-11th century the emperors engaged in a great struggle with the papacy for dominance, and, particularly under the powerful Hohenstaufen dynasty (1138–1208, 1212–54), they fought with the popes over control of Italy. Rudolf I became the first Habsburg emperor in 1273, and from 1438 the Habsburg dynasty held the throne for centuries. Until 1356 the emperor was chosen by the German princes; thereafter he was formally elected by the electors. Outside their personal hereditary domains, emperors shared power with the imperial diet. During the Reformation the German princes largely defected to the Protestant camp, opposing the Catholic emperor. At the end of the Thirty Years' War, the Peace of Westphalia (1648) recognized the individual sovereignty of the empire's states; the empire thereafter became a loose federation of states and the title of emperor principally honorific. In the 18th century, issues of imperial succession resulted in the War of the Austrian Succession and the Seven Years' War. The greatly weakened empire was brought to an end by the victories of Napoleon.

these bishops were based on the right of immunity that their churches exercised over their properties, and that meant that, within the areas of their properties, the counts and their subordinates had little or no opportunity to carry out their functions. The bishops' power was consolidated when the kings decided to transfer to the bishops the powers of counts in certain areas that were not covered by immunity.

Certain bishops, such as those of Liège and Utrecht, were able to combine their rights of immunity, certain jurisdictional powers, regalia, and ban-immunities into a unified secular authority, thus forming a secular principality called a *Sticht* (as distinct from the diocese) or—where the power structure was very large and complex, as in the case of the bishop of Liège—a prince-bishopric. As princes, the bishops were vassals of the king, having to fulfill military and advisory duties in the same way as their secular colleagues. The advantage of this system to the kings lay in the fact that the bishops could not start a dynasty that might begin to work for its own ends, and its smooth running stood and fell with the authority of the kings to nominate their own bishops.

Thus the spiritual-territorial principalities of the bishops of Liège and Utrecht emerged—the prince-bishopric of Liège and the *Sticht* of Utrecht. In Liège this development was completed in 972–1008 under the guidance of Bishop Notger, appointed by Otto I. As early as 985 he was granted the rights of the count of Huy, and the German kings made use of the bishopric of Liège to try to strengthen their positions in Lorraine. Utrecht, which lay more on the periphery of the empire, developed somewhat later. It was principally the kings Henry II, Conrad II, and Henry III who strengthened the secular power of the bishops through privileges and gifts of land.

STRUGGLE FOR INDEPENDENCE

Thus, the Low Countries during the 10th and 11th centuries saw the development of the pattern of a number of more or less independent feudal states, both secular and ecclesiastical, each of which was struggling for more freedom from the king's authority, the enlargement of its sphere of influence, and the strengthening of its internal power. Flanders led the way. In the 10th and 11th centuries it needed to pay only scant attention to the weak French kings of the Capetian dynasty and was thus soon able to exercise its power farther south— in Artois—and was even able to play an important part in a political power struggle around the French crown. In 1066 the count of Flanders lent his support to the expedition to England of his son-in-law, William, duke of Normandy. The counts of Flanders built up a strong administrative apparatus—the *curia comitis*, based on central officials and on local rulers called burgraves, or castellans (*castellani*), who were in charge of districts known as castellanies, where they had extensive military and administrative powers. The reclamation of land from the sea and from marsh and wasteland in the coastal area, which began in earnest in the 11th century, enlarged the estates and the income of the counts and brought about the need for a rational administrative system. The nobles were a power to be reckoned with, but Count Robert I (ruled 1071–93) and his successors were able to find support and a balancing force in such developing towns as Brugge, Ghent, Ypres, Courtrai, and Cassel. The murder of the powerful and highly respected Count Charles the Good (ruled 1119–27), who was childless, plunged Flanders into a crisis that involved not only the nobles and the towns but also, for the first time, the French king.

About 1100 such other territories as Brabant, Hainaut, Namur, and Holland began to expand and form principalities, helped by the weakening of the German crown during the Investiture Contest (a struggle between civil and church rulers over the right to invest bishops and abbots). The Concordat of Worms (1122) ruled that bishops were to be chosen by the chapter of canons of the cathedral; thus, the German king was obliged to transfer the secular powers to an *electus*, who was then usually ordained bishop by the metropolitan. Although the king still exercised some influence over the elections, the local counts were able to make their voices heard the loudest in the chapter, so that Utrecht, for example, soon had bishops from the families of the counts of Holland and Guelders. This was the end of the strong influence that German imperial power exercised through the bishops in the Low Countries. Thenceforth, the spiritual and secular princes stood together, although the death of a bishop still tended to plunge the principality into a crisis.

FRENCH AND ENGLISH INFLUENCE

As their power declined, the Holy Roman emperors could do little more than involve themselves almost incidentally in the affairs and many conflicts of the Low Countries. The German decline went hand in hand with the increasing influence of the French and English kings, particularly after 1200; this applied especially to French power in Flanders. A struggle for the throne that broke out in Germany at the death of Henry VI (1197) found the two powerful factions— the Ghibellines and Guelfs—on opposite

sides; in the Low Countries, a game of political chance developed, in which the duke of Brabant (Henry I) played an important role, alternately supporting both parties. The French king, Philip Augustus, and his opponent, King John of England, both interfered in the conflict, which polarized into Anglo-Guelf and Franco-Ghibelline coalitions, each looking for allies in the Low Countries. A victory won by the French king at the Battle of Bouvines, east of Lille (1214), put the count of Flanders at his mercy. The southern parts of the county were split off and incorporated into the county of Artois.

Throughout the 13th century, the French kings increased their influence in Flanders, which was joined to Hainaut by personal union. The power of the counts diminished during the reign of two countesses from 1205 to 1278 because of the increasing pressure of the kingdom and the growing power of the cities. The counts' efforts to control the urban elites (the patriciate) by controlling the cities' finances and the appointment of the magistrates (aldermen, or *schepenen*) failed because the French king supported the patricians. King Philip IV, who was successful in his territorial expansion in Champagne and Gascony, also tried to incorporate the county of Flanders by a military invasion, in which he was supported by his patrician partisans. By 1300 the annexation of Flanders was almost complete. Resistance by Count Guy, which was supported by the crafts

BATTLE OF THE GOLDEN SPURS

The Battle of the Golden Spurs (also called the Battle of Courtrai or the Battle of Kortrijk) was fought on the outskirts of Kortrijk in Flanders (now in Belgium) on July 11, 1302. In it an untrained Flemish infantry militia, consisting mainly of members of the craft guilds (notably that of the weavers) defeated a professional force of French and patrician Flemish cavalry, thus checking the growth of French control over the area. It is so named for the spurs supposedly taken from the vanquished. The towns of Flanders rebelled against the occupying French army and besieged the French garrison at Courtrai castle. France then sent a relief army. The ill-armed militia prevailed over the mounted force by making its stand on a patch of ground surrounded by streams and moats, thus frustrating any attempt at a rapid cavalry charge; the marshy terrain also impeded other efforts of the horsemen. This victory led to a generation of political ascendancy of the weavers' guild in the urban centres and ended the threat of French annexation. It also began the "infantry revolution" of the 14th century. The Scots, at the Battle of Bannockburn (1314), consciously emulated the Flemings, and their victory led the English to fight on foot—and win—against the French at the Battle of Crécy (1346) and the Battle of Poitiers (1356).

in the towns, culminated in a resounding victory by the Flemish army (which consisted largely of citizens of the towns fighting on foot) over the French knights at Courtrai (the Battle of the Golden Spurs, 1302) and prevented total annexation.

French influence remained strong during the 14th century, however, as the counts saw themselves repeatedly opposed by a mighty coalition of subjects in revolt. An early case was the peasant revolt in the western part of the county, supported by Brugge and lasting from 1323 to 1328; it was provoked by heavy taxation as a consequence of the French-imposed peace conditions of 1305. Only the massive help of a French army enabled the count to impose his heavy repression. Then the outbreak

of the Hundred Years' War about 1337 tempted the Flemish to take sides with the English, whose wool imports they needed for their large-scale textile industry. From 1338 until his death in 1346, Count Louis I of Nevers sought the protection of the French king, to whom he fled, leaving his county virtually in the hands of the three major cities of Ghent, Brugge, and Ypres, which had developed as city-states. Again in 1379–85 a new revolt of the major cities against the count's son, Louis II of Male, provoked French military intervention, which, however, did not resolve the situation. Louis of Male also fled to France, and peace with the Flemings could only be negotiated favourably for the cities by their new prince, Philip, duke of Burgundy, youngest son of the French king, John II.

SOCIAL AND ECONOMIC STRUCTURE

To obtain some insight into the social structure of the Low Countries between 900 and 1350, it is important to realize that, although the territorial princes wielded supreme power, the people were in fact directly dependent on an elite that, by virtue of owning land and possessing certain powers of jurisdiction and administration, had formed seigneuries, in which they held considerable effective power. These lords could control their dependents by demanding agricultural services, exercising certain rights over dependents' inheritances, levying monies in return for granting permission to marry, and forcing them to make use of the lords' mills, ovens, breweries, and stud animals. In the main, the owners of these seigneuries were treated as nobles and were often, though not always, bound to the territorial prince by feudal ties. A separate class was formed by the knights, who in the 12th century were usually *ministeriales* (servants who had originally been bondsmen) and were used by their lords for cavalry service or for higher administrative duties, for which they received a fief. It was not until the 13th century and, in many places, even later that the feudal nobility and ministerial knights became unified in a single aristocracy. Apart from these nobles, there were also freemen who owned their own land (*allodium*), but little is known about them; they were present, however,

in large numbers in the cattle-breeding regions of Flanders, Zeeland, Holland, and Friesland, where the numerous rivers and streams must have split up the land into many small farms. The descendants of noble families who were no longer able to live as richly as the nobles and who were known as *hommes de lignage* (in Brabant), *hommes de loi* (Namur), or *welgeborenen* (Holland), must have been very close in status to the freemen. In the agricultural areas of Hainaut, Brabant, Guelders, and the Oversticht were dependents whose legal status is difficult to determine, though they may be classed as bondsmen because of their being liable for various services and payments.

A factor of great, if not decisive, importance for social and economic relations, not only in the Low Countries but in all of western Europe, was the growth of the population. There is no direct statistical information but only a certain amount of indirect knowledge—after about 1050, it can be seen in the internal colonization (in the form of reclamation of such waste ground as woods and bogs), in the building of dikes and polders, in the expansion of agricultural land, and in the growth of the villages (new parishes) and towns.

The opening up of extensive areas of wood and heathland led to the foundation of new settlements (known in the French-speaking areas as *villes neuves*), to which colonists were attracted by offers of advantageous conditions—which were also intended to benefit the original estates. Many of these colonists were younger sons who had no share in the inheritance of their fathers' farms. The Cistercian and Premonstratensian monks, whose rules prescribed that they must work the land themselves, played an important part in this exploitation of new land. In the coastal regions of Flanders, Zeeland, and Friesland, they were very active in the struggle against the sea, building dikes both inland and on the coast itself. At first these dikes were purely defensive, but later they took on an offensive character and wrested considerable areas of land from the sea.

Especially important was the reclamation of marshland in the peat-bog areas of Holland and Utrecht and in the coastal regions of Flanders and Friesland. The Frisians had specialized in this work as early as the 11th century; Flemings and Hollanders soon adopted their methods, even applying them in the Elbe plain in Germany. The system, which consisted of digging drainage ditches, lowered the water table, leaving the ground dry enough for cattle grazing and, later, even for arable farming. The colonists, who were freemen, were given the right to cut drainage ditches as far back from the common watercourse as they wished. Certain restrictions were later imposed by the lords, however, who regarded themselves as the owners of these waste areas and demanded tribute money as compensation. Reclamation work was organized by a contractor (*locator*), who was responsible to the count and often carried out the function of local judge.

Thus, in the 12th and 13th centuries, a large area of land in the Holland-Utrecht peat-bog plain was made available for agriculture, facilitating the rise of nonagricultural communities (i.e., the towns). In Flanders, Zeeland, Holland, and Utrecht this struggle against the sea and the inland water was particularly noteworthy in that it led to the foundation of water boards, which in the 13th and 14th centuries were amalgamated to form higher water authorities (the *hoogheemraadschappen*). Mastery over the water had to be carried out on a large scale and in an organized fashion; the building of dikes required a higher authority and coordinated labour. Thus, various organizations emerged, acting independently in the field of canal and dike building and maintenance and responsible only to the government itself. These were *communitates*, with their own servants and their own managements (dike reeves and *heemraden*) and empowered to take necessary measures to maintain the waterworks, administer justice, and issue proclamations. This included the levy of taxes for this purpose, under the exclusive control of the landholders, who had to contribute proportionally to the area they possessed. The need of absolute solidarity, imposed by geography, thus created a system of communal organization based on full participation and equality exceptional in European terms. In the core of Holland, three large *hoogheemraadschappen* controlled the whole territory. They were headed by dike reeves who also were the count's bailiffs and thus functioned as high judges and administrators. They were assisted by *heemraden* elected by the landholders.

The increase in the population and the reclamation of land from the sea and marshes, as well as the fight to keep the sea out, all helped change the social and economic structures of the Low Countries. For centuries, the southern and eastern areas had been agricultural, often making use of the domain system. In the coastal areas, however, reduced labour requirements of cattle raising could be combined with fishing, weaving, and overseas trading. Dorestad, the centre of the Frisian trade, fell into decay not so much as a result of Viking raids (it was rebuilt after each one) as of a change in the course of the river upon whose banks the town was situated. Dorestad's leading position in trade was then taken over by Tiel, Deventer, Zaltbommel, Heerewaarden, and the city of Utrecht. Wheat was imported from the Rhine plain, salt from Friesland, and iron ore from Saxony, and, before long, wine, textiles, and metal goods were brought along the Meuse and Rhine from the south. The IJssel in Guelders also began to carry trading traffic through Deventer, Zutphen, and Kampen and, on the coast of the Zuiderzee (now IJsselmeer), through Harderwijk, Elburg, and Stavoren.

GROWTH OF FLANDERS

In the south, commercial developments were concentrated in two areas: one was the Artois-Flanders region, which profited from the shipping facilities of a river system providing access to the sea and to the wide Schelde plains; the other was the Meuse corridor. For centuries, sheep farming on chalky soils and coastal marshlands had produced the wool needed in the cloth industry; but to meet an increased demand wool was imported from England, for which purpose merchants from various Flemish towns joined together in the Flemish Hanse, a trade association, in London. Flemish cloth produced in fast-growing cities such as Arras, Saint-Omer, Douai, Lille, Tournai, Ypres, Ghent, and Brugge found its buyers throughout Europe. Notary's registers in Genoa and Milan, preserved since about 1200, mention many transactions of different varieties of Flemish cloth and indicate the presence of Flemish and Artesian (from Artois) merchants. The fairs (markets) in the Champagne region linked northern Italy with northwestern Europe; in Flanders a series of similar fairs was set up to facilitate contacts and credit operations among merchants of different nationalities.

To a large extent, the Flemish economy became dependent on the import of English wool, while its exports of finished cloth were directed mainly to the Rhineland, northern Italy, the French west coast, the northern Low Countries, and the Baltic. Flanders' early dominant position was possible owing to a favourable combination of geographic and economic factors. Because Flanders had the first large export industry in northern Europe, its production centres attained the highest levels of quality through specialization and diversification.

For the cloth industry itself, Ghent and Ypres were among the most important towns. In Ghent the production process was run by drapers (*drapiers*), who bought the raw material, had it treated by spinners, weavers, fullers, and dyers, and eventually sold the final product. A drop in wool imports from England could therefore cause immediate social and political upheavals in the city.

The area of the Meuse also carried on considerable trade and industry; merchants from Liège, Huy, Namur, and Dinant are named in 11th-century toll tariffs from London and Koblenz. This trade was supplied mainly by the textile industry of Maastricht, Huy, and Nivelles and by the metal industry of Liège and Dinant. Trade in Brabant, actively supported by the dukes, used the road, or system of tracks (medieval road systems were not advanced), that ran from Cologne through Aix-la-Chapelle, Maastricht, Tongres, Leuven, and Brussels to Ghent and Brugge. Four major trade routes thus developed before 1300 in the Low Countries, favouring the growth or even the emergence of cities; these were between the Rhine and the Zuiderzee, along the Meuse, along the land route

from Cologne through Brabant to the sea, and through Flanders. Only the latter displayed a spectacular growth during this period, taking advantage of its proximity to the sea to build up a massive export industry of labour-intensive, high-quality consumer products.

Since prehistoric times, fishing, particularly for herring, had been important in the coastal regions of Zeeland and Flanders. Since the 5th century BCE, archaeological evidence shows that the people produced salt, important in fish preservation, by boiling seawater. In later centuries, a more sophisticated technique was devised by burning peat, from which salt could be refined. This industry was located along the coast and near Biervliet and Dordrecht on the major rivers. It evidently was established to support the fisheries. The fishing industry was given added stimulus by the shift of the herring shoals from the coast of Schonen (Sweden) to the North Sea. The ships, however, were increasingly placed at the disposal of general trade and, in particular, of the wool trade with England. The German merchants also turned their attention to Holland, where Dordrecht became the most important centre. Because of its central position in the rivers area, this town offered the counts the chance to raise tolls on all traffic in the neighbourhood; moreover, all cargoes had to be unloaded and offered for sale—wine, coal, millstones, metal products, fruit, spices, fish, salt, grain, and wood.

NIJMEGEN

Founded on the Waal River (southern arm of the Rhine) in the eastern Netherlands, Nijmegen originated as the Roman settlement of Noviomagus and is the oldest town in the country. Often an imperial residence in the Carolingian period, it became a free city and later joined the Hanseatic League. In 1579 it subscribed to the Union of Utrecht against Spain. It was taken by the French (1672) in the third of the Dutch Wars, and the treaties—between Louis XIV, the Netherlands, Spain, and the Holy Roman Empire—that ended the hostilities were signed there in 1678–79. Nijmegen was the capital of Gelderland until its capture in 1794 by the French, who moved the capital to Arnhem. It served as a frontier fortress until its defenses were dismantled in 1878. Occupied by the Germans during World War II, the town was badly damaged and was the scene of an Allied airborne landing in 1944, during which the city centre was entirely destroyed. Rebuilt, Nijmegen is now an important focus of industry, a rail junction, and an inland shipping centre.

A scenic park, the Valkhof ("Falcon's Court"), contains ruins of Charlemagne's castle, which was destroyed by the Vikings but rebuilt by Frederick Barbarossa in 1155 before being demolished by French Revolutionary troops in 1796; a 16-sided baptistry (consecrated in 799) and the choir of its 12th-century church remain. The fine Renaissance Grote Kerk ("Great Church") of St. Stephen and the town hall (1554) both suffered war damage but have been restored. Other notable buildings include the Latin School (1544–45), the Weighhouse (1612), and the modern Church of St. Peter Canisius (1960). Nijmegen is the home of the Museum Het Valkhof (1999), which has a notable collection of Roman antiquities.

THE TOWNS

The towns gave the Low Countries a special character of their own. Apart from some towns that had existed even in Roman times, such as Maastricht and Nijmegen, most towns arose in the 9th century; in the 11th and 12th centuries, they expanded and developed considerably.

The emergence of the towns went hand in hand with the population increase and the extension of cultivable land, which made possible higher production. The population centres that emerged were not primarily agrarian but specialized in industry and trade.

The oldest towns were in the regions of the Schelde and Meuse. Near existing counts' castles or walled monasteries, merchants formed settlements (*portus*, or *vicus*). In some cases, like that of Ghent, for instance, the commercial *portus* was older than the count's castle and grew purely because of its advantageous location. The *portus* gradually merged with the original settlements to form units that both economically and in their constitutions took on their own characters with respect to the surrounding country—characters that were later manifested by defensive ramparts and walls. The cities in the Meuse valley (Dinant, Namur, Huy, Liège, and Maastricht) had already developed in the 10th century, owing to the heritage of this region as the core of the Carolingian empire. Maastricht in particular played a prominent role as one of the main seats of the German imperial church. In the Schelde valley a dense urban network had also developed. A later group (though not much later) was formed by the northern towns of Deventer and Tiel, while Utrecht had long been a town in the sense of a commercial centre. Zutphen, Zwolle, Kampen, Harderwijk, Elburg, and Stavoren are other examples of early towns. Much younger (13th-century) are the towns of Holland—Dordrecht, Leiden, Haarlem, Alkmaar, and Delft.

All the towns formed a new, non-feudal element in the existing social structure, and from the beginning merchants played an important role. The merchants often formed guilds, organizations that grew out of merchant groups and banded together for mutual protection while traveling during this violent period, when attacks on merchant caravans were common. From a manuscript dated about 1020, it appears that the merchants of Tiel met regularly for a drinking bout, had a common treasury, and could clear themselves of a charge by the simple expedient of swearing an oath of innocence (a privilege they claimed to have been granted by the emperor). Thus, there and elsewhere, the merchants constituted a horizontal community formed by an oath of cooperation and with the maintenance of law and order as its goal.

In contrast, therefore, to the vertical bonds in the feudal world and within the manors, horizontal bonds emerged between individuals who were naturally aiming at independence and autonomy. The extent to which autonomy was achieved varied greatly and depended on the power exercised by the territorial prince. Autonomy often developed spontaneously, and its evolution might have been accepted either tacitly or orally by the prince, so that no documentary evidence of it remains. Sometimes, however, certain freedoms were granted in writing, such as that granted by the bishop of Liège to Huy as early as 1066. Such town charters often included the record of a ruling that had been the subject of demands or conflicts; they frequently dealt with a special form of criminal or contract law, the satisfactory regulation of which was of utmost importance to the town involved. Indeed, the first step a town took on the road to autonomy was to receive its own law and judicial system, dissociated from that of the surrounding countryside; a natural consequence of this was that the town then had its own governing authority and judiciary in the form of a board, whose members were called *schepenen* (*échevins*), headed by a *schout* (*écoutète*), or bailiff. As the towns grew, functionaries appeared who had to look after the town's finances and its fortifications. They were often called burgomasters (*burgemeesters*).

TOWN OPPOSITION TO THE PRINCE

The development of a town's autonomy sometimes advanced somewhat spasmodically as a result of violent conflicts with the prince. The citizens then united, forming *conjurationes* (sometimes called communes)—fighting groups bound together by an oath—as happened during a Flemish crisis in 1127–28 in Ghent and Brugge and in Utrecht in 1159. The counts of Flanders from the house of Alsace (Thierry, ruled 1128–68, and Philip, 1168–91) kept careful watch, supporting and aiding the towns in their economic development but otherwise keeping the process in check.

In their struggle for autonomy, the towns had to fight for financial freedom, such as for the lessening or abolition of the taxes and tolls they had to pay to the prince but also and principally for the right to impose their own taxes, usually in the form of indirect taxation (e.g., excise duties), in order to raise money for necessary public works. Especially important to them was the right to frame their own laws; this legislative right (the *keurrecht*) was in most towns originally restricted to the control of prices and standards in the markets and shops but was gradually extended to cover civil and criminal law.

The extent of a man's obligation to serve in the prince's armed forces was often fixed or limited or both (sometimes by the provision for payment in lieu, sometimes by a legal definition of the number of foot soldiers or manned ships to be made available).

Thus, the town in the Low Countries became a *communitas* (sometimes called *corporatio* or *universitas*)—a community that was legally a corporate body, could enter into alliances and ratify them with its own seal, could sometimes even make commercial or military contracts with other towns, and could negotiate directly with the prince. Land within the town's boundaries usually became its property or its burghers' by redemption, and the town's inhabitants were usually exempt from any dependent relationship with outsiders.

A town's population usually had a distinct social structure. The merchants, the oldest and leading group, soon emerged as a separate class (the patriciate); they generally managed to gain control of the offices of *schepen* and burgomaster and thus controlled the town's finances. Sometimes the *homines novi*, a new class of up-and-coming merchants, tried to become part of the patriciate, as in Dordrecht and Utrecht. Beneath the patriciate a lower class formed, called the *gemeen* ("common," in the strict sense of the word), which embraced the artisans and organized into crafts such tradesmen as butchers, bakers, tailors, carpenters, masons, weavers, fullers, shearers, and coppersmiths. These crafts, or guilds, originally developed out of charitable organizations of people in the same profession and had to adhere to regulations laid down by the authorities. Gradually, however, they tried to obtain their independence, exercise influence in politics, cut themselves off from outsiders by means of compulsory membership, and introduce their own regulations regarding prices, working hours, quality of products, apprentices, journeymen, and masters. During the second half of the 13th century, class antagonism rose in the main industrial cities in Flanders. The political conflict between the count of Flanders, the king of France, and the patriciate opened the way for the craftsmen to score a military victory in 1302. This led to the constitutional recognition of the guilds as autonomous organs with the right of considerable participation in the cities' administration. The achievements of the Flemish artisans inspired their colleagues in Brabant and Liège to revolt and raise similar demands; Flemish military incursions provoked the same reaction in Dordrecht and Utrecht. In Brabant, the concessions were only short-lived, but their effects were more durable in the other places, although never undisputed by the old elites.

In Flanders and in the bishopric of Liège, the towns rapidly attained such power that they constituted a threat to the territorial prince, a situation that often resulted in violent conflicts. In contrast to this, relations between the prince and the towns of Brabant were more harmonious; the political interests of the prince and the economic interests of the towns coincided for the most part during the 13th century, while John I, Duke of Brabant, sought expansion toward the Rhine valley, which offered protection for the growing trade that moved from Cologne overland through Brabant. Duke John II, however, left such formidable debts that Brabant merchants were arrested abroad, which made them claim control over the duke's finances during Duke John III's minority (1312–20). The fact that from 1248 to 1430 only two dynastic successions involved a direct adult male heir gave the cities (which had incurred massive debts) recurrent opportunities to intervene in the government and to impose their conditions on the successors in the form of public testaments called *joyeuse entrée* acts, which were delivered at all successions from 1312 until 1794. The acts, which also applied to Limburg, contained dozens of ad hoc regulations besides a few more general and abstract notions, such as the indivisibility of the territory, a nationality requirement for the officials, approval of the cities before embarking on a war, and the subjects' right of resistance in case of violation of any stipulation of the acts. In Holland the towns did not really develop until as late as the 13th century, when they were helped by the counts.

During this period, when foundations were being laid for the dominant role the towns would later play in the Low

Countries, a decisive change also took place in the authority of the territorial prince. Originally he regarded his powers mainly as a means of increasing his income and of extending the area over which he could exercise power. He felt little duty toward his subjects or desire to further the welfare of the community as a whole. At best there were religious as well as material motives in his dealings with the churches and monasteries. There were no direct relations between the prince and all his subjects, for he was primarily lord of his vassals. The political, social, and economic developments discussed above, however, brought a change in this situation. In the first place, the prince's increasing independence meant that he himself began to behave like a king or sovereign lord. His authority was then referred to as *potestas publica* ("public authority"), and it was believed to be granted by God (*a Deo tradita*). The area over which he ruled was described as his *regnum* or *patria*. This implied not only the duty of a lord toward his vassals but also that of a prince (*princeps*) toward his subjects. This duty included as its first priority the maintenance of law and order (*defensio pacis*) by means of laws and their administration. He had further to protect the church (*defensio* or *advocatio ecclesiae*), while his involvement in land reclamation and in the building of dikes and with the development of the towns brought him into direct contact with the non-feudal elements of the population, with whom his relations were no longer those of a lord toward his vassals but took on a more modern aspect—that of a sovereign toward his trusted subjects. He became, according to the 14th-century lawyer Philip of Leiden, the *procurator rei publicae* ("he who looks after the matters of the people"). Contact with his subjects was through the representatives of the *communitates* of the water boards and *heemraadschappen* and through the towns and non-urban communities, which were legally corporate bodies in dealings not only with outsiders but also with the prince. Sometimes the towns expressly placed themselves under the protection of the prince and declared themselves committed to loyalty to him. Such a town was Dordrecht, which, in a document dated 1266, expressed its loyalty and at the same time described the count of Holland as *dominus terrae* ("lord of the land"). These new notions point to a more modern conception of a state, to a growing awareness of territoriality, and to new possibilities of collaboration between prince and subjects.

CHAPTER 4

CONSOLIDATION OF TERRITORIAL STATES (1384–1567)

Among the many territorial principalities of the Low Countries, Flanders, Brabant, Hainaut-Holland, and Gelderland (Guelders) in the mid-14th century had a dominating military and diplomatic position. Flanders had already arrested the course of French domination, and its feeling of territoriality was strengthened by this and by many minor wars between the principalities as well as by three major revolts of large segments of the population against the principality's count. This antagonism displayed some early expressions of Flemish nationalism against the count and the nobility, who were backed by France and were French-speaking. In Brabant, national feelings were similarly fostered by fears of foreign invasions in the 1330s. In many respects, Flanders was the real territorial leader during the late Middle Ages. Its population was by far the largest of the principalities, its economic development the strongest, and its institutions the most elaborate. The extraordinary size of the largest cities made it impossible to rule the county without their collaboration. Thus during the 13th century, the *scabini Flandriae*, uniting delegations from the governments of the main cities, intervened in various political matters of the principality, especially concerning economic policy. During the 14th century, the three largest cities, Brugge, Ghent, and Ypres, formed a nearly permanent consultation committee called the three members of Flanders on which was bestowed decisive powers in most political matters, including taxation, legislation, and justice; it also wielded a strong influence in international relations. During the repeated periods of revolt or of absence of the count, the three members automatically extended their functions to the overall exercise of power. This experience explains why in Flanders, in contrast to Brabant and Hainaut, a system of representation by three estates (clergy, nobility, and the burghers) did not develop spontaneously. The power of the cities proved so overwhelming that they did not have to share control with the clergy and the nobility. It was the duke of Burgundy who introduced assemblies of three estates from 1385 onward, as a means to contain the cities, just as he imposed the addition of a fourth member to the consultation committee, which provided rural representation. These moves, however, did not profoundly alter the balance of power, which remained intact until the prince expanded his territory during the 15th century.

In the county of Holland, power relations were balanced between the count, the nobility, and the burghers; the clergy played almost no role, since there were few important abbeys. The cities were much smaller than those of Flanders; a group of the six largest cities (Dordrecht, Leiden, Haarlem, Amsterdam, Gouda, and Delft) wielded the greatest influence and power. From 1349 onward a deep cleavage among the Dutch nobility over the succession to the throne led to the formation of two parties, the Kabeljauwen (Cods) and the Hoeken (Hooks); most cities were also divided

along these party lines. Feuds on a local basis took the shape of the party antagonisms, which during certain periods of crisis spread over the whole county and over neighbouring Zeeland and Utrecht as well. During the years after 1392, the periods from 1419 to 1427, 1440 to 1445, and again in the 1470s and '80s, there was a high degree of discord in which the prince and his high officials saw their prerogatives seriously challenged. The relatively small size of the cities, close links between noble and patrician families, a weak administrative organization, and dynastic rivalries for the throne contributed to the ongoing party strife until the end of the 15th century.

Gelderland was later in its development, partly because the powerful Duke William (ruled 1379–1402) of that principality had his own financial resources as a result of his military activities in the service of the English and, later, French kings; under William's successors, however, the knights and the towns became more powerful and finally gained permanent representation as estates. In Utrecht, too, there was cooperation between the prince (the bishop) and the estates; and the clergy, particularly the collegiate churches of the town of Utrecht, played an important part: the Land Charter of Bishop Arnold in 1375 was inspired by the Joyeuse Entrée of Brabant. In the prince-bishopric of Liège, cooperation between prince and estates had to be won by violent conflicts between the towns and the bishop and, within the towns, between the patriciate and the crafts. It was mainly to these territorial estates that the princes had to turn for financial help, which was often voted to them only on limiting conditions.

THE BURGUNDIANS

In the second half of the 14th century, the dukes of Burgundy (princes of the French royal house of Valois) began to penetrate these territorial principalities in the Low Countries, whose feelings of territoriality made them regard the dukes of Burgundy with suspicion. The marriage in 1369 of Philip II the Bold of Burgundy to the heiress of the count of Flanders (Margaret) signified the beginning of this Burgundian infiltration, which was repeatedly furthered by marriages, wars, and such tricks of fate as inheritances.

Through his marriage Philip gained possession, after the death of his father-in-law in 1384, of the counties of Flanders, Artois, Rethel, Nevers, and the free county of Burgundy (Franche-Comté), the latter being within the Holy Roman Empire. He thus not only gained a large and powerful part of the Low Countries but was also able to extend his Burgundian property. Though it seemed at first that French power might again become the dominant force in the Low Countries, it soon became clear that the Burgundian dukes, while happy to continue taking part in French politics, were extremely independent and more interested in forging

a single powerful empire out of the Low Countries and Burgundy. Duke John the Fearless succeeded to all his father's lands in 1404, while his younger brother Anthony was given Brabant, where the childless Duchess Joanna had named him as her successor, which was accepted by the estates. Anthony's branch of the Burgundians died out as early as 1430, so that Brabant fell to the other branch under Philip III (Philip the Good; ruled 1419–67), who also gained possession—through war, family relations, and purchase—of Hainaut-Holland, Namur, and Luxembourg. This Burgundian power structure was not a state but was founded on a personal union among the various principalities, each of which jealously guarded its own freedom and institutions. The Burgundian dukes did, however, attempt to set up central organizations to bridge the differences among the principalities and to keep the various regions under stricter control by appointing governors (stadtholders).

Regional courts and exchequers increasingly enforced the central government's control in administrative, political, and judicial fields. Some principalities, such as Brabant and Hainaut, claimed that their privileges disallowed any foreign interference in their territories; in Flanders and Holland, however, the dukes introduced officials from their Burgundian homeland. In the long term, this policy of bringing in foreign administrators raised serious resistance against the central government, especially

Philip III, also known as Philip the Good. Archive Photos/Getty Images

because it tended to make French the only administrative language, while the majority of the population in the Low Countries was Dutch-speaking. To further central control, Duke Philip extended his court in order to incorporate regional nobilities, and in 1430 he created the Order of the Golden Fleece, to which he brought the highest nobles from his principalities.

In addition, the judicial tasks of his Great Council were entrusted from 1435 to a special group of councillors who steadily increased the weight of the central jurisdiction over local and regional customs and privileges. The ambitions of the Burgundian dukes finally ran aground on the forced and overly hasty centralization and expansion of power carried out by Charles the Bold (ruled 1467–77), who was able, nevertheless, to annex Gelderland. Charles imposed increasingly high financial demands, which were put before the States-General—an assembly that united the delegates from the various states at meetings called by the duke and held at regular intervals; he tried to constitute a kingdom in the Low Countries with himself as regent, an endeavour that failed in 1473. Charles did manage, however, to elevate the central law court to the rank of the royal Parliament of Paris—an obvious defiance of the king of France's prerogatives.

THE ORDER OF THE GOLDEN FLEECE

The Order of the Golden Fleece was founded by Philip III at Bruges in Flanders in 1430 to commemorate his wedding there to Isabella of Portugal. Its first chapter was held at Lille in 1431, and in 1432 its seat was fixed at Dijon, capital of the duchy of Burgundy. Dedicated to the Blessed Virgin and to St. Andrew, it was first constituted to have a grand master (the sovereign duke) and 23 knights, but membership was subsequently increased to 31 and eventually to 51. The order—founded to defend the Roman Catholic religion, to uphold the usages of chivalry, and to increase the prestige of the dukes of Burgundy—was ideally supposed to settle all disputes between its knights, whose actions were to be appraised, commended, or censured at its chapters; the knights had the right to trial by their fellows on charges of rebellion, treason, or heresy.

Through the marriage of Mary of Burgundy to the Austrian archduke Maximilian (1477), the grand mastership passed to the house of Habsburg. The Holy Roman emperor Charles V (Charles I of Spain), who granted the order exclusive jurisdiction over all crimes that might be committed by its members, left the grand mastership to his son Philip II of Spain, to whose successors it was confirmed by Pope Clement VIII in 1600; but, following the extinction of the Spanish Habsburgs (1700), it was disputed between the Bourbon kings of Spain and the Austrian Habsburgs. The emperor Charles VI instituted the order in Vienna in 1713, and thenceforward both the Austrian and the Spanish sovereigns and pretenders continued to award the Golden Fleece as their principal order of knighthood. It was exclusively reserved to Roman Catholics of the highest nobility.

After his defeat and death in battle to French-supported forces, a movement for regional and local rights arose and won a series of privileges from his daughter Mary (ruled 1477–82) that halted the previous centralization movement. Moreover, the duchy of Burgundy itself was taken over by the French crown, so that the Burgundian union, as it was reformed by the States-General from 1477, became a union without Burgundy. The pressure of French incursions brought the members of the States-General into closer collaboration. While ensuring their loyalty to the Burgundian dynasty and organizing a defense against France, they obtained the first written constitution (Groot-Privilege, 1477) for the whole of the principalities in the Low Countries. It recognized extensive rights for the States-General, such as control over the waging of war, currency, taxation, and tolls; furthermore, it prescribed the use of the legal language to be used in the courts. This text remained for centuries a point of reference for the rights of the subjects, granting to individuals the right of resistance in cases where tenets of the document were seen to be violated.

THE HABSBURGS

After Mary's position had become more firmly established by her marriage to Maximilian of Habsburg (the son and future successor of the Holy Roman emperor), the States-General, because of its internal particularism, proved unable to provide a lasting administration.

Gradually, a restoration took place, at first under the regency of Maximilian after Mary's death in 1482. Maximilian, however, lacked the political skills to deal with the various social forces in the Low Countries. His political strategy was aimed simply at a thorough recovery of the territorial and institutional losses since 1477, but his policy of high taxation, debasement, warfare, and violation of privileges, during a period of deep general economic crisis, provoked opposition and revolt, first in Flanders but also later in Holland, Brabant, and Utrecht. His answer was, as it had been in the past, the brutal use of military force, which plunged these regions into 10 years of devastating internal war. When his and Mary's son Philip I the Handsome (ruled 1493–1506) took over the government, he smoothly resumed the centralization process by refounding the central law court (then known as the Great Council of Malines) and set up within the duke's council permanent commissions to discuss important political and financial questions.

The fate of the Low Countries was already closely bound up with that of Austria by virtue of the Habsburg marriage; in 1504, this situation was intensified when Philip and his wife, Joan, inherited the Spanish crown. From then on, the Low Countries were merely a part of a greater whole, and their fate was principally decided by the struggle of this Spanish-Austrian empire for European hegemony. They repeatedly had to make sacrifices for the many wars waged against France, particularly under Emperor Charles V, who in 1519 had added the German imperial crown to his many possessions. The emperor, who was almost always out of the country, placed the Low Countries under the rule of governors-general—first his aunt Margaret and later his sister Mary, who retained control and worked toward further centralization even when he was in the country.

The States-General could do little more than offer passive resistance, principally through financial manipulations. As a meeting place for the regional deputies, the States-General did have a certain influence and, by its opposition, strengthened a sort of negative feeling of unity. That the emperor himself also saw the Low Countries as a unit can be seen in his incorporation of the territories in the north and east, including Groningen and Friesland (1522–28). A remarkable step was the imposition of temporal power over the bishop of Utrecht (1528); full power was also acquired over the duchy of Gelderland in 1543. Consequently, Charles took measures to separate his so-called Seventeen Provinces of the Low Countries from the empire as "Burgundian Kreis" ("Circle") (1548) and in the Pragmatic Sanction (1549), which stated that succession would be regulated in identical fashion in all the regions of the Low Countries that he had included in his empire. The Low Countries were thus prevented from being split up.

In the meantime, the process of centralization had reached a decisive phase with the foundation of the collateral councils (1531), which were separate from the Great Council. They were the Council of Finance, which had in effect already existed for some time; the Council of State, in which members of the high nobility could advise the governess; and the Secret Council, in which permanent officials dealt with everyday administration and composed ordinances without having to wait for advice. All the government organs, except for the central law court in Malines, were in Brussels, which from that time became the capital of the Low Countries. The States-General and territorial states were still a stumbling block in the acquisition of financial resources, so that Charles V was never able to provide himself with a standing army.

Under Charles's son Philip II, who in 1555–56 succeeded as king of Spain and prince of the Netherlands, the policy of centralization was continued. It culminated in the introduction of a new ecclesiastical hierarchy. The Low Countries, which formerly had been, ecclesiastically speaking, merely an extension of the archbishoprics of Cologne and Reims, became by virtue of a papal bull of 1559 a directly governed region of the church under three archbishops and 15 bishops. There was fierce resistance to this by the high nobles, who saw the high positions in the church slip from their grasp; by the abbots, who feared the incorporation of their monasteries for the maintenance of new bishoprics; and by a number of territories, which were afraid of greater inquisitorial activities under new bishops. The high nobles, who were often excluded from the activities of the Secret Council, led the resistance under the capable Prince William of Orange (1533–84) and the popular Count of Egmond. Resistance increased when the Burgundian Antoine Perrenot de Granvelle (bishop of Arras and virtually prime minister under the Netherlands' governor Margaret of Parma) was appointed archbishop of Malines and then cardinal and primate of the Netherlands. The government gave way, and Granvelle was forced to leave the country; yet the high nobles themselves hardly knew how to run affairs. The initiative was thus transferred to the low nobility, who in 1565 united by bond of oath in the so-called Compromise, and in 1566 presented to the governor a petition requesting the relaxation of edicts and ordinances against the Calvinists and other Protestants. At the same time, they adopted the name Geuzen (*gueux*, "beggars"), originally a term of abuse.

As the resistance grew stronger, the Protestants became more confident, and fanatics started a violent campaign against churches—the "breaking of the images" (August 1566)—against which the governor took powerful measures, but only in the first few months of 1567 was peace restored. King Philip II, however, whose information concerning these events was somewhat out of date because of slow communications and who was uneasy because of the "breaking of the images," decided to take stern measures.

He sent his trusted general, Fernando Álvarez de Toledo, Duke of Alba, to the Netherlands. Alba's strict regime precipitated a revolt that eventually led to the partition of the Netherlands.

ECONOMIC STRUCTURE

The economic structure of the Low Countries underwent far-reaching changes in the 14th–16th centuries. The growth in population, which in western Europe had begun in the 10th century, ceased with relative suddenness after 1300. The European famine of 1315–17 had dramatic effects in the cities; in Ypres 10 percent of the population died, had to be picked up off the streets, and were buried by public means. Social tensions, insurrections, and internal wars also cost numerous lives during the 14th century, especially in the rebellious cities of Flanders and Liège. Many Flemish weavers and fullers fled to England, helping there to build up an English cloth industry, which came to compete with that of the Low Countries. The effects of recurrent plagues from 1349 onward, raging once in each decade until the early 15th century, must have been devastating as well. The population as a whole was seriously diminished, but in the cities, where overpopulation had been developing since the late 13th century, the losses were replaced by rural surpluses, leaving somewhat easier living conditions in the cities for the survivors.

Generally, the standard of living in the Low Countries improved in the second half of the 14th century.

In the 14th and 15th centuries, Brugge became the main international market of northwestern Europe. Colonies of foreign merchants installed their offices: Italians, Catalans and other Iberians, French and English, and above all the German Hanse, for whom Brugge was the most important *Kontor* (office). Southern and northern Europe met at Brugge, and their exchange networks were linked there. An intensive movement of bills of exchange converged there and helped to balance the region's export deficit with the Mediterranean states. The densely populated Low Countries evidently formed an important market for imported goods such as wine, Mediterranean fruits, and Eastern spices and silk; grain was also an important import. The relatively affluent population could afford expensive goods, but it also produced labour-intensive, high-quality objects, including fashionable clothing and various works of art and applied art, such as paintings, jewelry, woodcuts, and pottery. The trade network helped to spread these works throughout Europe.

On the other hand, the loss of some one-third of the European population, mostly to plague, had severely reduced the export markets, causing competition to intensify. The Brabantine cities had developed their own textile industry, competing internationally. Since the guilds held a firm grasp on wages and regulations from 1302 onward in Flanders,

they raised the production costs higher than those in Brabant and much higher than those in England and Holland. The Flemish had to become reoriented toward ever more sophisticated methods and higher-quality products in that state's large, old cities. Improvements in linen and tapestry weaving exemplified new innovations. Entrepreneurs now shifted their production toward villages, unrestricted by guild regulations, where wages were lower and quality controls weaker. These rural manufacturers used cheaper wools from local areas and (from the 15th century) Spain, and they produced lighter, less refined cloth, which found a wide middle-class market.

Holland became the site of marked economic change during the second half of the 14th century. The drainage of the peat bogs had produced land that was not well suited to the cultivation of bread grains, and cattle raising had become the major means of subsistence. That occupation's reduced labour requirements drove a portion of the rural population into the cities, where some found jobs in crafts and seafaring. Dairy products continued to be exported to the larger cities in Flanders and Brabant, but grain now had to be imported, largely from Artois and, increasingly from the 15th century, the Baltic region. The Dutch also learned the technique of preserving herring common to that region; the shift of the herring shoals to the North Sea had helped the Dutch take the lead in this trade. In addition, they developed a shipbuilding industry for which they again needed imports, this time of wood, iron, tar, and pitch from the Flemish Hanse area. They succeeded in building a competitive fleet that could offer transportation at a lower cost than that of the Hanse. The Dutch then were able to penetrate the Baltic Sea region, not only to buy sorely needed raw materials but increasingly also to sell and transport. None of the Dutch products were exclusive to them, the goods being often of even lesser quality than those offered by their competitors; their price, however, was always more advantageous, thanks to their excellent cargo facilities. Apart from the herring industry, the Dutch competed in cloth and, even more effectively, in beer: their quality of barley, clear water, and hops enabled them to brew a product of distinctive character for which demand grew. The cities of Delft, Gouda, and Haarlem became major beer-exporting centres, shipping to the southern Netherlands and to the Baltic regions as well. The Dutch also exported some bulk salt. When the production of salt derived from peat proved to be of insufficient quantity and quality for salting fish, the Dutch imported raw maritime salt from the French Atlantic coasts and refined it in their peat-fueled ovens. This was suitable for the fish industry and could also be exported to the Baltic area, the traditional production from Lüneburg, Germany, having slowed down.

While Holland thus laid the basis for its remarkable 17th-century prosperity, the southern Netherlands showed a shift of commercial leadership from Brugge to Antwerp. During the 15th century, Antwerp developed strongly thanks to its free entrepreneurial climate and its two annual fairs, which were combined with two more in the nearby Schelde harbour city of Bergen-op-Zoom. At that time, the fairs still functioned as subsidiaries to the Brugge market, but they nevertheless attracted merchants from central and southern Germany. While Brugge lived through a deep political crisis in the 1480s, Antwerp attracted the new colonial trade, especially that of the Portuguese, and the important Augsburg, Frankfurt, and Nürnberg merchant and banking houses. They imported new textiles in return for copper, silver, and other metal products. The Italians soon left Brugge for Antwerp, belatedly followed by the increasingly regressing German Hanse. The fast expansion of the Antwerp market was supported by excellent relations with the monarchy that, in turn, could finance its hegemonistic policy through loans from Antwerp merchants. A special innovation was financial techniques developed at the Antwerp *beurs* (stock exchange), created in 1531. While Brugge remained a clearing house for international commercial debts, where exchange rates for bills were determined, the Antwerp exchange specialized in transferable, usually discounted, public debts.

Generally speaking, a commercial capitalism was developing that stimulated the entire economy of the Netherlands. Competition in the cloth industry was growing especially strong between urban and expanding rural manufacturers. The towns battled these rural clothmakers in vain, though in 1531 Holland issued an edict to restrict them throughout the county, but with little success. Moreover, Holland itself had begun to play an increasingly important economic role; new industries were developing, but fishing, shipping, and trade remained its main means of support apart from arable farming and cattle breeding. Dordrecht, one of the major commercial centres of the Low Countries, was rivaled by Rotterdam and Gorinchem and, by the 16th century, was outstripped by Amsterdam, which cornered an increasing proportion of Baltic trade, as evidenced from the lists of the toll in the Sound (between Sweden and Denmark).

The regions along the Meuse and IJssel also maintained their commercial activity. In the bishopric of Liège there was even a metal industry with blast furnaces, paid for by capital raised by traders. Coal mining in the area between the Meuse and the Sambre was also organized according to modern capitalist methods.

The cultivation of commercially exploitable crops also developed in country areas—hemp for rope making, hops and barley for brewing, flax for the manufacture of linen. Yet all this was at the expense of wheat farming. Grain had to be imported in increasingly large quantities, and, whenever grain imports fell off, the people, particularly the lower classes, went hungry. The economic apparatus had become more versatile and brought greater prosperity, but at the same time, precisely because of this specialization, it had become more vulnerable. The distribution of prosperity was variable; the great mass of the people in the towns suffered the consequences and bore the main burden of the rise in prices occasioned by inflation.

POPULATION GROWTH

It is impossible to estimate the population of the Low Countries before about 1470, and even for that date complete data are not available. Figures are often not available for all areas at a given date in the Middle Ages. An acceptable figure for the Low Countries in the late 15th century might be about 2,400,000 inhabitants. Flanders was by far the most populated and most densely inhabited principality, with about 750,000 people and a density of 30 persons per square mile (77 per square kilometre). It was followed by Brabant with 413,000 people and about 15 persons per square mile (40 per square kilometre) and Holland with 268,000 people and 25 per square mile (66 per square kilometre), although the latter data are from the year 1514. The other principalities counted far fewer inhabitants—for example, 209,000 in Hainaut, 180,000 in Artois, and 140,000 in Gelderland, Liège, and Luxembourg.

After 1470 the population must have declined generally, owing to wars, bad harvests, and epidemics. From 1490 a new period of growth especially favoured Brabant and Holland. About 1570 the duchy of Brabant counted about 500,000 inhabitants, which was still less than the more densely populated Flanders. One-quarter of the Flemish peasants farmed plots of only 5 to 12 acres (2 to 5 hectares), and nearly half had even less than 5 acres. The level of urbanization was growing extremely fast in the Low Countries, especially in the largest principalities. In 1470, 36 percent of Flanders' population and 31 percent of Brabant's were city dwellers, while in Holland the proportion reached 45 percent in 1514. It should be noted, however, that the cities of Holland were still relatively small, the largest being Leiden with 14,000. In the southern Low Countries in the mid-14th century, Ghent and Brugge attained populations of 64,000 and 46,000, respectively, while Brussels counted 33,000 in 1482 and Malines (Mechelen) grew to 25,000 around 1540. Antwerp showed spectacular growth, from 15,000 in 1437 to nearly 40,000 around 1500, and more than 100,000 in 1560, its peak for this period.

CULTURE

The Low Countries played an important part in the artistic, scientific, and religious life of Europe. In the late Middle Ages, when prosperity was increasing and the princely houses, particularly that of the Burgundians, as well as the middle classes in the towns, were encouraging progress, the Low Countries began to make independent contributions to cultural life.

The most original of these were in the field of visual and applied arts. From the late 14th century the Low Countries produced sculptors like Claus Sluter, whose most famous works are the funerary monuments for the duke of Burgundy, Philip the Bold, and his wife at Dijon, France, and painters like Melchior Broederlam who also served the duke. In the 15th century, however, the cities in the southern Low Countries became the core of cultural activity, because the duke's court resided mostly in that region and because the local bourgeoisie, clergy, and noblemen profited from the Burgundian prosperity and could invest in works of art, which allowed them to share somewhat in the splendour of the court. The main centres were Ghent (Jan and Hubert van Eyck and Hugo van der Goes), Leuven (Dieric Bouts), Brussels (Rogier van der Weyden), and Brugge (Hans Memling and Gerard David). Each of these masters stands for a school of followers. Miniature painting similarly was a most flourishing activity, reaching its first height in the northern Low Countries (Utrecht) about 1400, but rising also in the south through the 15th century. Tapestry weavers in Arras attained a unique quality, which was imitated in Tournai, Brussels, Oudenaarde, Brugge, Ghent, and elsewhere. Brabant was famous for its woodcut triptychs made in Leuven and Antwerp (then in Brabant), Brugge for its lace, jewelry, and fashionable clothing. All

THOMAS À KEMPIS

About 1392 Thomas à Kempis (born Thomas Hemerken 1379/80, Kempen, near Düsseldorf, Rhineland [Germany]—died August 8, 1471, Agnietenberg, near Zwolle, Bishopric of Utrecht [now in the Netherlands]) went to Deventer, Netherlands, headquarters of the learned Brethren of the Common Life, a community devoted to education and the care of the poor. There he studied under the theologian Florentius Radewyns, who in 1387 had founded the Congregation of Windesheim, a congregation of Augustinian canons regular (i.e., ecclesiastics living in community and bound by vows). Thomas joined the Windesheim congregation at Agnietenberg monastery, where he remained almost continually for over 70 years. He took his vows in 1408, was ordained in 1413, and devoted his life to copying manuscripts and to directing novices.

Although the authorship is in dispute, he probably wrote the *Imitatio Christi* (*Imitation of Christ*), the devotional book that, with the exception of the Bible, has been considered the most influential work in Christian literature. Remarkable for its simple language and style, it emphasizes the spiritual rather than the materialistic life, affirms the rewards of being Christ-centred, and supports Communion as a means to strengthen faith. His writings offer possibly the best representation of the *devotio moderna* , the Roman Catholic movement that stressed meditation and the inner life. Thomas stresses asceticism rather than mysticism, and moderate—not extreme—austerity.

these extraordinary works were exported through Europe, where they won the appreciation of princes, aristocrats, and rich burghers.

In the southern Low Countries, mysticism reached its zenith in the 13th and 14th centuries in the poems of Sister Hadewych and the prose of the prior Joannes Ruusbroec (Jan van Ruysbroeck). Ruusbroec's writings were founded on a considerable knowledge of theology; it is not certain whether his work had a direct influence on the founding of the religious movement along the IJssel—the modern devotion (*devotio moderna*)—or whether mysticism merely created the intellectual climate in which the new school of thought could develop.

The modern devotion was inspired by Geert Groote (Gerard Groote, 1340–84) of Deventer, who preached, as did many others, the ascetic and pious life and resistance to the secularization of the church. His message was well received, and many lay people found in themselves a desire to live in communities devoted to the service of God; these were the Brethren and Sisters of the Common Life, who later organized themselves into the Windesheim monasteries and convents, which followed Augustinian rules. Their communities were extremely important for both education and religion; they were industrious copyists and brought a simple piety to the lower classes. Their work, like that of the mendicant orders, was a typical product of life in the towns. The movement reached its peak in Thomas à Kempis, from Zwolle, whose *Imitatio Christi* (*The Imitation of Christ*) became quite widely read, not least in Dutch versions.

DEVELOPMENT OF DUTCH HUMANISM

Within the modern devotion, where great importance was attached to good teaching, Dutch humanism was able to develop freely. Of importance was the foundation in 1425 of the Catholic University of Leuven (Louvain); it received in 1517 the Collegium Trilingue where Latin, Greek, and Hebrew were taught. The greatest Dutch humanist was Erasmus, whose fame spread throughout the world and who had been taught in the schools of the Brethren of the Common Life. He drew his inspiration, as did many other humanists, from antiquity and was famed for his pure Latin. He was in touch with the greatest minds of his time, visited England (Cambridge) and Italy, and worked for some years in Basel and in Freiburg. Erasmus' greatest achievement was to turn the science of theology, which had degenerated into meaningless Neoscholastic disputes, back to the study of sources by philological criticism and by publishing a new edition of the Greek New Testament. Although he vociferously criticized the church and even the princes, he avoided

DESIDERIUS ERASMUS

The illegitimate son of a priest and a physician's daughter, Desiderius Erasmus (born October 27, 1469, Rotterdam, Holland—died July 12, 1536, Basel, Switzerland) entered a monastery and was ordained a priest in the Augustinian order in 1492. Having found no satisfaction in his priestly duties, he won a release in 1494, and from that time he was a traveling scholar. He studied at the University of Paris and traveled throughout Europe, coming under the influence of St. Thomas More and John Colet. The book that first made him famous, the *Adagia* (1500, 1508), was an annotated collection of Greek and Latin proverbs. Erasmus became noted for his editions of Classical authors, Church Fathers (including Jerome, Augustine of Hippo, Cyprian, Irenaeus, and Origen), and the Greek New Testament, which was a landmark achievement for its time, enabling scholars to examine a more accurate text than had been available for centuries. Among his own books the most popular and enduring are *Handbook of a Christian Knight* (1503) and *Praise of Folly* (1509). Using the philological methods pioneered by Italian humanists, he helped lay the groundwork for the historical-critical study of the past. By criticizing ecclesiastical abuses, he encouraged the growing urge for reform, which found expression both in the Protestant Reformation and in the Catholic Counter-Reformation. Though he saw much to admire in Martin Luther, he came under pressure to attack him; he took an independent stance, rejecting both Luther's doctrine of predestination and the powers claimed for the papacy.

out of conviction a break with the church and pleaded for religious tolerance.

The humanists were principally intellectuals, however, expressing themselves in literary and scientific treatises and having little impact on the broad masses of the people. Many of them, like Erasmus, desired no break with the church and did not accept that break when it became a fact by the appearance of Martin Luther. Instead, they wanted reformation within the church. It was otherwise for the reforming movements that brought turmoil to the Low Countries in the first half of the 16th century. Even Lutheranism had few followers, despite its early appearance (Luther's dogmas were condemned by the Catholic University of Leuven as early as 1520). There was a Lutheran community in Antwerp; but otherwise, support was limited to individual priests and intellectuals. Another Protestant group, the Sacramentarians, differed with Luther over the question of the Eucharist; they denied the consubstantiation of Christ in the Eucharist, although their stance enjoyed little support from the people.

An uproar was caused by the Anabaptists (so called because they rejected the baptism of infants and therefore had themselves rebaptized as adults), who refused to swear the oath of allegiance to the prince or to serve in the armed forces or in government per se and who believed in a *lumen internum* ("inner light"). This baptist movement won great popularity in the Low Countries after 1530; from the very beginning there were two branches—the social revolutionaries and the "quiet baptists." The first of these was characterized by a lively enthusiasm and a willingness, once the external trappings of the church had been rejected, to organize itself into communities, which soon formed close ties with each other. Prophesies by the social-revolutionary branch of the imminent coming of Christ and of a New Jerusalem fascinated the masses, while their fanaticism and readiness to sacrifice themselves made a deep impression on a population suffering poverty and misery. In 1534 a section of the Anabaptists moved to Münster in Westphalia, where they supposed that the New Jerusalem would be built; and in 1535 an abortive attempt was made to take over the town hall in Amsterdam. After a long siege, the bishop of Münster succeeded in reconquering his town, and the Anabaptists suffered terrible vengeance. Only the "quiet baptists" were able to continue, under the leadership of the Frisian pastor Menno Simons (these Mennonites are even today strongly represented in the provinces of Groningen, Friesland, and Noord-Holland).

The future of the movement for reformation in the Netherlands was assured, however, not by the biblical humanists nor by the Anabaptists but by a movement less intellectual than the first and more realistic than the second—Calvinism.

The theology of John Calvin (1509–64) was radical, strict, logical, and consistent. Its central theme was the absolute might and greatness of God, which made man a sinful creature of no significance who hoped merely to win God's grace by honouring him in daily hard work. Calvinism found its way to the Netherlands by way of France, though there may have been some direct influence from Geneva, Calvin's town. Calvinist writings were known in Antwerp as early as 1545, while the first translation into Dutch of his *Christianae religionis institutio* is dated 1560, which was also the year in which support for him spread in the Netherlands, largely because the Calvinists preached their creed in public and held open-air services.

Calvinist teaching appealed not only to the lower classes but also to the intellectual and middle classes because of its glorification of work, its discipline, its organization into communities, and its communal singing of the psalms. The government, however, saw the movement as a threat to its plans for unity and centralization, which were supported by the Roman Catholic church, and it took stern measures against Calvinism. Calvinists forcibly removed their coreligionists from prisons and occasionally even attacked monasteries. This group's rejection of icons, paintings, statues, and valuables in churches sometimes led them to remove them and hand them over to the town magistrates. But this idealism became corrupted, and the leaders were unable to retain control of the movement.

It should be noted that Calvinism and other forms of Protestantism had spread rapidly among the urban middle classes after 1550 in defiance of rule by Roman Catholic Spain. From 1551 to 1565 the number of persons persecuted in the county of Flanders for heresy rose from 187 to 1322. In Antwerp, the largest city of the Low Countries, with some 100,000 inhabitants around 1565, one-third of the population openly declared for Calvinist, Lutheran, or other Protestant denominations; another third declared itself to be Roman Catholic, while the last third was undeclared. Similar proportions are assumed to have existed in the other main cities, while the rural textile area in southwest Flanders counted large numbers of Anabaptists and Calvinists. It was among these Calvinists that an iconoclast movement to desecrate churches and destroy church images began in August 1566, spreading within a week to more than 150 villages and towns in the southern principalities.

The movement was weakened, however, when it lost the support of the nobility, and especially the lower nobility, which had been sympathetic to Calvinism. The government now besieged and captured the Calvinist centre, Valenciennes, by defeating a Calvinist army at Oosterweel (1567), near Antwerp. The result was a great exodus of Calvinists. Nevertheless, Calvin's ideas had penetrated deeply, and his supporters, who had emigrated to England, East Friesland, and the Pfalz of Germany, were able to maintain their unity and support their coreligionists in the Low Countries. The Calvinists were to become the driving force behind the revolt against Spanish rule.

CHAPTER 5

THE REVOLT AND THE FORMATION OF THE REPUBLIC (1567–79)

The forcible measures taken by the central government against the "breaking of the images" were followed by a brief period of peace. The Duke of Alba (who became governor after the departure of Margaret of Parma on the last day of 1567) introduced stern measures at the express command of the king. These provoked a resistance to the government (often referred to as the "revolt") that triggered the Eighty Years' War (1568–1648). The iconoclast movement itself, which had raged across the country like a storm, had already shown a deep-rooted resistance that had many causes and was brought to a head by Alba's measures.

CAUSES OF THE REVOLT

It is impossible to label any of the causes of the revolt as the decisive factor. An important one, however, was a religious motive. Criticism of the structure of the Roman Catholic church and the riches and worldly way of life of its prelates and the accompanying desire for reform had always been strong in the Low Countries; and Protestantism, through the teaching of Luther, the Sacramentarians, the Anabaptists, and, above all, the Calvinists, had gained a firm foothold. The measures taken against the resistance—harsh edicts, prison sentences, torture, and death sentences, carried out with great cruelty—fanned the flames all the more and among all classes. Social and economic causes, however, also lay behind the resistance, especially among the lower classes—the wars with France, the epidemics, poor harvests, hard winters, floods, and a frightening inflation and consequent rise in prices all combined to cause despair and misery among the masses and made them susceptible to radical ideas. At the same time, in the upper classes of the nobility and the urban patriciate, there was a sharply felt reaction against the absolutist policy of the king, who lived far away in Spain and yet whose wish was law in the Low Countries. Towns felt their privileges being threatened, and the nobles found their independent status being undermined by the ever-increasing activities of the Secret Council. The mercenaries, who were often stationed in a town as a garrison and acted as occupying forces, also aroused hostility. The fact that the resistance did not present a united front may be ascribed to the particularism among the territories—Holland, with its commercial interests, could hardly be expected to be enthusiastic on behalf of typically agrarian feudal provinces such as Hainaut or Artois.

The main cleavage in the opposition groups, however, was social as well as religious: the high nobility and richest merchants mostly remained Roman Catholic, as did the peasants and the urban poor living on the church's alms. The lower nobility, the urban middle classes, and the rural textile workers massively opted for one or the other form of religious, political, and social protest against the prevailing order. This fundamentally explains the earlier accommodation of the rural provinces of Artois, Hainaut, Namur, and Luxembourg under Spanish rule, while opposition was fierce in the urbanized provinces of Flanders, Brabant, Holland, and Zeeland. The rural northeast also remained predominantly Roman Catholic until well into the 17th century.

It is clear, however, that the terror organized by Alba burst like a bombshell in this political, social, economic, and religious climate. William, the prince of Orange, with sharp political insight, had decided not to wait for Alba's arrival; he had managed to escape in time to his birthplace in Nassau-Dillenburg, leaving behind all his possessions, which were promptly confiscated. His son, Philip William, was taken prisoner to Spain. Alba sent his troops to the principal towns and set up the Council of Troubles (or Council of Blood), which imposed severe penalties, often including the death sentence or confiscation of property, sparing nothing and nobody, not even the most powerful—the counts of Egmond and Hoorne were publicly beheaded in Brussels in June 1568.

Alba also rushed through installation of the new ecclesiastical hierarchy, which had not been completed. Furthermore, he attempted to make the central government independent of the provincial states by means of new taxes on property, on the sale of land or building, and on the sale of goods. This met with violent resistance because the taxes were to be general and permanent, so that the separate states would no longer have the means to make conditions for the furnishing of taxes (although they themselves already levied taxes on the sale of goods) and, more important, because a permanent tax system would make the king independent of his subjects. The taxes were the final link in the policy of absolutism and centralization, which would lead to a unified state controlled by a prince with unlimited power.

The severity with which Alba ruled was not able to prevent the immediate appearance of resistance. The Geuzen (guerrilla forces) conducted pillaging raids in the country and piracy at sea, for which they had "authority" in the form of letters of marque issued by William of Orange in his capacity as sovereign of the principality of Orange. Attacks took place as early as 1568. A small force led by Louis of Nassau, William's brother, enjoyed a modest victory over the Spaniards at Heiligerlee (in the province of Groningen), considered the beginning of the Eighty Years' War; but shortly afterward Louis was defeated near Jengum in East Friesland. A greater setback, however, was the complete failure, due to lack of funds, of a campaign led by William himself in Brabant. During the sombre years of

1568–72 the "Wilhelmus" was written—a song of faith, hope, and trust that was to become the Dutch national anthem. Other songs written by the Geuzen lifted the spirits of the people during this period and in later years.

During these years, William negotiated for help from Germany, England, and, above all, the French Huguenots. A large-scale attack was planned for the summer of 1572. Before William could carry it out, the Geuzen seized the port of Brielle (April 1, 1572), west of Rotterdam. This was a move of considerable strategic importance because the port controlled the mouth of both the Meuse and the Waal, and the prince immediately supported the movement. The Geuzen then took Flushing, Veere, and Enkhuizen, so that William had useful bases in Holland and Zeeland. The help that the Geuzen received from the Calvinists in these towns was striking— the Calvinists, a radical minority, were again and again able to force the more conservative town magistrates either to cooperate or to resign. Oudewater, Gouda, Dordrecht, Leiden, Hoorn, and Haarlem followed, only Amsterdam keeping the Geuzen out. The purposeful activities of the Calvinists also led to their gaining churches, often the principal church of a town, for their services; they closed monasteries, and Roman Catholic services were soon forbidden.

The revolt was at first successful only in Holland because of its unique position. As a commercially oriented province, it had been more inclined to look after its own interests than to cooperate with other provinces. Trade had been seriously threatened by the Geuzen but was now free again. Moreover, the province lay in a strategically favourable position—difficult to reach from the central government in Brussels and almost inaccessible to the Spanish armies by virtue of its many rivers, lakes, drains, and bogs.

To give the revolt a legal basis, the fiction was invented that it had been a revolt not against the king but against his evil advisers, particularly the governor. By their own authority, in July 1572 the states of Holland gathered in Dordrecht, where William of Orange was proclaimed stadtholder of Holland and Zeeland. The prince himself went to Holland and, realizing that the Calvinists had been the driving force behind the revolt, became a member of the Calvinist church. But he repeatedly expressly avowed his ideal of the United Netherlands, in which there would be room for Catholics and Calvinists alike.

Alba, disappointed by his failure to push through the tax reforms and about to return to Spain, learned of the fall of Brielle and decided to stay and start a counteroffensive. The south was immediately brought under control with the occupation and plundering of Malines; then Zutphen and Naarden in the north were taken and likewise plundered. This provoked stronger resistance, and Haarlem was retaken only after a long siege, which not only demoralized and decimated Alba's troops but also strengthened the other towns in their decision to offer resistance (1573). Thus, the Spaniards were unable to take Alkmaar, their fleet suffered a heavy defeat in the Zuiderzee, and a long siege of Leiden was relieved by flooding the surrounding country (1574). (As a reward, the town later was given a university, where Calvinistic theology was to be a principal subject for study.) Spanish troops never again forced their way into Holland—a heavy blow for the most powerful monarchy in the world.

UNIFICATION AFTER ALBA

Alba left on December 18, 1573, and his successor, Don Luis de Requesens, was unable to prevent further secessions in the north. Even the south, which had been loyal to Spain until then but where active Calvinist movements existed (especially in Ghent), became amenable to William's ambition for a united resistance to the Spanish regime. Problems involved were considerable, with one of the most contentious points being the question of religion—the more radical north demanded the total abolition of Roman Catholicism in Holland and Zeeland and the acceptance of Calvinism by the southern provinces. William, however, was diplomatic enough not to make this demand. It was finally agreed that the States-General

PACIFICATION OF GHENT

The Pacification of Ghent was the first major expression of the Netherlands' national self-consciousness. It called for the expulsion of Spanish troops from the Low Countries, the restoration of provincial and local prerogatives, and an end to the persecution of Calvinists or anyone else for religious reasons. While the signatories did not abjure their allegiance to King Philip II of Spain, it was clear that they wished any reconciliation to be on their own terms. It was a document very much in line with William I of Orange's beliefs.

The religious clauses of the pacification implicitly recognized the right of the largely Calvinist provinces of Holland and Zeeland—the centres of the military resistance—to order their own house as long as they did not attempt to advance their faith beyond their borders. The Catholic (i.e., southern) provinces, on the other hand, were to leave their Protestants unmolested.

A new royal governor was allowed to assume his duties only after he accepted the pacification and ordered the Spanish troops out of the country (February 1577). Based on the pacification,

Late 16th-century engraving by Frans Hogenberg of the Pacification of Ghent. Gianni Dagli Orti/ The Art Archive at Art Resource, NY

organs of national government were reconstituted and reasserted. The Spanish governor, however, chafing at the limitations on his power, soon resumed hostilities, and Spanish troops reentered the provinces.

This external threat to the prescribed union was accompanied by internal violations of the document's religious clauses. Calvinists, especially, forced their creed on large areas of Flanders and Brabant. Catholic faith in the union was thus seriously undermined. A further blow was the formation, in January 1579, of "closer unions" within the larger grouping. The Union of Arras, joining the southern provinces, based itself on a Catholic reading of the pacification and tended toward reconciliation with Spain; the Union of Utrecht joined the northern provinces for continued and improved resistance. The general union of the pacification was tenuously maintained until 1584, but by then its spirit had long since been vitiated.

would deal with the question later, and until such time the Calvinists would be masters only of Holland and Zeeland. A new governor (Requesens died in March 1576) was to be accepted only if he approved the pacification and sent away the foreign troops, who, because they had received no pay, were beginning to mutiny and plunder and were becoming an increasing nuisance. Another condition of his acceptance was that he govern with native officials and in close consultation with the states. On this basis, delegates from all the provinces came to an agreement, and on November 8, 1576, they signed the Pacification of Ghent.

Their sense of unity was further strengthened by the news that on November 4 Antwerp had been invaded by mutinying Spanish troops, who had slaughtered 7,000 citizens in a massacre that came to be known as the "Spanish Fury."

William's idealism, his desire for unity, and his tolerant ideas had apparently triumphed. Unity of thought, however, did not last long; and within three years signs of a split appeared between the urbanized and rural provinces (which later became a permanent split). It was immediately obvious that within the United Netherlands there were opposing powers of radicalism and reaction. For various reasons, they could not maintain equilibrium; the reactionaries tried to force their ideas on the country with the help of the new governor, Don Juan of Austria, a half-brother of the king, and the Calvinists continued their radical program to make theirs the official and only religion. In Ghent, Malines, and Brussels, radical Calvinists took over the city governments, while in Antwerp, the magistrates displayed a conspicuous tolerance toward the Protestants.

Many intractable factors underlay these conflicts—deep-running religious differences between regions; a deeply rooted particularism that hindered cooperation; and structural and economic differences between Holland and Zeeland on the one hand (commerce and industry) and Hainaut and Artois on the other (agrarian economy and feudal possession of land). It is impossible to point to any one factor that was of paramount importance. William did his utmost to save the pacification, and he found support for his ideas of tolerance among the rich burghers; yet he was unable to bridge the differences between rich and poor, Roman Catholics and Calvinists. Moreover, Don Juan died in 1578 and was succeeded by Alessandro Farnese (duke of Parma and son of the earlier governess Margaret), who was conspicuous for his military and diplomatic gifts, which made him a worthy opponent for William and who may be credited with removing Calvinist control in the south and with the return of loyalty to the king in the southern provinces.

Notable, too, was the appearance in the north and south of movements toward "closer unions," which within the whole of the United Netherlands were to bring about greater community of interests between certain provinces. On January 6, 1579, the Union of Arras (Artois) was formed in the south among Artois, Hainaut, and the town of Douay, based on the Pacification of Ghent but retaining the Roman Catholic religion, loyalty to the king, and the privileges of the estates. As a reaction to the accommodation of Artois and Hainaut, the Union of Utrecht was declared, at first including northern principalities but later drawing signees from parts of the south as well. The participation of the south was eventually broken by military force.

CHAPTER 6

BELGIUM

Belgium is one of the smallest and most densely populated countries in Europe, and it has been, since its independence in 1830, a representative democracy headed by a hereditary constitutional monarch. Initially, Belgium had a unitary form of government. In the 1980s and '90s, however, steps were taken to turn Belgium into a federal state with powers shared among the regions of Flanders, Wallonia, and the Brussels-Capital Region.

Culturally, Belgium is a heterogeneous country straddling the border between the Romance and Germanic language families of western Europe. With the exception of a small German-speaking population in the eastern part of the country, Belgium is divided between a French-speaking people, collectively called Walloons (more than one-third of the total population), who are concentrated in the five southern provinces (Hainaut, Namur, Liège, Walloon Brabant, and Luxembourg), and Flemings, a Flemish- (Dutch-) speaking people (more than one-half of the total population), who are concentrated in the five northern and northeastern provinces (West Flanders, East Flanders [West-Vlaanderen, Oost-Vlaanderen], Flemish Brabant, Antwerp, and Limburg). Just north of the boundary between Walloon Brabant (Brabant Walloon) and Flemish (Vlaams) Brabant lies the officially bilingual but majority French-speaking Brussels-Capital Region, with approximately one-tenth of the total population.

The country has a total of 860 miles (1,385 km) of land boundaries with neighbours; it is bounded by the

Belgium. Olinchuk/Shutterstock.com

Netherlands to the north, Germany to the east, Luxembourg to the southeast, and France to the south. Belgium also has some 40 miles (60 km) of shoreline on the North Sea.

Belgium and the political entities that preceded it have been rich with historical and cultural associations, from the Gothic grandeur of its medieval university and commercial cities and its small, castle-dominated towns on steep-bluffed winding rivers, through its broad traditions in painting and music that marked one of the high points of the northern Renaissance in the 16th century, to its contributions to the arts of the 20th century and its maintenance of the folk cultures of past eras. The Belgian landscape has been a major European battleground for centuries, notably in modern times during the Battle of Waterloo (1815) and the 20th century's two world wars. Today, the European Union (EU) and the North Atlantic Treaty Organization (NATO) have headquarters in or near Belgium's capital city of Brussels.

Guild houses along the Lys River in Ghent, Belgium. Encyclopædia Britannica

RELIEF, DRAINAGE, AND SOILS

Belgium generally is a low-lying country, with a broad coastal plain extending in a southeasterly direction from the North Sea and the Netherlands and rising gradually into the Ardennes hills and forests of the southeast, where a maximum elevation of 2,277 feet (694 metres) is reached at Botrange.

The main physical regions are the Ardennes and the Ardennes foothills; Côtes Lorraines (Belgian Lorraine), the intrusion of the Paris Basin in the south; and the Anglo-Belgian Basin in the north, comprising the Central Plateaus, the plain of Flanders, and the Kempenland (French: Campine).

The Ardennes region is part of the Hercynian orogenic belt of mountain ranges, which reaches from western Ireland into Germany and was formed roughly 300 to 400 million years ago, during the Paleozoic Era. The Ardennes is a plateau cut deeply by the Meuse River and its tributaries. Its higher

Flat reclaimed farmland near the border of the Netherlands in the maritime Flanders region of northern Belgium. © SuperStock.

points contain peat bogs and have poor drainage; these uplands are unsuitable as cropland.

A large depression, known east of the Meuse River as the Famenne and west of it as the Fagne, separates the Ardennes from the geologically and topographically complex foothills to the north. The principal feature of the area is the Condroz, a plateau more than 1,100 feet (335 metres) in elevation comprising a succession of valleys hollowed out of the limestone between sandstone crests. Its northern boundary is the Sambre-Meuse valley, which traverses Belgium from south-southwest to northeast.

Situated south of the Ardennes and cut off from the rest of the country, Côtes

MEUSE RIVER

The Meuse (Flemish: Maes; Dutch: Maas) River rises at Pouilly on the Langres Plateau in France and flows generally northward for 590 miles (950 km) through Belgium and the Netherlands to the North Sea. In the French part, the river has cut a steep-sided, sometimes deep valley between Saint-Mihiel and Verdun, and beyond Charleville-Mézières it meanders through the Ardennes region in a narrow valley. Entering Belgium at Givet, it continues northward to Namur, where it is joined on the left (west) bank by the Sambre River and then turns eastward to Liège. The Meuse there forms a natural routeway for river transport and is the centre of industrial development. At Liège it is deep and narrow and lies about 450 feet (137 metres) below the plateau tops. The river turns north and, from Maastricht (Netherlands) to Maaseik (Belgium), forms the frontier between the Netherlands and Belgium. From Venlo (Netherlands) it curves gradually west, reaches sea level, and divides, one branch flowing into the Hollandsch Canal (an outlet of the North Sea) while another joins the Waal River (a channel of the Rhine) near Gorinchem to become the Merwede. Near Dordrecht the Merwede divides into the Noord to the north, which joins with the Lek River to become the Nieuwe Maas, and the Oude Maas to the south. The Nieuwe Maas and the Oude Maas come together at the Nieuwe Waterweg (New Waterway), which leads to the North Sea.

The Meuse River is navigable for most of its length and is one of the more important waterways of western Europe. In the vicinity of Maastricht, the Albert Canal extends northwestward from the Meuse to reach Antwerp, while the Juliana Canal parallels the Meuse's course northward into the southern part of the Netherlands. The Meuse and its canals are heavily traveled by small cargo ships and barges.

The valley of the Meuse River is a natural barrier that has historically formed part of the defenses on the approach to the heart of the Paris Basin from the east. Its line has given great strategic importance to the fortress of Verdun and was the scene of heavy fighting in World War I. During World War II, the crossing of the Meuse River capped the successful German breakthrough into France in May 1940.

Lorraines is a series of hills with north-facing scarps. About half of it remains wooded; in the south lies a small region of iron ore deposits.

A region of sand and clay soils lying between 150 and 650 feet (45 and 200 metres) in elevation, the Central Plateaus cover northern Hainaut, Walloon Brabant, southern Flemish Brabant, and the Hesbaye plateau region of Liège. The area is dissected by the Dender, Senne, Dijle, and other rivers that enter the Schelde (Escaut) River; it is bounded to the east by the Herve Plateau. The Brussels region lies within the Central Plateaus.

Bordering the North Sea from France to the Schelde is the low-lying plain of Flanders, which has two main sections. Maritime Flanders, extending inland for about 5 to 10 miles (8 to 16 km), is a region of newly formed and reclaimed land (polders) protected by a line of dunes and dikes and having largely clay soils. Interior Flanders comprises most of East and West Flanders and has sand-silt or sand soils. At an elevation of about 80 to 300 feet (25 to 90 metres), it is drained by the Leie, Schelde, and Dender rivers flowing northeastward to the Schelde estuary. Several shipping canals interlace the landscape and connect the river systems. Lying between about 160 and 330 feet (50 and 100 metres) in elevation, the Kempenland contains pastureland and is the site of a number of industrial enterprises; it forms an irregular watershed of plateau and plain between the extensive Schelde and Meuse drainage systems.

CLIMATE

Belgium has a temperate, maritime climate predominantly influenced by air masses from the Atlantic. Rapid and frequent alternation of different air masses separated by fronts gives Belgium considerable variability in weather. Frontal conditions moving from the west produce heavy and frequent rainfall, averaging 30 to 40 inches (750 to 1,000 mm) a year. Winters are damp and cool with frequent fogs; summers are rather mild. The annual mean temperature is in the low 50s °F (about 10 °C). Brussels, which is roughly in the middle of the country, has a mean minimum temperature of just below 32 °F (0 °C) in January and a mean maximum in the low 70s °F (about 22 °C) in July.

Regional climatic differences are determined by elevation and distance inland. Farther inland, maritime influences become weaker, and the climate becomes more continental, characterized by greater seasonal extremes of temperature. The Ardennes region, the highest and farthest inland, is the coldest. In winter, frost occurs on about 120 days, snow falls on 30 to 35 days, and January mean minimum temperatures are lower than elsewhere. In summer, the elevation counteracts the effect of distance inland, and July mean maximum temperatures are the lowest in the country. Because of the topography, the region has the highest rainfall in Belgium. In contrast, the Flanders region enjoys generally higher temperatures throughout the year. There are fewer than 60 days of frost and fewer than 15 of snow. On the seacoast these figures are reduced to below 50 and 10, respectively. There are a few hot days, especially on the coast, where the annual rainfall is the lowest in the country.

PLANT AND ANIMAL LIFE

All of Belgium except the Ardennes lies within the zone of broad-leaved deciduous forestation. The dominant tree is the oak; others include beeches, birches, and elms. Little remains of the forest that covered this area 2,000 years ago. Most of lowland Belgium is now used for agriculture or human settlement; small clumps of deciduous trees and grasses dominate the remaining open spaces. In the Kempenland, however, significant areas are devoted to planted forests of silver birch and Corsican pine.

The Ardennes lies within the zone of mixed deciduous and coniferous forestation. The area has been heavily logged for centuries. Hence, little old-growth forest remains. The Ardennes is dominated now by coniferous forests in the higher elevations and by zones of mixed coniferous and deciduous trees, especially beeches and oaks, in the foothills. Hautes Fagnes, which is located at the northeastern edge of the Ardennes, has many peat bogs. Drainage has improved, however, and the area, forested with spruce, is part of a nature reserve.

Forest and grassland dominate the landscape south of the Sambre-Meuse valley. Meadows, with a few orchards, occur near the Fagne depression and in the Herve Plateau, whereas forest occupies a significant portion of the land along both edges of the Ardennes and in the heart of Côtes Lorraines.

The animal population, greatly reduced by human activities, is Eurasian. Most remaining wild animals are found in the Ardennes; wild boars, wildcats, deer, and pheasant are among the more common animals of the region. A number of birds can be found in the Belgian lowlands, including sandpipers, woodcocks, snipes, and lapwings. The Anglo-Belgian Basin north of the Ardennes is home to a considerable population of muskrats and hamsters.

ETHNIC GROUPS AND LANGUAGES

The population of Belgium is divided into three linguistic communities. In the north the Flemings, who constitute more than half of Belgium's population, speak Flemish, which is equivalent to Dutch (sometimes called Netherlandic). In the south the French-speaking Walloons make up more than one-third of the country's population. About one-tenth of the people are completely bilingual, but a majority have some knowledge of both French and Flemish. The German-language region in eastern Liège province, containing a small fraction of the Belgian population, consists of several communes around Eupen

The ethnic and linguistic composition of Belgium. Encyclopædia Britannica

and Saint-Vith (Sankt-Vith). The city of Brussels comprises a number of officially bilingual communes, although the metropolitan area extends far into the surrounding Flemish and Walloon communes. The French-speaking population is by far the larger in the capital region. Bruxellois, a regionally distinct dialect influenced by both French and Flemish is also spoken by a small segment of the city's inhabitants.

During the 19th and early 20th centuries, Belgium's managerial, professional, and administrative ranks were filled almost entirely by the French-speaking segment of the population, even in Flanders. The Flemings long protested what they felt was the exclusion

FLEMING AND WALLOON

The Flemings, who constitute more than half of the Belgian population, speak Flemish (Dutch) and live mainly in the north and west. The Walloons, who make up more than one-third of the Belgian population, speak dialects of French and live in the south and east. The vast majority of both groups are Roman Catholic.

Originally, the area of Belgium was a part of Gaul in Roman times and was inhabited by Romanized Celts. Gradually the land was infiltrated by groups of Gothic Germans, until finally in the 3rd and 4th centuries CE, a new wave of Germans, the Salic Franks, began pressing down from the northeast. Eventually they pushed back the Romans and took up a line generally corresponding to the present north-south division between Flemings and Walloons, a natural line of formerly dense forests. Only later, in the 5th century, after the withdrawal of the Roman frontier garrisons, did many Franks push on southward and settle much of Gaul proper. The northern Franks retained their Germanic language (which became modern Dutch [sometimes called Netherlandic]), whereas the Franks moving south rapidly adopted the language of the culturally dominant Romanized Gauls, the language that would become French. The language frontier between northern Flemings and southern Walloons has remained virtually unchanged ever since.

This linguistic boundary is minutely demarcated by law and passes roughly east-west across north-central Belgium on a line just south of the capital city, Brussels. North of the line, all public signs and government publications must be in Flemish, which has official status; the same situation prevails for French south of the line. In Brussels, which is officially bilingual, all signs and publications must be in both languages.

Much of the history of modern Belgium consists of the struggle of the country's Flemish-speaking community to gain equal status for its language and to acquire its fair share of political influence and economic opportunity in a society that was dominated largely by Walloons after the country achieved independence in 1830. In the 20th century the Flemings were successful in obtaining legislation to further these aims, but their linguistic and other differences with the Walloons remain a source of social friction.

of the average nonbilingual Fleming from effective participation in everyday dealings concerning law, medicine, government administration, and industrial employment. The Flemings, after gradually gaining greater numerical and political strength, eventually forced reforms that established Flanders as a unilingual Flemish-speaking area, provided Flemings with access to political and economic power, and established a degree of regional autonomy. Many disputes and much rancour remain between Flemish- and French-speaking Belgians, however.

Foreign-born residents make up less than one-tenth of the population. Citizens of the EU constitute much of the foreign-born population, but there is also a large number of immigrants from other parts of the world—particularly North and Central Africa, the Middle East, and Southwest Asia.

RELIGION

The great majority of Belgians are Roman Catholic, but regular attendance at religious services is variable. Although it is marked in the Flemish region and the Ardennes, regular attendance at church has decreased in the Walloon industrial region and in Brussels. The relatively few Protestants live mostly in urban areas in Hainaut, particularly in the industrial region known as the Borinage, and in and around Brussels. Several municipalities on the north and west sides

of Brussels—notably Schaerbeek—are home to many Muslim immigrants. The country's small Jewish population is concentrated in and around Brussels and Antwerp.

SETTLEMENT PATTERNS

The ecological resources of the several natural regions and the consequent variations in land use have been major factors in determining patterns of rural settlement. The nature of the urban developments is derived mainly from the patterns of mining, manufacturing, commerce, and related enterprises throughout the country.

The population is sparse in the Ardennes region in the south, the Herve Plateau in the east, and the western Entre-Sambre-et-Meuse region in the southwest. The open landscape of maritime Flanders and the lower Schelde, intersected by dikes and canals, is dotted with farms and residential areas. Interior Flanders is a region of scattered habitation and market towns. However, Belgium is one of the world's most heavily urbanized countries, and the vast majority of its inhabitants live in cities.

In the Walloon coalfields—roughly in and to the north of the Meuse valley across south-central Belgium—coal mining, glass manufacturing, iron production, zinc metallurgy, and the chemical and electrical industries in the 19th and 20th centuries gave rise to a number of large cities with widely varying characteristics.

Liège (Flemish: Luik) has been the regional economic and cultural capital since the Middle Ages. Namur (Flemish: Namen), an ancient city that expanded significantly with industrialization, is the capital of the administrative region of Wallonia. Charleroi, the heart of a large urban industrial area, is a newer city dominated by commerce and industry. La Louvière, founded during the 19th-century industrial development, is a burgeoning metropolitan centre. The Borinage, an area of high population density without a central city, comes under the influence of the city of Mons (Flemish: Bergen).

In Flanders the ancient city of Antwerp (Flemish: Antwerpen; French: Anvers) and its metropolitan area, the second largest in the country, extend along the east bank of the Schelde. The city's port, one of the largest in Europe, is formed by the base of the estuary and the concave riverbank. The existence of the port has favoured the establishment of important and diverse industries: petroleum refining, chemical and metallurgical industries, food processing, and electronics manufacturing. The city is also well known for its diamond-cutting industry.

Ghent (Flemish: Gent; French: Gand), a historic university town, is another of Belgium's important ports. Long a centre of the textile industry, Ghent in the 20th century experienced an industrial regeneration characterized especially by steel production along the Ghent-Terneuzen Canal, connecting the port to the Schelde.

A third busy port, Zeebrugge (French: Bruges-sur-mer), is connected by canal to the inland city of Brugge (French: Bruges), meaning "bridge." Brugge is a city of medieval aspect, resplendent with cathedrals, late medieval public buildings, and ancient homes. As its name implies, the city has many bridges spanning the several canals and the canalized Reie River. Mentioned as early as the 7th century, Brugge became an important trading centre for the Hanseatic League and reached its zenith during the 15th century, when the dukes of Burgundy held court there.

Louvain (Flemish: Leuven), about 16 miles (26 km) east of Brussels, is the site of the Catholic University of Louvain (founded 1425), the first university to be established in the Low Countries. The institution was damaged severely during both world wars, but it was rebuilt, and many countries, the United States in particular, helped it to restock its libraries.

Belgium's largest city, Brussels (Flemish: Brussel; French: Bruxelles), the capital of both the country and the administrative region of Flanders, has suburbs that spread into Walloon Brabant and Flemish Brabant. It is the centre of commerce, industry, and intellectual life in Belgium. It is also a city of international importance. The headquarters of the EU and NATO are located in Brussels, infusing the city with a very multicultural and cosmopolitan air. It is home to embassies

BRUGGE: "VENICE OF THE NORTH"

Brugge (French: Bruges) is located about 10 miles (16 km) south of Zeebrugge, its port on the North Sea. Originally a landing place on the Zwijn estuary, into which the Reie River flowed, it was mentioned in the 7th century as the Municipium Brugense (a name derived from a Roman bridge over the Reie). Brugge's intricate network of canals has led many to describe the city as the Venice of the North. After it was evangelized by St. Eloi, bishop of Noyon-Tournai, the first counts of Flanders built their castle there (9th century) against Norman invaders. By the 13th century the town held a monopoly on English wool, was a leading emporium for the Hanseatic League, and, with the other "members from Flanders" (Ghent and Ypres), virtually governed the entire province. After maintaining its independence despite an attack by France in 1302, it reached its commercial zenith in the 14th century. At that time it was one of the largest and most important cities in northern Europe. As the Zwijn estuary silted up in the 15th century, the city began

Market Hall belfry towering above rooftops along the Groenerei canal, Brugge, Belgium. R. Kord/H. Armstrong Roberts

to decline as a trade centre but remained brilliant and powerful as the court of the dukes of Burgundy (counts of Flanders from 1384) and as the artistic centre of the Flemish school of painting, until the religious and political struggles of the 16th century completed its eclipse.

It remained a sleepy medieval town until the construction of the port of Zeebrugge and the cutting of a connecting canal (opened 1907) revived trade and stimulated industry and tourism. It was occupied by the Germans in World Wars I and II; the harbour of Zeebrugge was raided by the British in 1918, and blockships were sunk in the canal to deny the use of the port to German submarines.

As a rail and canal junction, Brugge depends largely on tourism, but a relatively new industrial area in the north produces ships, electronic equipment, dies, yeast, and industrial glass. Spinning, weaving, and lace making are traditional.

Medieval remains in the city include the old Market Hall (13th–15th century), with a famous 47-bell carillon in the belfry, and the Town Hall (1376–1420). The Chapel of the Holy

Aerial view of Brugge, Belgium. © Corbis

Blood (14th–16th century) contains the Chapel of St. Basil (1150) and a gold casket that is reputed to hold a few drops of Christ's blood brought from the Holy Land in 1150. Other notable churches include the Cathedral of St. Salvator (12th–16th century); the Church of Notre Dame, containing the tombs of Mary of Burgundy and her father, Charles the Bold; and the Church of Jerusalem (1428), a replica of the Church of the Holy Sepulchre. Notable among numerous museums with collections of Flemish art and history are the Memling Museum in the 12th-century Hospital of St. John, the Groeninge Museum, and the 15th-century Gruuthuse mansion. The béguinage (a retreat for secular nuns; 1245) is one of the finest in Belgium. The medieval atmosphere of Brugge lends itself to pageantry, a notable example of which is the Procession of Holy Blood (on Ascension Day).

and consulates of most of the world's countries, offices housing delegations from most of Europe's major substate regions (e.g., Catalonia and Bavaria), and more than 1,000 nongovernmental organizations associated with the United Nations. Many of the inhabitants of Brussels distance themselves from the debates between Flemish and French speakers and see themselves as living in a distinct cultural region.

DEMOGRAPHIC TRENDS

The annual growth rate of the Belgian population is very low; overall birth rates and immigration exceed death rates and emigration only slightly. Population growth rates, which were markedly higher in Flanders than in Wallonia prior to the 1980s, became nearly equivalent by the end of the 20th century. There was considerable rural-to-urban migration throughout the 20th century. The institution of policies that made Wallonia and Flanders officially unilingual regions greatly reduced migration between those two regions, but there is considerable migration within language regions. The emigration rate is low. Most of those who emigrate go to other EU countries or to the United States.

Since World War II the foreign-born population has increased at a rate higher than that of Belgian nationals, owing to continued immigration and a higher birth rate among immigrants. The largest concentrations of foreigners are found in the cities of the Walloon mining and industrial areas, in Brussels, and in Antwerp. Foreign workers are largely of Mediterranean origin (mostly Italian, Middle Eastern, and North African). A modest number of these guest workers return to their countries of origin each year.

CHAPTER 7

THE BELGIAN ECONOMY

Belgium has a free-enterprise economy, with the majority of the gross domestic product (GDP) generated by the service sector. The Belgian economy also is inextricably tied to that of Europe. The country has been a member of a variety of supranational organizations, including the Belgium-Luxembourg Economic Union (BLEU), the Benelux Economic Union, and the EU. The first major step Belgium took in internationalizing its economy occurred when it became a charter member of the European Coal and Steel Community in 1952. On January 1, 1999, Belgium also became a charter member of the Economic and Monetary Union (EMU), paving the way for the introduction of the euro, which became the country's sole currency in 2002, replacing the Belgian franc.

Historically, Belgium's national prosperity was mainly dependent on the country's role as a fabricator and processor of imported raw materials and on the subsequent export of finished goods. The country became a major steel producer in the early 19th century, with factories centred in the southern Walloon coal-mining region, particularly in the Sambre-Meuse valley. Rigorous monetary reform aided Belgium's post-World War II recovery and expansion, particularly of the Flemish light manufacturing and chemical industries that developed rapidly in the north, and Belgium became one of the first European countries to reestablish a favourable balance of trade in the postwar world. By the late 20th century, however, coal reserves in Wallonia were exhausted, the aging steel industry had become inefficient, labour costs had risen dramatically, and foreign investment (a major portion of the country's industrial assets are controlled by multinational companies) had declined.

The government, in an effort to reverse the near-depression levels of industrial output that had developed, subsidized ailing industries, particularly steel and textiles, and offered tax incentives, reduced interest rates, and capital bonuses to attract foreign investment. These efforts were moderately successful, but they left Belgium with one of the largest budget deficits in relation to gross national product in Europe. The government was forced to borrow heavily from abroad to finance foreign trade (i.e., importing of foreign goods) and to sustain its generous social welfare system. In the early 1980s the government attempted to reduce the budget deficit; the debt-to-GDP ratio decreased as tighter monetary and fiscal policies were implemented by the central bank. Moreover, in the early 1990s the government decreased its subsidy to the social security system. By the early 21st century, Belgium had diversified its sources of social security funding and succeeded in balancing its budget. Regionally, Flanders has attracted a disproportionate share of investment, but the national government has offered subsidies and incentives to encourage investment within Wallonia. Unemployment also has been less of a problem in Flanders, which has experienced significant growth in service industries, than in Wallonia, where the negative consequences of deindustrialization remain.

AGRICULTURE, FORESTRY, AND FISHING

Only a small percentage of the country's active population engages in agriculture, and agricultural activity has continued to shrink, both in employment and in its contribution to the GDP. About one-fourth of Belgium's land area is agricultural and under permanent cultivation; more than one-fifth comprises meadows and pastures. Major crops are sugar beets, chicory, flax, cereal grains, and potatoes. The cultivation of fruits, vegetables, and ornamental plants also is important, particularly in Flanders. However, agricultural activity in Belgium centres primarily on livestock; dairy and meat products constitute more than two-thirds of the total farm value.

Forage crops, barley, oats, potatoes, and even wheat are grown everywhere, but especially in the southeast. The region is one of striking contrasts: in the Condroz farms range in size from 75 to 250 acres (30 to 100 hectares), whereas in the Ardennes they are between 25 and 75 acres (10 to 30 hectares).

The open countryside of north-central Belgium—Hainaut, Flemish Brabant, Walloon Brabant, and Hesbaye (the region of rolling land southwest of Limburg)—includes pastureland as well as intensive diversified cultivation of such crops as wheat, sugar beets, and oats; local variations include orchards in northern Hesbaye. Farms, with their closed courts, range in size from 75 to 250 acres (30 to 100 hectares).

Most farms in the far north—maritime Flanders and the lower Schelde—range in size from 25 to 75 acres (10 to 30 hectares), some of which are under pasture, while the remainder are cultivated, with wheat and sugar beets again the dominant crops. Interior Flanders is devoted to grazing. Intensive cultivation is confined to gardens and small farms, which are usually smaller than 10 acres (4 hectares). Oats, rye, and potatoes are the chief crops; wheat, sugar beets, chicory, hops, flax, and ornamental plants (e.g., azaleas, roses, and begonias) also are grown in southwestern Flanders.

The planted forests of the Ardennes and the Kempenland support Belgium's relatively small forest-products industry. Growth of the forest industry after World War II has been aided by mechanization, allowing Belgium to reduce its reliance on imported timber.

Belgium's fishing industry is relatively small; almost all fish are consumed within the country. Zeebrugge and Ostend, the main fishing ports, send a modest fleet of trawlers to the North Sea fishing grounds. The harvesting of mussels is also an important industry in Belgium, with the mollusks being a popular menu item in restaurants throughout the country.

RESOURCES AND POWER

Historically, coal was Belgium's most important mineral resource. There were two major coal-mining areas. The coal in the Sambre-Meuse valley occurred in a narrow band across south-central Belgium from the French border through Mons, Charleroi, Namur, and Liège. Mined since the 13th century, these coal reserves were instrumental in Belgium's industrialization during the 19th century. By the 1960s the easily extractable coal reserves were exhausted, and most of the region's mines were closed. By 1992 mining had ceased there and in the country's other major coal-mining area, in the Kempenland (Limburg province) in northeastern Belgium. Belgium now imports all its coal, which is needed for the steel industry and for domestic heating.

During the 19th century, iron ore and zinc deposits in the Sambre-Meuse valley were heavily exploited. They, too, are now exhausted, but the refining of imported metallic ores remains an important component of Belgium's economy. Chalk and limestone mining around Tournai, Mons, and Liège, which supports a significant cement industry, is of greater contemporary importance. In addition, sands from the Kempenland supply the glass-manufacturing industry, and clays from the Borinage are used for pottery products and bricks. Stones, principally specialty marbles, also are quarried.

Belgium's water resources are concentrated in the southern part of the country. Most streams rise in the Ardennes and flow northward; three-fourths of the country's groundwater originates in the south. Since the largest concentration of population is in the north, there is a marked regional

An example of high-quality lace being hand crafted in Belgium. Steven Poh/ Shutterstock.com

heavy demands from industrial and domestic consumers. Moreover, water pollution is a serious problem. In the south a modest hydroelectric power industry has developed along fast-moving streams. However, as nuclear reactors generate more than half of Belgium's electricity, the use of water for cooling in nuclear power stations is much more significant. With the expansion of domestic and commercial needs in the late 20th and early 21st centuries, increasing attention focused on problems of water quality and supply.

MANUFACTURING

The manufacturing sector accounts for about one-sixth of the GDP. Manufacturing is the major economic activity in the provinces of East Flanders, Limburg, and Hainaut. The corridor between Antwerp and Brussels also has emerged as a major manufacturing zone, eclipsing the older industrial concentration in the Sambre-Meuse valley.

Metallurgy, steel, textiles, chemicals, glass, paper, and food processing are the dominant industries. Belgium is one of the world's leading processors of cobalt, radium, copper, zinc, and lead. Refineries, located principally in the Antwerp area, process crude petroleum. Antwerp is also known for diamond cutting and dealing. The lace made in Belgium has been internationally renowned for centuries. To combat the slow decline of this

disjunction between water supply and demand. This problem is addressed through elaborate water-transfer systems involving canals, storage basins, and pipelines. Although reasonably plentiful, existing water supplies incur

BRUSSELS LACE

Named for the Belgian capital city, Brussels lace became distinguished from other bobbin laces made in Flanders during the second half of the 17th century. Brussels laces were of high quality, popular at court, and made professionally at workshops called béguinages (often associated with convents) by unmarried women whose lives were dedicated to the work. The laces were of the non-continuous-thread technique, the richly delicate designs near-naturalistic, almost weightless, and at times breathtakingly beautiful. The ground could be a meshwork of drochel (hexagonal forms) or bars or a mixture of the two. Through the 19th century the laces became heavier, and the designs, though still beautiful, became rather crowded, frequently sprinkled with numerous dots and flourishes in keeping with the taste of the period.

The name Brussels came to include application laces and embroidered nets. From roughly 1720 a very fine, lightweight needle lace was made, in appearance like a very opulent Alençon lace, the stitches so minute that in some examples 10,000 can be counted per square inch. Examples are rare, but in 1851 needle lace was revived in the form of the immediately popular *point de gaze*, made of fine-quality cotton thread. Its packed designs incorporated roses with tiered petals, and its caskets of jewel-like filling stitches made it the prime choice for court wear and other special occasions. It was succeeded after World War I by the much heavier *point de Venise*, used mostly for table mats and runners. The quality of the bobbin laces also deteriorated as the costs of manufacture soared. A bolder bobbin lace, sometimes with needle-lace inclusions, of variable quality and known as *duchesse* was made in both Brussels and Brugge and was fashionable for collars and even dresses until the 1930s.

industry, which has been dependent on the handiwork of an aging population of skilled women, specialized schools were established in Mons and Binche to train younger workers.

Foreign investment led to considerable growth in the engineering sector of Belgium's economy in the late 20th century. The country has assembly plants for foreign automakers, as well as for foreign firms manufacturing heavy electrical goods. Moreover, Belgium has a number of important manufacturers of machine tools and specialized plastics.

FINANCE

The economic importance of the financial sector has increased significantly since the 1960s. Numerous Belgian and foreign banks operate in the country, particularly in Brussels. The National Bank, the central bank of Belgium, works to ensure national financial security, issues currency, and provides financial services to the federal government, the financial sector, and the public. The European Central Bank is now responsible for the formulation of key aspects of monetary policy. An important stock exchange was founded in Brussels in the early 19th century. In 2000 it merged with the Amsterdam and Paris stock exchanges to form Euronext—the first fully integrated cross-border equities market. Belgium has long been a target of significant foreign investment. Foreign investments in the energy, finance, and business-support sectors are of particular significance in 21st-century Belgium.

TRADE

Among Belgium's main imports are raw materials (including petroleum), motor vehicles, chemicals, textiles, and food products. Major exports include motor vehicles, chemicals and pharmaceutical products, machinery, plastics, diamonds, food, and iron and steel.

Belgium's principal trade partners are the member countries of the EU, particularly Germany, France, the Netherlands, and the United Kingdom.

SERVICES

Spurred by the expanding needs of international business and government as well as the growth of tourism, especially in western Flanders and the Ardennes, the service sector grew tremendously in the second half of the 20th century. Flanders in particular enjoyed an economic boom because of the growth of service industries. Today, the overwhelming majority of the Belgian labour force is employed in private and public services.

LABOUR AND TAXATION

After the service industries, manufacturing and construction enterprises are the largest employers. Agriculture and mining employ only a tiny percentage of the labour force. About half of Belgian workers belong to labour unions.

The Belgian government levies taxes on income as well as on

Central Liège, Belgium, cut by the Meuse River.
Photo Research International

goods and services. These taxes, along with social security contributions, provide the bulk of the national revenue. Regions and local units of government also may levy taxes.

TRANSPORTATION AND TELECOMMUNICATIONS

Belgium has an extensive system of main roads, supplemented by modern expressways that extend from Brussels to Ostend by way of Ghent and Brugge, from Brussels to Antwerp, from Brussels to Luxembourg city by way of Namur, and from Antwerp to Aachen (Germany) by way of Hasselt and Liège. Other expressways include those from Antwerp to Kortrijk by way of Ghent and from Brussels to Paris through Mons and Charleroi.

The railway network, a state enterprise, is one of the densest in the world. Brussels is the heart of the system, the centre of a series of lines that radiate outward and link the capital to other cities both inside and outside the country. The heaviest traffic is between Brussels and Antwerp.

Antwerp handles a major portion of the country's foreign trade through its port. Other important ports are Zeebrugge-Brugge, Ostend, Ghent, and Brussels. Navigable inland waterways include the Meuse and the Schelde, which are navigable throughout their length in Belgium. A canal from Charleroi to Brussels links the basins of the two main rivers through the Ronquières lock. The Albert Canal links Antwerp with the Liège region. A maritime canal connects Brugge and Zeebrugge; another connects Ghent and Terneuzen (Netherlands), on the Schelde estuary; and a third links Brussels and Antwerp.

The Brussels international airport is the centre of Belgian air traffic. Smaller international facilities are maintained at Antwerp, Liège, Charleroi, and Ostend. Partly owned by the state, an international airline, SABENA, operated from 1923 to 2001. Its place has been taken by Brussels Airlines.

Belgium's technologically advanced telecommunications network is well developed, with a number of companies offering traditional telephone, cellular telephone, cable, and other telecommunications services. Cellular telephone and Internet usage in Belgium is similar to that of other western European countries, although Belgians own fewer personal computers than their immediate neighbours.

CHAPTER 8

BELGIAN GOVERNMENT AND SOCIETY

Belgium is a constitutional monarchy. The Belgian constitution was first promulgated in 1831 and has been revised a number of times since then. A 1991 constitutional amendment, for instance, allows for the accession of a woman to the throne.

Under the terms of the Belgian constitution, national executive power is vested in the monarch and his Council of Ministers, whereas legislative power is shared by the monarch, a bicameral parliament comprising the Chamber of Representatives and the Senate, and the community and regional councils. In practice, the monarch's role as head of state is limited to representative and official functions; royal acts must be countersigned by a minister, who in turn becomes responsible for them to the parliament.

The prime minister is the effective head of government; the position of prime minister was created in 1919 and that of vice prime minister in 1961. Typically the leader of the majority party or coalition in the parliament, the prime minister is appointed by the monarch and approved by the parliament.

LOCAL GOVERNMENT

Prior to 1970 Belgium was a unitary state. An unwritten rule prevailed that, except for the prime minister, the government had to include as many Flemish- as French-speaking ministers. Tensions that had been building throughout the 20th century between the two ethnolinguistic groups led to major administrative restructuring during the 1970s, '80s, and '90s. A series of constitutional reforms dismantled the unitary state, culminating in the St. Michael's Agreement (September 1992), which laid the groundwork for the establishment of the federal state (approved by the parliament in July 1993 and enshrined in a new, coordinated constitution in 1994). National authorities now share power with executive and legislative bodies representing the major politically defined regions (Flemish: gewesten; French: régions) of Belgium—the Flemish Region (Flanders), the Walloon Region (Wallonia), and the Brussels-Capital Region—and the major language communities of the country (Flemish, French, and German). The Flemish Region—comprising the provinces of Antwerp, Limburg, East Flanders, West Flanders, and Flemish Brabant—and the Flemish Community are represented by a single council; the Walloon Region—comprising the provinces of Hainaut, Namur, Liège, Luxembourg, and Walloon Brabant—and the French Community each have a council, as do the Brussels-Capital Region and the German Community. The regional authorities have primary responsibility for the environment, energy, agriculture, transportation, and public works. They share responsibility for economic matters, labour, and foreign trade with the national government, which also retains responsibility for defense, foreign policy, and justice. The community councils have authority over cultural matters, including the use of language and education.

Farther down the administrative hierarchy are the provinces (Flemish: provincies), each of which is divided into arrondissements and further subdivided into communes (gemeenten). The provinces are under the authority of a governor, with legislative power exercised by the provincial council. The Permanent Deputation, elected from the members of the provincial council, provides for daily provincial administration. Each commune is headed by a burgomaster, and the communal council elects the deputy mayors.

JUSTICE

Judges are appointed for life by the monarch; they cannot be removed except by judicial sentence. At the cantonal, or lowest, judicial level, justices of the peace decide civil and commercial cases, and police tribunals decide criminal cases. At the district level, judicial powers are divided among the tribunals of first instance, which are subdivided into civil, criminal, and juvenile courts and commercial and labour tribunals. At the appeals level, the courts of appeal include civil, criminal, and juvenile divisions that are supplemented by labour courts. Courts of assizes sit in each province to judge crimes and political and press offenses. These are composed of 3 judges and 12 citizens chosen by lot.

The Supreme Court of Justice is composed of three chambers: civil and commercial, criminal, and one for matters of social and fiscal law and the armed forces. The last court does not deal with cases in depth but regulates the application of the law throughout all jurisdictions. The military jurisdictions judge all cases concerning offenders responsible to the army and, in time of war, those concerning persons accused of treason. The State Council arbitrates in disputed administrative matters and gives advice on all bills and decrees. The Arbitration Court, established in 1984, deals with disputes that develop between and among national, regional, and community executive or legislative authorities.

POLITICAL PROCESS

Communal and provincial elections take place every six years; regional and community council elections occur every five years; and national elections are held at least every four years. Deputies to the Chamber of Representatives are elected directly, as are certain senators, while other senators are either designated by the community councils from their ranks or selected by the rest of the Senate. Each deputy and senator has a language community and a regional affiliation.

Belgium's leading political parties were long divided into French- and Flemish-speaking wings; however, as the country moved toward federalism, the differences between these wings became more pronounced, and they became increasingly discrete organizations. The traditional parties include the Social Christians—that is, the Flemish Christian Democrats and their French counterpart, the Humanist and Democratic Center; the Socialist Party (divided into Flemish- and French-speaking branches); the Flemish Liberals and Democrats; and the French-speaking Reform Movement. Other ethnic and special-interest parties also have emerged, including French- and Flemish-speaking Green parties, Flemish separatist parties, and the right-wing National Front in Wallonia. Because representatives are elected on the basis of proportional representation, recent governments have been dominated by coalitions of the strongest parties. The Vlaams Belang, a party with a strong anti-immigrant message that succeeded the right-wing Vlaams Block, had notable electoral success in Flanders in the late 1990s and early 2000s, while the separatist New Flemish Alliance made its mark in the 2010 federal legislative elections.

All citizens age 18 and older are required to vote in national elections. They are informed of political events through the press, but, as press ownership increasingly is concentrated in fewer hands, many persons consider the medium to be unamenable to the expression of a wide range of opinions.

CATHOLIC UNIVERSITY OF LEUVEN

The original Catholic University of Leuven was founded in 1425 in Leuven (Louvain), Brabant (now in Belgium), by Pope Martin V at the behest of Duke John (Jean) IV of Brabant, who modeled its constitution after the University of Paris. In 1517 the Dutch scholar Desiderius Erasmus became involved with the founding of Leuven's Trilingual College, "the school of the new learning in Europe," for the study of Greek, Latin, and Hebrew. During the 16th century Justus Lipsius and Gerard Mercator were also on the faculty. At that time Leuven was the chief centre of anti-Reformation thought. The forces of the French Revolution suppressed the university in 1797, but in 1834 the Belgian episcopate reestablished it as a French-language, Roman Catholic university.

The university's famous library was burned during the German invasion in 1914, and a new library was built (1921–28) with American funds and books donated by many nations. The library was again destroyed by fire during the German invasion in 1940 but was subsequently restored.

In the 1930s the university began to teach some courses in Flemish. Although the Belgian government had previously forbidden the use of Flemish in universities, it changed its policy in 1932 in response to growing pressure from Belgium's sizable Flemish-speaking population. In 1969, after student riots, ethnic protests, and government upheavals, the Catholic University was reorganized into separate Flemish- and French-language divisions. Each of the two divisions was given separate legal status in 1970, and the first faculties were installed in Louvain-la-Neuve in 1972. In the one university (Katholieke Universiteit Leuven) the language of instruction is Flemish (Dutch), and its site remains in Leuven. In the other university (Université Catholique de Louvain) the language of instruction is French, and the site is the newly created town Louvain-la-Neuve ("New Louvain"), about 15 miles (24 km) south-southwest of old Leuven.

Radio and television often organize debates and discussions that provide political information. In spite of these efforts, a degree of disaffection exists among the citizens with regard to politics. Conflicts over the competencies of different levels of government life tend to foster this sense of antipathy and often serve to heighten tensions between Flemish- and French-speaking Belgians.

SECURITY

The Belgian armed forces include land, air, and naval components, as well as reserve forces and a medical service. Belgium was one of the founding members of the military alliance NATO, and the organization's headquarters are located in Brussels. A federal police force and numerous local police forces carry out law enforcement in the country.

Arenberg Castle, Catholic University of Leuven. Evgeny Murtola/Shutterstock.com

HEALTH AND WELFARE

A great improvement in health conditions after World War II was due as much to the programs of social insurance, covering nearly the entire population, as to advances in medical science. In addition to the many hospitals, hundreds of centres offer specialized help in medical, psychological, and geriatric areas as well as in physical rehabilitation. Under a 1925 statute, each commune has a commission of public assistance that is represented on the communal council and provides aid to the indigent. Belgium's welfare system, though comprehensive, has placed great strain on the national budget.

HOUSING

Building is encouraged in a number of ways, including government-guaranteed mortgage loans that have low interest rates. Most Belgians prefer to live in single-family houses. The rate of home ownership in Belgium is among the highest in western Europe, though the cost of housing increased significantly in the late 1990s and early 2000s. There are some shortages in housing supply, but the situation is not acute. The National Housing Society oversees public housing construction for low-income families. The state also sponsors programs to alleviate slum conditions.

EDUCATION

Freedom of education is a constitutional guarantee in Belgium, but conflicts between public and confessional (i.e., Roman Catholic) schools date almost to the founding of the kingdom and remain a delicate problem within the social fabric. A dual system of state-run schools and religious "free" schools (the latter are nearly all Roman Catholic) exists on the primary and secondary levels, with the "free" schools subsidized by the state to compensate for the abolition of fees in 1958. The language of instruction is either French, Flemish, or German, depending on the region. Secondary schools are graded into two types, one that is staffed by graduates from teachers colleges and offers technical and vocational education and another that is staffed by university graduates and offers either a classical or a modern curriculum.

In addition to numerous specialized institutions for advanced training, Belgium has several universities. The Catholic University of Leuven (Louvain; 1425) and the Free University of Brussels (1834), both formerly bilingual, were each divided into independent Flemish- and French-speaking universities (thereby creating four universities) in 1969–70. The University of Liège (1817) and the University of Mons-Hainaut (1965) teach in French, and Ghent University (1817) teaches in Flemish.

CHAPTER 9

BELGIAN CULTURAL LIFE

Belgium's long and rich cultural and artistic heritage is epitomized in the paintings of Pieter Bruegel, the Elder, Jan van Eyck, Hans Memling, Dieric Bouts, Peter Paul Rubens, René Magritte, and Paul Delvaux; in the music of Josquin des Prez, Orlando di Lasso, Peter Benoit, and César Franck; in the dramas of Maurice Maeterlinck and Michel de Ghelderode and the novels of Georges Simenon and Marguerite Yourcenar; in the mapmaking of Gerardus Mercator; and in the many palaces, castles, town halls, and cathedrals of the Belgian cities and countryside.

The federal structure of Belgium encourages the drawing of cultural distinctions among and between Flanders, Wallonia, and the small German-speaking minority—institutionalized as formally empowered "communities." Through educational initiatives, language promotion, and patronage of the arts, these communities see to it that regional cultures do not lose their distinctiveness. In addition, some regions are more strongly associated with particular cultural attributes than others. Flanders is particularly noted for its visual art, and various schools of painting have arisen there. In music, avant-garde tendencies have become influential in Brussels, Liège, Ghent, and Antwerp, while Hainaut remains the centre of the classical and popular traditions.

DAILY LIFE AND SOCIAL CUSTOMS

Belgium's strong tradition of fine cuisine is expressed in its large number of top-rated restaurants. The country is known for moules frites (mussels served with french fries) as well as waffles, a popular snack item. Belgian chocolate is renowned around the world and may be considered a cultural institution. Chocolatiers such as Neuhaus, Godiva, and Leonidas, among others, are internationally acclaimed for their truffles and candies sold in small, distinctive cardboard boxes. Chocolate is one of Belgium's main food exports, with the majority being shipped to other EU countries.

Beer is Belgium's national beverage; the country has several hundred breweries and countless cafés where Belgians enjoy a great array of local brews, including the famed Trappist and lambic varieties. While the reputation of Belgian beer is often overshadowed by that of its larger neighbour, Germany, the brewing and consuming of beer within the country is a cultural institution in and of itself. Most beers have particular styles of glasses in which they are served, and a variety of seasonal brews are synonymous with various holidays and celebrations. It is also common for special brews to be created for occasions such as weddings, a tradition that is reported to have begun in the early 1900s, when nearly every village had a brewery. In many small Belgian villages, the brewer was also the mayor.

Festivals focus on regional history and the celebration of the seasons. In the Walloon area there are joyous spring festivals, such as the carnivals of Binche and Stavelot; summer festivals, such as the procession of giants at Ath and the dragon battle in Mons; and the winter festivals of St. Nicholas, Christmas, and the New Year. In Flanders these festivals have become folkloric celebrations

PIETER BRUEGEL, THE ELDER

Not much is known of the early life of Pieter Bruegel, the Elder (born c. 1525, probably Breda, duchy of Brabant—d. September 5/9, 1569, Brussels), but in 1551 he set off for Italy, where he produced his earliest signed painting, *Landscape with Christ and the Apostles at the Sea of Tiberias* (c. 1553). Returning to Flanders in 1555, he achieved some fame with a series of satirical, moralizing prints in the style of Hiëronymus Bosch, commissioned by an Antwerp engraver. He is best known for his paintings of Netherlandish proverbs, seasonal landscapes, and realistic views of peasant life and folklore, but he also took a novel approach to religious subject matter, portraying biblical events in panoramic scenes, often viewed from above. He had many important patrons; most of his paintings were commissioned by collectors. In addition to many drawings and engravings, about 40 authenticated paintings from his enormous output have survived. His sons, Peter Brueghel the Younger and Jan, the Elder Brueghel (both of whom restored to the name the *h* their father had abandoned), and later imitators carried his style into the 18th century.

with a religious or historical character. Notable events include the Festival of Cats in Ypres, which is held once every three years and commemorates a practice from earlier centuries of tossing cats from the tower of the Cloth Hall to keep their numbers under control. (The cats helped guard textiles kept in the Cloth Hall from rodents, but once the textiles were sold, the cats tended to proliferate.) Today the festival recreates this practice with toy cats and, more generally, celebrates cats as a species. Another popular event is the Procession of the Holy Blood; held in Brugge, it is the modern continuation of a medieval tradition of parading through the city with what was said to be the coagulated blood of Christ—taken from his body after the descent from the cross. According to legend, the relic at the centre of the ceremony was brought back to Brugge by Thierry, the crusading count of Flanders, in the 12th century. Finally, marionette shows survive in the Toone Theatre in

Participants known as Gilles perform during the Carnival of Binche. Benoit Doppagne/AFP/Getty Images

Brussels. The traditional folk culture is in marked contrast to modern forms of popular culture, which, as everywhere in the West, are dominated by television, cinema, and popular music.

THE ARTS

Belgium's rich heritage makes it an artistic centre of considerable importance. The paintings of the Flemish masters are on display in museums and cathedrals across the country; Belgium's contribution to Art Nouveau is clearly evident in the Brussels cityscape, and folk culture is kept alive in a variety of indoor and outdoor museums. Among the most celebrated examples of Art Nouveau architecture in Brussels are the home of architect Baron Victor Horta, which is now a museum, and the Stoclet House,

designed by Josef Hoffmann. The latter was designated a UNESCO World Heritage site in 2009.

Belgium holds several significant annual musical events, including the Queen Elisabeth International Music Competition. Belgians also have taken a foreign musical form, American jazz, and made it very much their own. The style owes much to Antoine-Joseph Sax, the Belgian-born instrument maker who invented the saxophone. Practitioners of homegrown jazz have included cabaret singer Jacques Brel, jazz harmonica player Jean ("Toots") Thielemans, and the legendary Django Reinhardt, a Belgian-born Rom (Gypsy) who mastered a guitar style that wedded Duke Ellington to flamenco. Belgium teems with jazz clubs and bistros and hosts a number of respected jazz festivals each

DJANGO REINHARDT

Django Reinhardt (born Jean-Baptiste Reinhardt, January 23, 1910, Liberchies, Belgium—died May 16, 1953, Fontainebleau, France) was of Gypsy parentage and traveled through France and Belgium as a boy and young man, learning to play the violin, guitar, and banjo. The loss of the use of two fingers of his left hand after a caravan fire in 1928 did not impair his remarkable aptitude for the guitar. In 1934 he became coleader, with violinist Stéphane Grappelli, of the Quintette du Hot Club de France, a group whose many records are greatly prized by connoisseurs. In his only visit to the United States, in 1946, Reinhardt toured with the Duke Ellington orchestra.

For most of his career Reinhardt played in the swing style that reached its peak of popularity in the 1930s. Perhaps his most lasting influence on jazz was the introduction of solos based on melodic improvisation, at a time when guitarists generally played chorded solos. His inimitable improvisations, particularly those in slow tempos, were often a curious but beguiling blend of Gypsy and jazz sounds. Among his guitar compositions transposed into orchestral works are "Nuages" and "Manoir des mes rêves."

year. Belgians also played an important role in the creation of techno music late in the 20th century.

Literary works produced in Flanders have a style peculiar to the region, whereas in the Walloon area and in Brussels most authors write for a larger French readership that is inclined especially toward Parisian tastes. Moreover, some works that are thought of as French are written by Belgian authors living in France, and others are by writers living in Belgium who are considered French.

In Belgium the comic strip is a serious and well-respected art form that has become part of the country's modern cultural heritage. Children throughout the world became familiar with the adventures of the boy hero Tintin, who was created by Hergé (Georges Rémi) and was featured in a comic strip that first appeared in 1929. The Smurfs, created in 1958 by Peyo (Pierre Culliford),

TINTIN

One of the world's most familiar comic book characters, Tintin is something of a Belgian national treasure. Accompanied by his faithful fox terrier, Snowy (Milou in the original French), Tintin, an intrepid young investigative reporter, began traveling the world in the service of truth and justice in 1929. In his debut story, *Tintin in the Land of the Soviets*, which began as a serial in the children's weekly *Le Petit Vingtième*, Tintin travels to Soviet Russia, exposing nefarious dealings by the Bolsheviks. In subsequent tales his inquisitive spirit takes him to the Belgian Congo, China, the United States, the high seas, and even the Moon. In humorous adventures that often reflected contemporary events, Tintin explored an increasingly complex world and always stood up for what was right.

Tintin and his creator, Hergé (pen name of Belgian cartoonist Georges Rémi), have been subject to controversy over the years. The first few Tintin stories were viewed by some as expressing a simplistic, prejudiced, at times even racist view of the world. Later in life, Hergé reworked some elements to be less offensive. Beginning with *The Blue Lotus* (1936), in which Tintin traveled to China, Hergé committed to intensively researching the stories in order to accurately portray locales and characters. The cartoonist's decision to continue publishing *Tintin* in a German-approved newspaper throughout the Nazi occupation of Belgium was viewed in some corners as collaboration, although the stories were largely apolitical.

When Hergé died in 1983, the 24th album in the Tintin series had been only roughly sketched. The unfinished volume was published posthumously. At the beginning of the 21st century, Tintin remained a beloved character, his stories having been translated into more than 80 languages. In June 2009 a museum dedicated to the work of Hergé and the character Tintin opened in Louvain-la-Neuve, Belgium. *The Adventures of Tintin* (2011), an animated film directed by Steven Spielberg, was among several screen adaptations of the series.

became world famous as a television cartoon series. Brussels is home to a large comic-strip museum that attracts visitors from throughout Europe.

CULTURAL INSTITUTIONS

The Belgian artistic heritage is represented in major museums in Brussels, Ghent, Brugge, Antwerp, Charleroi, and Liège. Traditional art and architecture are preserved in a large outdoor museum near Hasselt. The most extensive collection of Central African art in the world is housed in a museum in Tervuren, a suburb of Brussels. The National Orchestra and the National Opera in Brussels enjoy world fame. The Museum of Musical Instruments, also in Brussels, has a fine collection. War monuments at Waterloo, Ypres, and Bastogne, among others, attract

EDDY MERCKX

Belgian champion bicycle racer Eddy Merckx (born Edouard Louis Joseph Merckx, June 17, 1945, Meensel-Kiezegem, Belgium) is arguably the greatest professional rider ever. In a professional career stretching from 1965 to 1978, he recorded 445 victories in 1,585 races. During his peak years (1969–75), he won some 35 percent of the races he entered. Because the focus of the sport has become specialized since Merckx's era—the stars of one-day classics do not usually shine in multiday stage races, and vice versa—nobody is likely to approach his total wins. He was nicknamed "the Cannibal" for his voracious appetite for victories.

Merckx won the men's amateur division of the Union Cycliste Internationale (UCI) Road World Championships, also known as the World Cycling Championships, in 1964. With 80 wins as an amateur, he turned professional the next year and won the open (professional) division of the UCI Road World Championships in 1967, 1971, and 1974. He was highly successful in the three great stage races, winning the Vuelta a España (1973), the Giro d'Italia (1968, 1970, 1972–74), and the Tour de France (1969–72, 1974). He also won lesser stage races such as the Tour of Switzerland, the Dauphiné-Libéré, and Paris-Nice.

Merckx was a strong climber, winning the polka-dot jersey of the Tour de France's "King of the Mountains" in 1969 and 1970, and a formidable time trialist, breaking the world record for distance covered in a one-hour ride in 1972. Moreover, Merckx set a record for the most days as leader of the Giro (72) and of the Tour de France (96).

Merckx also excelled in the great one-day classics, winning Milan-San Remo (1966–67, 1969, 1971–72, 1975–76), Paris-Roubaix (1968, 1970, 1973), Liège-Bastogne-Liège (1969, 1971–73, 1975), the Tour of Flanders (1969, 1975), the Amstel Gold Race (1973, 1975), and the Tour of Lombardy (1971–72).

After retiring as a racer in 1978, Merckx opened a bicycle factory near Brussels that designs and supplies custom bicycles, including those for several professional teams.

visitors and history buffs to Belgium from around the world.

SPORTS AND RECREATION

If Belgians could play only one sport, it probably would be football (soccer). The Royal Belgian Football Association encompasses thousands of teams and clubs. Belgian's national team, known as the Red Devils, has long been a power in international competitions. Cycling, too, has numerous enthusiasts, many inspired by the example of Eddy Merckx, who dominated international cycling during the 1960s and '70s, winning the Tour de France and the Giro d'Italia five times each.

Belgium also has produced a number of Olympians, including Hubert van Innis, who won six medals in archery events at the 1920 games; Ulla Werbrouck and Robert van der Walle, who dominated women's and men's judo in the later 20th century; and swimmer Frederik Deburghgraeve, who set a world record and won a gold medal in the men's 100-metre breaststroke at the 1996 Olympic Games in Atlanta.

For daily recreation, most of the major cities have accessible parks. The Ardennes and the North Sea coast are major destinations for Belgians on vacation.

MEDIA AND PUBLISHING

The many daily newspapers published in Belgium are controlled by press consortiums. Among the most influential and widely read newspapers are *Le Soir*, *De Standaard*, and *Het Laatste Nieuws*. A German-language daily, *Grenz-Echo*, is published in Eupen. The majority of newspapers have some political affiliation, but only those of the socialist press are linked to a political party. Belgium has several magazines, but these face strong foreign competition.

Radio broadcasting was born in Belgium. As early as 1913, weekly musical broadcasts were given from the Laeken Royal Park. Radio-Belgium, founded in 1923, was broadcasting the equivalent of a spoken newspaper as early as 1926. Belgian Radio-Television of the French Community (Radio Télévision Belge Francophone; RTBF), which broadcasts in French, and the Flemish Radio and Television Network (Vlaamse Radio en Televisie; VRT, formerly Belgian Radio and Television [BRTN]), in Flemish, were created as public services. Both are autonomous and are managed by an administrative council. Radio Vlaanderen International (RVI) serves as an important voice of the Flemish community in Belgium.

CHAPTER 10

BELGIUM: PAST AND PRESENT

After the Burgundian regime in the Low Countries (1363–1477), the southern provinces (whose area roughly encompassed that of present-day Belgium and Luxembourg) as well as the northern provinces (whose area roughly corresponded to that of the present-day Kingdom of the Netherlands) had dynastic links with the Austrian Habsburgs and then with Spain and the Austrian Habsburgs together. Later, as a consequence of revolt in 1567, the southern provinces became subject to Spain (1579), then to the Austrian Habsburgs (1713), to France (1795), and finally in 1815 to the Kingdom of the Netherlands. While Luxembourg remained linked to the Netherlands until 1867, Belgium's union with the Netherlands ended with the 1830 revolution. Belgian nationality is generally considered to date from this event. Throughout the long period of foreign rule, the southern part of the Low Countries generally preserved its institutions and traditions, and only for a short interval, under the First French Republic and Napoleon, could integration with an alien system be enforced.

The Burgundian period, from Philip II (the Bold) to Charles the Bold, was one of political prestige and economic and artistic splendour. The "Great Dukes of the West," as the Burgundian princes were called, were effectively considered national sovereigns, their domains extending from the Zuiderzee to the Somme. The urban and other textile industries, which had developed in the Belgian territories since the 12th century, became under the Burgundians the economic mainstay of northwestern Europe.

The death of Charles the Bold (1477) and the marriage of his daughter Mary to the archduke Maximilian of Austria proved fatal to the independence of the Low Countries by bringing them increasingly under the sway of the Habsburg dynasty. Mary and Maximilian's grandson Charles became king of Spain as Charles I in 1516 and Holy Roman emperor as Charles V in 1519. In Brussels on October 25, 1555, Charles V abdicated the Netherlands to his son, who in January 1556 assumed the throne of Spain as Philip II.

THE SPANISH NETHERLANDS

Under Spanish rule, discontent increased in the Netherlands and revolution broke out in 1567, but the union between the south and the north could not be maintained after the first years of conflict.

The formation of the Union of Arras (January 6, 1579) by the conservative Catholic provinces of Artois and Hainaut (fearing the dominance of more urban, more commercial, and therefore more progressive provinces) enabled the Spanish commander Alessandro Farnese to resume war against the rebellious Protestants. William I (of Orange) emerged as the leader of the latter group, supported by the Union of Utrecht (January 23, 1579), and rallied the numerous provinces that opposed a return to Spanish rule. After a series of

sieges, however, Farnese made himself master of many towns in the southern part of the country and finally, on August 17, 1585, recaptured Antwerp, which had closed its gates to rebels and government forces alike. Antwerp's surrender incited the still resisting northern provinces to close the Schelde River to foreign shipping. From this time onward, the whole of the southern part of the Netherlands once more recognized Philip II as its sovereign. In 1598 Philip II granted the sovereignty of the Netherlands to his daughter Isabella Clara Eugenia and her husband, Archduke Albert VII of Austria.

The United Provinces of the north, also known as the Dutch Republic, were never recovered, and in 1609 Albert was even forced to join them in a 12-year truce. He died in 1621, the same year that the war was resumed. Isabella was, from that time on, nothing more than a governor-general. During the resumed course of the war (1621–48), the region to the east of the Meuse, northern Brabant, and Zeeland were lost. Philip IV of Spain agreed to the new northern boundary of the Spanish Netherlands in the Peace of Westphalia (1648). Hostilities between France and Spain persisted, marked by further losses of territory on the southern border (Artois in 1640 and parts of Flanders in the later 17th century).

ADMINISTRATION

The government of the Spanish Netherlands, though not independent, enjoyed a large degree of autonomy. A governor-general, usually a member of the Spanish royal family, represented the king in Brussels. Local leaders held most positions on the three councils that assisted the governor (the Council of State, the Privy Council, and the Council of Finances). The president of the Privy Council became a kind of prime minister; although holders of this office did not hesitate to show independence of Madrid in order to protect their interests, they remained supporters of absolutism, regularly asserting the authority of the royal government at the expense of regional and local rights. After 1664 the Council of Finances, under its chief official, the treasurer-general, began to function as a sort of ministry of economic affairs. The councils exercised considerable autonomy domestically. With respect to foreign policy, however, they were controlled less by the governor-general than by a Spanish official in Brussels called the secretary of state and war. In Madrid there was a council of state for the Netherlands made up of natives of the Belgian provinces.

The bishopric of Liège (in present-day eastern Belgium) was ruled as a separate principality by its prince-bishops, as had been the case since the Middle Ages. During the revolt against Spain, Liège maintained a strict neutrality and continued to do so through most of the 17th and 18th centuries. Its institutional development paralleled that of the neighbouring regions.

The most important of various representative bodies in the Spanish Netherlands were the provincial estates or assemblies. Their authority to levy and collect taxes enabled them to ensure that a considerable portion of the revenue was spent within the country. A permanent deputation drawn from the estates supervised public works. The States General, consisting of delegates from all the provincial estates, had enjoyed great influence before and during the revolt against Spain. From that time their role diminished, and after 1632 the States General no longer met. Regionalism, deep-rooted in the provinces during the 16th century, gave way in the 17th century to a wider unity. The aristocratic provincial governors revolted against the government's centralizing policy in the early 1630s but were forced to flee the country for lack of urban support. By 1700 only Hainaut, Luxembourg, Namur, Limburg, and south Gelderland, all of which had proved their loyalty, still had provincial governors.

The supreme authority in judicial matters was the Great Council of Malines, founded in 1504. This body, however, had to defend its jurisdiction against the encroachments of the Privy Council. The provincial courts of justice were the councils of Flanders, Brabant, Namur, Luxembourg, southern Gelderland, Hainaut, and Artois (until 1659). The unique autonomy of the Council of Brabant had been granted by the king in conformity with the provincial liberties of that region. Nevertheless, after 1603 the king was represented in Brabant by financial officials under a procurer-general. In addition to their judicial duties, all these magistrates had increasing administrative functions.

Nearly constant warfare made the administration of the country increasingly difficult. Foreign troops manned the fortresses of Antwerp, Ghent, Ostend, and Charleroi, and other armed forces were raised locally. Government finances, weakened by the loss of revenues from the northern provinces, suffered still further from the enormous military expenditures.

ECONOMIC DEVELOPMENTS

The revolt against Spain in 1567 and the military campaigns it provoked in the following years were detrimental to industrial activity in the southern provinces. Moreover, the Spanish reconquest of the territory caused a major emigration of merchants and skilled artisans. Amsterdam replaced Antwerp as the chief trading centre of Europe. Many towns facing industrial decline reacted by restructuring their economic bases. Antwerp fostered new enterprises in silk weaving, diamond processing, and the production of fine linen, furniture, and lace; in addition, it resuscitated many old export products, such as musical instruments, tapestries, embroidery, and brass. Although English competition had crippled the Flemish woolen industry, Ghent developed a specialization in luxury fabrics, and Brugge in cloth for everyday use.

From the end of the 16th century on, import and export duties provided a new source of revenue. Taxes on foreign trade originated from permits allowing commerce with the rebellious United Provinces of the north. By the middle of the 17th century, these taxes had become real customs tariffs. The financial problems of the government also made the sale of public offices a common practice.

The commercial revitalization of the southern Low Countries, particularly of Antwerp, was gradual, but it no doubt partly explains the flourishing artistic life during the period. This was chiefly evident in the works of the Flemish school of 17th-century painters—among them Peter Paul Rubens, Anthony Van Dyck, and Jacob Jordaens. The ongoing Counter-Reformation stimulated demand for art in the triumphant Baroque style. Rubens, court painter to Isabella and Archduke Albert, made Antwerp one of the cultural capitals of Europe. In the area of scholarship, the Bollandists, a group of Antwerp Jesuits, made valuable contributions to historical methodology.

The Peace of Westphalia (1648), which ended the Eighty Years' War between Spain and the Dutch and the German phase of the Thirty Years'

War, stimulated economic competition between the countries of northern Europe. As a result, Flemish textile manufacture once again shifted from the towns to the countryside, where production costs were lower. In addition, the burgeoning bureaucracies and new mercantilist policies of rival capitals attracted many Flemish artisans. Emerging fashions abroad, particularly the Enlightenment Classicism and colonial exoticism of France and England, were soon to overtake the Baroque style of the Spanish Netherlands.

THE AUSTRIAN NETHERLANDS

In 1700 the Spanish Habsburg dynasty died out with Charles II, and a new conflict with France arose. By the Treaty of Utrecht (1713), ending the War of the Spanish Succession, the territory comprising present-day Belgium and Luxembourg (the independent principality of Liège not included) passed under the sovereignty of the Holy Roman emperor Charles VI, head of the Austrian branch of the house of Habsburg.

Under the Austrians, as under the Spanish Habsburgs, the southern Netherlands enjoyed political autonomy. The Austrian government initially modernized the Spanish institutions internally by introducing a new working spirit and more efficient administrative methods. To a greater degree than under Spanish rule, appointments to public offices depended upon competence and dedication. Apart from attempting to subject the provinces and the class-ridden society to absolute imperial power, the Austrian government focused in particular on rationalizing public finances at all levels, on the formation of a dynamic, well-documented bureaucracy, and on the improvement of the country's infrastructure.

WAR OF THE SPANISH SUCCESSION

Habsburg Charles II had named the Bourbon Philip, duke d'Anjou, as his successor as the ruler of Spain, but when Philip took the throne as Philip V, his grandfather Louis XIV invaded the Spanish Netherlands. The former anti-French alliance from the War of the Grand Alliance was revived in 1701 by Britain, the Dutch Republic, and the Holy Roman emperor, who had been promised parts of the Spanish empire by earlier treaties of partition (1698, 1699). The English forces, led by the duke of Marlborough, won a series of victories over France (1704–09), including the Battle of Blenheim, which forced the French out of the Low Countries and Italy. The imperial general, Eugene of Savoy, also won notable victories. In 1711 conflicts within the alliance led to its collapse, and peace negotiations began in 1712. The war concluded with the Peace of Utrecht (1713), which marked the rise of the power of Britain at the expense of both France and Spain, and the Treaties of Rastatt and Baden (1714).

Emperor Charles VI attempted to relieve the economic distress in the southern Netherlands by founding the Ostend Company (1722) to trade with Asia, but England and the United Provinces forced him after a few years to abandon the project. At the death of Charles VI in 1740, the southern Netherlands passed to his daughter Maria Theresa. The War of the Austrian Succession, however, resulted in a new French occupation in 1744. Austrian rule was restored by the Treaty of Aix-la-Chapelle (1748).

The regime of the empress Maria Theresa of Austria enjoyed popularity as the economic situation began to improve again toward the middle of the 18th century. As in contemporary England, an increase in agricultural productivity stimulated a population increase, especially in rural areas. This, in turn, spurred the development of various industries. The agricultural transformation occurred mainly on the small farms of Flanders; one of its main features was the spread of potato cultivation, which added an important element to the diet of the rural population. In addition, in the French-speaking part of the country, a number of landed proprietors invested in mining enterprises, notably in the area between the Sambre and the Meuse rivers, which belonged to the principality of Liège. In the southern Netherlands, urban merchants and manufacturers had more in common with the rural landowning class than was usual in continental European countries in the 18th century. As in the case of Britain, this created an atmosphere favourable to the development of industrial capitalism. During this period Ghent, Antwerp, and Tournai had factories with more than 100 workers; wages, however, were poor. Verviers, in the principality of Liège, was an important centre for woolen manufactures, Ghent for cotton goods.

After 1750 the influence of the Enlightenment permeated government policy in the domains of demography, social relief, employment, public health, education, religion, culture, and art, mainly at the expense of the Roman Catholic Church. Religious suppression and administrative reforms, sponsored by Maria Theresa's son and successor, the emperor Joseph II, caused great dissatisfaction among the upper classes. The Austrian government was no longer inclined to maintain the remnants of feudal privilege. Reforms deepened to include replacement of the traditional provinces and their aristocracies by districts and newly appointed intendants. The proposal to suppress simultaneously the central councils and the provincial courts of justice constituted a clear threat to provincial autonomy. The governor-general of the Austrian Netherlands was reluctant to enforce the edicts involved, but other leading members of the administration, including the emperor's minister plenipotentiary, insisted upon the abolishment of the traditional bodies.

In 1789, stirred by the outbreak of revolution in neighbouring France, conservatives led by Henri van der Noot and progressives led by Jean-François Vonck

BRABANT REVOLUTION

Centred in the province of Brabant, the Brabant Revolution was precipitated by the comprehensive reforms of the Holy Roman emperor Joseph II (reigned 1765–90); these violated various medieval charters of provincial and local liberties, including Brabant's Joyeuse Entrée, which was abrogated by the emperor in 1789. The revolutionaries were at first successful in driving the Austrian forces out of the provinces. The revolutionary vanguard, which consisted of two groups—the conservative Statists, led by Henri van der Noot, and the progressive Vonckists, led by Jean-François Vonck—issued a republican declaration of independence on January 11, 1790. The Vonckists were dissatisfied with the constitution, which called for a loose confederation similar to that of the Dutch Republic; they were soon outlawed by the more popular Statists. The Brabant Revolution, which was largely a middle-class affair, was crushed by Austrian forces at the end of the year, but it inspired the Belgian quest for independence in succeeding decades.

united in opposition to the emperor and defeated an Austrian force at Turnhout. After their common victory, conservatives and progressives came into conflict. The conservatives, or Statists, in the end gained the upper hand and made a triumphant entry into Brussels. This "Brabant Revolution" (so called because most of its leaders came from Brabant) had widespread support in the towns. The peasants, on the other hand, had little in common with the middle-class revolutionaries and generally supported the Austrians. Thus, when Leopold II, successor to Joseph II, decided to reestablish imperial authority in 1790, he encountered no opposition from the mass of the people. On December 2, 1790, imperial troops reoccupied Brussels.

The discontented Statists now looked to revolutionary France for support, but enthusiasm waned when it became clear that a French military victory was the prelude to annexation. On October 1, 1795, the French National Convention voted to annex the southern Netherlands and the principality of Liège, where a revolution against the prince-bishop had prepared the country for assimilation into the French Republic. Thenceforth, the territory of Liège was amalgamated with the Belgian provinces.

FRENCH ADMINISTRATION

Under French rule there was no autonomy as there had been under the Spanish and Austrian regimes. The administration was centralized, aristocratic privileges abolished, and the church persecuted. Military conscription measures provoked a peasants' revolt (1798–99), but repression was extremely harsh. Under the Napoleonic consulate and empire (1799–1814), the position of the clergy was regulated by a concordat with the papacy.

Further changes included introduction of the French civil code and the decimal metric system and the reopening of the Schelde River to maritime traffic to and from the harbour of Antwerp.

The period of the Napoleonic empire may be considered the beginning of the Industrial Revolution in Belgium. Only at the very end of the 18th century, with the prospects of a wider market and under Napoleon's encouragement, did mechanization (i.e., the Industrial Revolution in its strictest sense) begin in the textile sector. Mechanization quickly made Ghent, with its cotton mills, and Verviers, with its woolen industry, the leading textile centres of the country. The coal and metal industries of Hainaut (under French rule, the *département* of Jemappes) and Liège also flourished. From the beginning of the 18th century, the coal industry had expanded production with the help of the Newcomen pump and systematically extended its export markets to France. Annexation of the Belgian provinces by France opened the market still further, hastening the modernization process in which Belgium already led the continent.

THE KINGDOM OF THE NETHERLANDS

After the defeat of Napoleon, the Allied powers were determined not to leave the Belgian territories in the hands of France. Under the influence of Great Britain, it was decided that the territories would be united in a single state with the old republic of the United Provinces, thus to constitute a better barrier against French expansion than that of 1715. The Kingdom of the Netherlands, the existence of which was confirmed by the Congress of Vienna (June 1815), was thus established for the convenience of Europe, regardless of the wishes of the Belgians and the Dutch. Prince William of Orange ascended the throne on March 16, 1815, under the title William I; he was crowned September 27.

The two parts of the Netherlands, which had been one country until the 16th century and were now reunited, had developed in markedly different ways during the two intervening centuries. The north was commercial and the south increasingly industrial; the north was Protestant and Flemish- (Dutch-) speaking and the south Roman Catholic and partly French-speaking (the elite was entirely French-speaking). Under the Dutch house of Orange, the north was to be predominant. Dutch, sometimes called Netherlandic, became the official language of the new kingdom; moreover, the fundamental law gave Belgium and Holland the same number of representatives in the States General, in spite of the fact that the population of Belgium was nearly twice that of the former United Provinces. Belgian representatives, members of the nobility, rejected the constitution, but it was promulgated by the king over their objections.

William I encouraged the industrialization of the south, commissioning the construction of new roads and canals and the establishment of new commercial and financial companies; he also

extended subsidies to promising industrial enterprises, frequently from his own
private fortune. In the beginning, the
favourable economic situation reinforced
the king's popularity among the middle
class. The mechanized textile industries
of Ghent and Verviers continued their
progress, while the modern coal mines
and forges of Liège and Hainaut prospered. Antwerp's role as an international
port was expanding rapidly.

King William I also created three
state universities: Ghent and Liège,
which were new, and Louvain, which he
put under state control to remove it from
Catholic influence. Secular academies
(athénées) were established at the secondary level, and state inspection was
mandated for church-controlled schools.
An attempt to interfere with the curriculum of the training schools for priests
(1825) brought clerical dissatisfaction
with the government to its height. In an
effort to disengage the Protestant monarch from the religious affairs of the
south, the clergy and traditional Catholic
elite began clamouring for freedom of
religion, education, and association.
This remarkable shift in mentality within
the ranks of the southern conservatives
was welcomed by the more progressive
merchants, who in their turn had grown
more critical toward the north and the
king's policy.

After 1821 the conflicting interests
of north and south also created an economic split. The commercial north,
having little industry, desired more
free trade; the industrial south sought
greater tariff protection in order to
compete against falling British export
prices. The king's unwillingness to
increase protection gave the industrial-
ists a grievance against the government.
Progressives and clericals now joined
forces. Both groups wanted to curtail the
personal power of the king in favour of
a true parliamentary system, based on
an expanded range of civil and political rights. In this new climate, Unionism
came into being in 1827, merging young
Catholics and liberals in the south into
a strong antigovernment coalition. The
king agreed to make concessions regarding matters of religion and language but
refused to relinquish his ultimate authority. This refusal generated the "Belgian
Revolution" of August–September 1830,
in the tracks of the July Revolution in
Paris the same year.

The revolutionaries at first demanded
separate administrations for the northern
and southern Netherlands. The actions of
the radical patriots in Liège, however, soon
aggravated the situation. The unyielding
attitude of the king now led to a complete
break. On September 25 a provisional
Belgian government was established,
and on October 4 it proclaimed the country's independence, a move reaffirmed by
the newly elected National Congress on
November 10. William I prepared for war,
but on December 20 the great powers
intervened, imposing an armistice on both
sides. On January 20, 1831, an international
conference in London (under the influence
of the new liberal governments in France
and Britain) recognized Belgium as an

independent, neutral state, its neutrality to be guaranteed by the European powers.

INDEPENDENT BELGIUM BEFORE WORLD WAR I

The National Congress had decided that Belgium should be a monarchy, but finding a king proved difficult. In the end, Prince Leopold of Saxe-Coburg, who was related to the British royal family and who became engaged to the daughter of the French king, was acceptable to both Britain and France. On July 21, 1831, Leopold ascended the throne, promising to support the liberal constitution, which gave the greater part of the governing power to a parliament elected by property owners. Some days later, the Dutch army invaded Belgium. The Belgians, who had no regular army, were defeated, but the London Conference agreed to intervention by the French army, which forced the Dutch to withdraw. The conference then decided to divide the provinces of Limburg and Luxembourg, assigning part to Belgium and part to the Netherlands. William I refused to accept this settlement. The Belgians, therefore, continued to occupy Dutch Limburg and Luxembourg until William finally relented in 1838. The eastern half of Luxembourg became the Grand Duchy of Luxembourg, while the western half became a Belgian province. In 1839 the Dutch government officially recognized Belgium in its borders of 1838.

In the short run, the revolution had a detrimental effect on the economy. Separation from the north resulted in the sudden loss of the large Dutch market, including the colonies. The Schelde River remained closed until 1839. The Belgian government addressed the crisis by launching a vigorous policy of internal investment. In 1835 it inaugurated a railroad line between Brussels and Malines, the first to operate on the continent. The Antwerp-Cologne line, completed in 1843, opened great prospects for the Belgo-German transit trade. In 1844 a favourable trade agreement between Belgium and the German Zollverein ("Customs Union") completed this strategy.

Private participation in the development program was encouraged. In the case of railroads, for example, the government restricted itself to the construction of main lines as an incentive for private enterprise to provide the secondary network. The modernization of the infrastructure, in turn, created a climate conducive to industrial investment. Belgian banks played a decisive role in the response, in particular the Société Générale, founded in 1822 by King William I, and the Banque de Belgique, founded in 1835 by Belgian liberals. Both companies provided extensive financing for the new mechanized sectors, especially those of the Walloon heavy industry. Converting these enterprises into limited companies, the banks sold shares to the public while holding enough shares in their own or their subsidiaries' portfolios to retain control. Through this and other measures, including extension of long- and short-term credit to developing companies and the establishment of savings banks to augment resources, the Brussels banks created a new type of financial organization, the industrial banking system, which would soon be imitated by the French, the Germans, and later the English-speaking world.

While the Walloon industrial economy expanded rapidly with the infusion of capital, the mechanized textile industry in Flanders remained less dynamic. The Brussels banks exhibited little interest in this industry in the region because it was splintered over many small family enterprises. Moreover, the Ghent cotton industry faced the formidable competition of the British, and Flemish woolen producers had lost the advantage to those of Verviers and northern France. The mechanized linen mills fared better but precipitated, along with their British counterparts, a disastrous decline in the traditional linen industry based on cottage spinning and weaving throughout rural Flanders. The crisis reached a climax with the famine of 1844–46, when poor grain harvests coincided with a potato blight. The deep impoverishment of the Flemish countryside retarded the full modernization of the region until the beginning of the 20th century.

LIBERAL DOMINANCE

After 1839, the Unionist coalition that had consolidated the revolution showed signs of falling apart. The progressives, especially, were unhappy with the growing influence of the Roman Catholic Church and with the government, which increasingly enacted the personal policy of the monarch. In 1846 middle-class anticlericals laid the foundation for a national liberal party independent of the Unionist movement, aiming in particular at the curtailment of the church's growing social position. Later, a Roman Catholic conservative party took shape in opposition. Thus, one of the ideological polarities of modern Belgian politics was born.

The first Liberal government came to power in 1847 and withstood the revolutionary shock wave that rocked Europe the following year. Electoral reforms, hastened by international circumstances, secured the long-standing political dominance of the Liberal urban bourgeoisie.

The Liberal governments broadened the free-trade policy in order to promote industrialization and commercial expansion and lifted a number of fiscal hindrances on internal trade. The great Liberal reformer Walthère Frère-Orban took special measures to reinforce Belgium's economic infrastructure: in 1850 he founded a central issuing bank (the National Bank of Belgium), in 1860 a public cooperative bank for municipal finances (the Communal Credit), and five years later a public savings bank (the General Savings Bank).

By 1863 the prosperity of the country permitted redemption of the

WALTHÈRE FRÈRE-ORBAN

An exponent of doctrinaire economic liberalism and a strong advocate of free trade, Walthère Frère-Orban (born Hubert Joseph Walthère Frère-Orban, April 24, 1812, Liège, French Empire [now in Belgium]—died January 1, 1896, Brussels, Belgium) played a prominent part in the Liberal movement while practicing law in Liège. He was sent in 1847 to the Chamber of Representatives as a member from that city. From 1847 to 1894 he served as the leading Liberal member of the lower house in addition to holding many ministerial posts. As minister of finance (1848–52), he founded the Banque Nationale, abolished the newspaper tax, reduced the postage, and modified the customs duties as a preliminary to a free-trade policy.

To facilitate negotiations for a new commercial treaty, he conceded to France a law of copyright, which proved highly unpopular in Belgium. He resigned and the rest of the Cabinet soon followed him. While serving again as finance minister in 1857, he embodied his free-trade principles in commercial treaties with Great Britain and France and abolished the *octroi* duties (local import taxes) and tolls on national roads. After becoming prime minister in 1868, he defeated a French attempt to gain control of the Luxembourg railways (1869). In his second term as prime minister, he provoked the bitter opposition of Belgium's Catholic party by establishing secular primary education (1879) and by breaking off diplomatic relations with the Vatican (1880). Although Frère-Orban grudgingly conceded an extension of the franchise (1883), the hostility of the Radicals and the discontent caused by a financial crisis resulted in the overthrow of his government in the elections of 1884. He continued to lead the Liberal opposition until 1894.

Netherlands' right to levy charges on ships entering the Schelde estuary, a right enacted in 1839. The port of Antwerp was the great beneficiary, able to compete strongly with Rotterdam (Netherlands) and Hamburg. Favourable trade agreements with France, Britain, and the Netherlands further stimulated the Belgian export and transit trade. The importation of grain was also fully liberalized, without noticeable objection from the agrarian pressure groups, as the prices of grain, rent, and land remained quite high until the 1870s.

On the political scene, the growing social influence of the church became a matter of passionate public debate. As the controversy mounted, the respective attitudes became more and more radicalized. Among the Liberals, anticlericalism frequently evolved into antireligiosity; among the Catholics, the defense of the church increasingly became a means to acquire political power. The Liberals, controlling the government, managed to curtail the church's influence in such crucial domains as public charity and public education. The church successively lost its influence in the state secondary schools and in

Walthère Frère-Orban. BAO Image Broker/ Newscom

precipitated a conservative landslide in the elections of 1884, which gave the Catholics a majority in both chambers of the parliament.

PERIOD OF CATHOLIC GOVERNMENT

Aside from the education controversy, the biggest factor in the Liberals' defeat was probably their advocacy of free trade, which was favoured by manufacturers but exposed farmers to ruinous foreign competition. In the early 1880s, when the Belgian market was flooded with American grain, the Catholic Party became the champion of the rural classes by promising to protect agriculture. It also espoused the cause of the nascent Flemish movement that sought to expand opportunities for Flemish-speaking Belgians in a country until then dominated by a French-speaking upper bourgeoisie.

The last years of the 19th century and the first of the 20th were years of social tension. In 1886 there was a disturbance among workers in Liège, followed by unrest in other industrial areas. The Catholic government of Auguste-Marie-François Beernaert suppressed this movement harshly, but, beginning in 1889, a series of laws were passed regulating workers' housing, limiting labour by women and children, and providing workmen's compensation. Because of the system of electoral property qualifications, the working class did not have the right to vote

the state universities. When the Liberal government eliminated religious education from public primary schools, the so-called School War erupted. This conflict strengthened the Catholics in their distrust of the state and prompted the development of a state-independent Catholic school network, which met with great success. The School War

CONGO FREE STATE

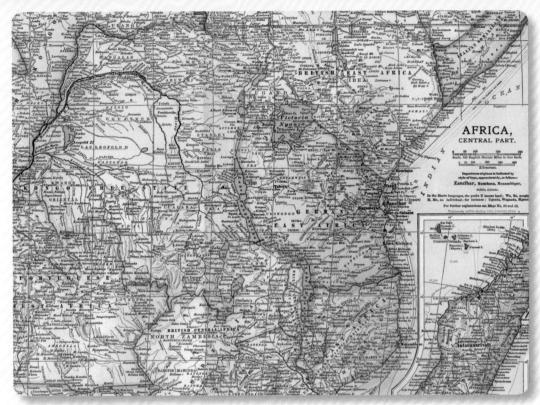

Map of Central Africa showing the Congo Free State, from the 10th edition of Encyclopædia Britannica, *published in 1902.* Encyclopædia Britannica

Occupying almost all of the Congo River basin and coextensive with the modern Democratic Republic of the Congo, the Congo Free State was created in the 1880s as the private holding of a group of European investors headed by Leopold II, king of the Belgians. The king's attention was drawn to the region during Henry (later Sir Henry) Morton Stanley's exploration of the Congo River in 1874–77. In November of 1877 Leopold formed the Committee for Studies of the Upper Congo (Comité d'Études du Haut Congo, later renamed Association Internationale du Congo) to open up the African interior to European trade along the Congo River. Between 1879 and 1882, under the committee's auspices, Stanley established stations on the upper Congo and opened negotiations with local rulers. By 1884 the Association Internationale du Congo had signed treaties with 450 independent African entities and, on that basis, asserted its right to govern all the territory concerned as an independent state. At the Berlin West Africa Conference of 1884–85, its name became the Congo Free State, and European powers recognized Leopold as its sovereign.

Leopold extended his military control over the interior in the early 1890s. The Arab slave traders of the Lualaba River region succumbed in 1890, when their leader Tippu Tib left for Zanzibar. Katanga, rich in copper and other minerals, fell in 1891 after Leopold's troops shot the ruler, Msiri. Later rebellions were repressed. Transportation links to the interior were established with the construction (1890–98) of a railway to bypass the Congo River rapids below Stanley (now Malebo) Pool; the upper course of the river and its tributaries were all navigable by steamboat.

The regime, under Leopold's unrestrained personal control, became notorious for its treatment of the Congolese. Forced labour was used to gather wild rubber, palm oil, and ivory. Beatings and lashings were used to force villages to meet their rubber-gathering quotas, as was the taking of hostages: one method employed by Leopold's agents was kidnapping the families of Congolese men, who were then coerced into trying to meet work quotas (often unattainable) in order to secure the release of their families. Rebellious actions by the Congolese elicited swift and harsh responses from Leopold's private army, the Force Publique (a band of African soldiers led by European officers), who burned the villages and slaughtered the families of rebels. Force Publique troops were also known for cutting off the hands of the Congolese, including children. This mutilation not only served as a punishment and a method to further terrorize the Congolese into submission, but it also provided a measure (the collection of severed hands) by which the soldiers could prove to their commanding officers that they were actively crushing rebellious activity. Brutality was widespread in mines and on plantations. The population of the entire state is said to have declined from some 20 million to 8 million.

The truth about Leopold's brutal regime eventually spread, largely owing to the efforts of the Congo Reform Association, an organization founded by British citizens in the early 20th century. Finally, indignation among people in Britain and other parts of Europe grew so great that Leopold was forced to transfer his authority in the Congo to the Belgian government. In 1908 the Congo Free State was abolished and replaced by the Belgian Congo, a colony controlled by the Belgian parliament.

until after the legislature revised the constitution in 1890; in 1893 universal suffrage was adopted for men age 25 and over. Though the effect of this law was weakened by giving a plural vote to electors fulfilling certain conditions of income, age, and education and to heads of families, it resulted in the election of the first Socialist deputies to the legislature. The Equality Law of 1898 made Flemish an official language, on a par with French. Social legislation benefited from the improving economic climate of the 1890s. The Flemish provinces were now fully engaged in the Industrial Revolution, the mechanization process having penetrated into the textile industries of the small towns and villages.

Belgian industry, dominated by powerful financial groups, began to assume worldwide importance and was active in Asia and Latin America, as well as in Europe. In Africa, King Leopold II acquired the Congo Free State as a personal possession in 1885. While employing brutal methods to suppress rebellion, Leopold's regime forced the Congolese to work in mines and to gather rubber, palm oil, and ivory for export. The completion in 1898 of the Matadi-Léopoldville (now Kinshasa) railroad, which facilitated access to the interior of the Congo River basin, prompted Belgian banks to push for annexation by the Belgian government. Mounting international indignation over Leopold's harsh rule of the Congo Free State eventually forced the king to hand over his control to the Belgian parliament in 1908.

The rivalry between France and Germany in the period 1870–1914 constituted a continuous danger to neutral Belgium. King Leopold II and his successor, King Albert I, sought vigorously to strengthen the Belgian armed forces but met resistance from the Belgian Catholic Party governments, which reflected the antimilitaristic sentiments of their grassroots constituency. In 1909 the army recruitment system, which until then had favoured the wealthy by allowing them to hire substitutes for military service, was finally reformed.

BELGIUM AND WORLD WAR I

As international tensions heightened during the summer of 1914, Germany made plans to besiege France by crossing Luxembourg and Belgium, despite their neutrality. The two countries refused free passage to the German troops and were invaded on August 2 and August 4, respectively. The Belgian army retired behind the Yser (IJzer) River in the west of Flanders and held this position until 1918. During the war, the Belgian government sat at Le Havre, France, while King Albert I, as commander in chief of the army, remained with his troops in unoccupied Belgium. In 1916 the Belgian Catholic Party government was enlarged to include some Socialists and Liberals. Germany attempted to profit from Flemish-Walloon antagonism in Belgium by supporting the Flemish Activists, a radical nationalist group that accepted the German offer of assistance. Most Flemings, however, were resolutely hostile to collaboration with the enemy and refused to recognize either the Council of Flanders, founded during the occupation, or the University of Ghent, changed during the occupation from a French-language to a Flemish-language institution. (Shortly after liberation, the

Belgian government made the State University of Ghent partially and then, in 1930, completely Flemish.)

THE INTERWAR PERIOD

The Treaty of Versailles (1919), ending World War I, abolished Belgium's obligatory neutrality and returned the cantons of Eupen and Malmédy to its territory. In 1920 a treaty of military assistance was signed with France. In 1921 an economic union was concluded with Luxembourg that tied the currencies of Belgium and Luxembourg together. Belgium's eastern frontier was guaranteed by the Pact of Locarno (1925). In Africa, Belgium received the mandate for Ruanda-Urundi, a part of German East Africa that Belgian colonial forces had occupied during World War I.

On the domestic front, political democratization and trade unionism, as well as social legislation and the Flemish movement, gathered momentum in postwar Belgium. Upon their return to Brussels in November 1918, the king and his government announced the introduction of absolute universal suffrage for all men over the age of 21, implying the abandonment of plural voting. The first elections held following this reform ended the Catholic domination of Belgian politics. Coalition governments, mostly Catholic-Liberal, were the rule in the interwar period. However, the Socialist Party, which had emerged during the social democracy movement of the late 19th century, became increasingly prominent. The anti-Bolshevist climate of the time, nonetheless, resulted in a persisting aversion to socialism among the middle class. The Belgian Socialists and the Liberals both opposed woman suffrage, regarding it as most advantageous to the Belgian Catholic Party. (Only in 1948 did Belgian women gain the right to vote in national elections.) Within the Belgian Catholic Party, the centre of gravity shifted during the interwar period from the old conservative camp to the Christian Democratic wing as Christian trade unionism experienced a significant upsurge. Both Christian Democrats and Socialists stimulated social legislation, especially during the years of Socialist participation in the government.

The Belgian economy of the interwar period faced serious difficulties. The war had caused a loss of 16 to 20 percent of the national wealth; not only had parts of the country been seriously damaged by combat, but the Germans had largely dismantled the Walloon heavy industry. Moreover, many Belgian investors had lost their capital in Russia, which had been transformed by revolution into the Soviet Union. Reconstruction proved difficult for other reasons as well. Germany was delinquent and inadequate in its payment of war reparations mandated by the Treaty of Versailles. The National Bank of Belgium, in an effort to redress the shortfall, advanced on behalf of the Belgian government the money needed for reconstruction. In so doing, however, the bank increased still further the money supply and the government's already massive short-term debt, which had originated from the conversion into Belgian francs of the German marks circulating in Belgium at war's end. Under such circumstances, inflation was inevitable. Soaring exchange rates generated an acute flight of capital and an imbalance of payments. Inflation also eroded the increase in real wages, which the Socialists and Christian Democrats had been able to obtain in the democratization euphoria of the immediate postwar years.

The government, which had originally hoped to restore the gold standard at its prewar parity level, soon realized that such a policy had become impossible. Increasing monetary and financial instability and fear of hyperinflation with possibly dangerous social consequences led to the formation in 1925 of a national union government, intent on restoring the gold standard but at a more realistic parity level. The reform failed, precipitating the fall of the government in March 1926. The subsequent Catholic-Liberal coalition government succeeded in restoring the gold standard on October 22, 1926, at 20 percent of its prewar level. Belgian capital returned to the country, and, because of the franc's undervaluation, much foreign capital flowed in as well. Belgian companies, infused with fresh capital,

LÉON DEGRELLE

After failing three times to pass his final law exams at the Catholic University of Leuven (Louvain), Léon Degrelle (born June 15, 1906, Bouillon, Belgium—died March 31, 1994, Málaga, Spain) entered politics. Using banking scandals and the corruption of national parties as issues, he organized the Rexist Movement in 1930, allegedly to cleanse the Roman Catholic religion of political contamination. Though originally a wing of the ruling Catholic Party, the Rexist Movement became an opposition party and, under Degrelle's guidance, elected 21 deputies to the Belgian Parliament in 1936. Subsidized by the Italian dictator Benito Mussolini, Degrelle turned the Rexists into a fascist organization. In alliance with the 16 deputies of the separatist Flemish Nationalist Party, the Rexists forced the formation of weak coalition governments in the late 1930s.

During World War II Degrelle collaborated with the German occupation forces. In August 1941 he formed and later commanded the Walloon and Flemish storm-trooper brigades that fought on the Russian front. Under his guidance the Rexists took control of local governments and newspapers in Belgium. After Belgium was liberated (September 1944) he was sentenced in absentia to death as a collaborator. Degrelle flew to Spain in the last days of the war after fighting the Soviet advance into eastern Germany. In Spain he was protected by Francisco Franco and became a Spanish citizen.

began to invest again outside Belgium, under the leadership of the mixed banks. The discovery of rich mineral deposits in the Belgian Congo made colonial development schemes increasingly attractive. Large-scale investments in southeastern and south-central Europe partly replaced the lost Russian accounts. Owing to the franc's undervaluation, the export industries in Flanders and Wallonia also were booming. The overall prosperity generated speculative excesses, particularly on the Brussels Exchange, which was now an important capital market.

The perceived neglect of and discrimination against Flemish soldiers at the Yser front during the war, coupled with the lack of official response to postwar Flemish demands, caused a marked shift to the right among many Flemings. In 1930 the Belgian government acquiesced somewhat to the pressure, making Flanders and Wallonia legally unilingual regions, with only Brussels and its surroundings remaining bilingual. The arrangement left the linguistic borders unfixed, the government's hope being that the Frenchification of central Belgium would continue and allow eventually for enlargement of the French-speaking region.

The Belgian economy was, of course, jolted by the stock market crash of 1929 in the United States, but Britain's decision two years later to abandon the gold standard and allow the pound to float affected the country much more severely. Still traumatized by the experience of the 1920s, the Belgian government decided to maintain the gold parity of 1926, which left the franc seriously overvalued as the pound sterling and dollar fell. Belgian exports declined sharply, as did business profits and investments, while unemployment soared, heightening the atmosphere of social unrest. Only in March 1935 would the government abandon its policy of maintaining the franc at its 1926 level; the gold value of the franc was devalued by 28 percent.

With the onset of the Great Depression, the Socialist Party advocated a program of economic planning in accordance with the ideas of the socialist theorist Hendrik de Man. At the same time, there emerged two Belgian parties: a strictly Flemish party that enjoyed little success and the broader-based Rexists under the leadership of Léon Degrelle. The latter party won 21 seats, more than 10 percent of the chamber, in the elections of 1936.

Strikes broke out in the same year and led the tripartite government of Paul van Zeeland to establish paid holidays for workers and a 40-hour workweek for miners. Also in 1936, the first National Labour Convention marked the starting point of an institutionalized dialogue between the so-called social partners (employers, trade unions, and government).

Meanwhile, King Leopold III, who succeeded his father, Albert I, in 1934, faced an increasingly tense international situation. Leopold advocated a policy of neutrality aimed at keeping Belgium from the seemingly inevitable conflict. Although this policy was approved by the parliament, Belgium, in its determination to resist all aggression, constructed a line of defense from Namur to Antwerp.

NAZI OCCUPATION

On May 10, 1940, Germany invaded Belgium, Luxembourg, and the Netherlands. The Netherlands capitulated after 6 days, Belgium after 18. France, which along with Britain had sent troops to Belgium, had to lay down arms three weeks later. The British troops, covered by the Belgian army, retreated from Dunkirk, France, in particularly dramatic circumstances. The Belgian government fled the country, first to France, in hopes of being able to return to occupied Belgium, and later to London. King Leopold III, commander in chief of the army, refused to follow the government and was taken prisoner by the Germans and confined to his palace at Laeken. The four years of ensuing Nazi occupation were distinguished by a growing resistance organization. When the Allied forces reached Belgium on September 3, 1944, the Belgian underground army was able to prevent the destruction of the port of Antwerp, which served as the most important continental provisioning point for Allied troops for the remainder of the war.

BELGIUM AFTER WORLD WAR II

Because of the limited extent of its war damage, estimated at only 8 percent of the national wealth, and the implementation of a vigorous government policy, Belgium experienced a remarkable economic resurgence in the early postwar years. Monetary reform kept inflation under control, and liberalization of the domestic economy quickly returned the market mechanisms to the centre of the industrial, agricultural, and commercial activities. In the climate of recovery, social legislation won the support of both unions and employers.

The investigation of wartime economic and especially political collaboration with Germany resulted in large-scale purges and the detention of many citizens. The extreme rightist parties disappeared from the political scene. The Communist Party, having identified very early with the resistance movement, experienced a short-lived growth, taking part in coalition governments between 1944 and 1947; the anticommunist reflex during the Cold War brought this interlude to an end.

Despite the economic revival, political stability deteriorated, notably over the "royal question." In 1944, at the time of the Allied offensive, the Germans had transferred King Leopold III to Austria, where he was held until 1945. The government, upon returning to Brussels in early September 1944, conferred the regency on the king's brother, Prince Charles. After the war Leopold remained in exile in Switzerland until the "royal question" could be resolved. Generally speaking, the Flemish were the king's partisans and the Walloons his opponents. The Christian Democrats favoured the king's return, while the Socialists and Liberals opposed it. In 1950 a referendum showed that nearly 58 percent of the voters approved of the return of the sovereign, but the king's arrival that year signaled virtual civil war in the Walloon country. In August 1950 Leopold appointed his eldest son, Prince Baudouin, to rule temporarily in his place. In July 1951 he abdicated, and Baudouin officially assumed the title of king.

The composition of the government continued to fluctuate, although from the 1950s onward the Christian Democrats maintained a continuous presence, often in coalition with the Socialists. Various nationalist parties emerged—a Flemish one in 1954 and two French-language parties in the 1960s. Eventually the three traditional parties—the Social Christians, the Liberals, and the Socialists—each split along linguistic lines, rendering the political decision-making process increasingly complicated.

The policy of the postwar Belgian governments, apart from the "royal question" settled in 1951, was dominated by five major issues: consolidation of the mixed economy, the ideological controversy concerning education, the process of decolonization, the matter of language

and regional autonomy, and Belgium's role in the new postwar supranational organizations. In 1948 Belgium joined with the Netherlands and Luxembourg in the Benelux Economic Union, which had been conceived in 1944 in London. The country became a signatory of the North Atlantic Treaty Organization (NATO) in 1949 and three years later joined the European Coal and Steel Community. In 1957 Belgium signed the Treaties of Rome, which it had helped to formulate, becoming a member of both the European Economic Community (later the European Community, which was embedded in and ultimately replaced by the European Union [EU]) and the European Atomic Energy Community.

During the late 1950s, growing opposition to colonial rule in the Belgian Congo led to large-scale demonstrations in Léopoldville. The Belgian government accelerated the process of political emancipation of its colonies, granting independence to the Congo (now the Democratic Republic of the Congo) in June 1960 and to Ruanda-Urundi (now the countries of Rwanda and Burundi) in July 1962.

The education controversy became critical once again in the second half of the 1950s. The Socialist-Liberal coalition simultaneously cut subsidies to private (mainly Catholic) secondary schools and promoted a major extension of the state's secondary education system. After the defeat of the Socialists and Liberals in the 1958 election, a "School Pact" was signed under the initiative of the new Social Christian prime minister, Gaston Eyskens. This compromise measure, which authorized extension of the state secondary schools while guaranteeing conditional state subsidies for their private counterparts, marked the onset of an enduring ideological pacification in the country.

Following the "miracle recovery" of the late 1940s, Belgium's economic surge subsided. The consolidation of the mixed economy, aimed at linking economic growth with a more equitable distribution of income and with an increase in the supply of public goods and social benefits, had been successful, but at the cost of rising wages and a heavier tax burden. Continued reliance on the aging Walloon heavy industry, coupled with a declining investment rate, seriously compromised the competitive power of the Belgian economy, reducing its growth rate to a level near that of Britain's.

Participation in the European customs union from 1958 gradually reversed the unfavourable economic trend by enlarging the market for Belgian products. An explicit expansion policy by the government was also a contributing factor. Prime Minister Eyskens reformed the state finances and launched an active policy of regional economic development in 1959. The Flemish sector, unencumbered by the rigid industrial structure that characterized Wallonia, attracted foreign investment on a large scale from the United States, from Belgium's European Community partners, and subsequently from Japan. Meanwhile, it was generous state subsidies that kept Walloon heavy industry alive.

The growing economic disparity between the two regions intensified dissatisfaction with the unitary state system. The Flemings opposed subsidizing an ailing regional economy that lacked any prospect of structural industrial reform. The Walloons, in turn, feared that the more numerous and prosperous Flemings would soon dominate the state. Linguistic and economic tensions were now inextricable. As a consequence of massive strikes in Wallonia in early 1961, an immovable linguistic border was defined by an act of parliament in 1962–63, and a new special arrangement was elaborated for the bilingual area around Brussels.

FEDERALIZED BELGIUM

After tensions led to the division of the still bilingual University of Louvain into a Flemish-speaking campus on Flemish territory and a French-speaking campus on Walloon territory in 1969–70, a slow but definitive process of federalization got under way. The parliament accorded cultural autonomy to the Flemish and Walloon regions in 1971. A revision of the constitution nine years later allowed for the creation of an independent administration within each region. Another revision of the constitution in 1988–89 extended regional autonomy to encompass the economy and education. It also

ALBERT II

The second son of King Leopold III, Albert II (born Albert Félix Humbert Théodore Christian Eugène Marie of Saxe-Coburg-Gotha, June 6, 1934, Brussels) was educated at home and in Geneva and Brussels and entered the Belgian navy in 1953. From 1962 until his ascension, he served as honorary chairman of the Belgian Office of Foreign Trade, leading some 70 important trade missions and becoming an expert on shipping. He also served as the longtime president of the Belgian Red Cross and as a member of the International Olympic Committee.

In 1959 he married Paola Ruffo di Calabria, an Italian princess. The couple had three children: Philippe (born 1960), Astrid (born 1962), and Laurent (born 1963). Albert succeeded his childless older brother Baudouin after the latter's death in July 1993. Though many had speculated he would abdicate in favour of his eldest son, Albert was sworn in as sixth king of the Belgians on August 9, 1993. An avid motorcycle rider, Albert in 2003 celebrated the 10th anniversary of his coronation by kickstarting a commemorative parade of some 20,000 bikers. While constitutional reform in 1993 had federalized the government and limited the power of the monarchy, Albert remained an important symbol of unity to the country as it faced growing political divisiveness between French-speaking Wallonia and Flemish-speaking Flanders. At times Albert's role as a unifier went well beyond the bounds of symbolism; indeed, in 2007–08 he played an active part in negotiations that led to the formation of a governing coalition after a protracted period of particular acrimony and instability in the Belgian parliament.

gave the bilingual metropolitan area of Brussels the status of a third independent region with its own administration and changed Belgium explicitly into a federal state. This transformation was finalized with the St. Michael's Agreement (September 1992), which also called for the division of Brabant into two provinces (Flemish Brabant and Walloon Brabant).

The acceleration of the federalization process during the 1980s was influenced to a large extent by economic factors. The oil crises of 1973 and 1979–80 and the ensuing world recession stunned Belgium's decidedly open economy. A coalition government formed in 1981 by the Liberals and the Social Christians pursued a program of restrictive monetarism and structural reform: the Belgian franc was devalued (1982), and the increase in the money supply was brought under control by cutting public services and by ending governmental subsidies to the old industries. Within three years Belgian industry had regained its competitiveness, owing to a combination of government policy, improvement in the world economy, and the dynamism of Europe as it moved toward a more complete economic unification.

King Baudouin, who played a role in maintaining national unity by pacifying the contentious Flemish- and French-speaking communities, died on July 31, 1993. He was succeeded by his brother, Albert II.

During the 1990s, Belgium continued to struggle with its so-called language problem. Struggles over the nature and form of power devolution to language regions and communities attracted significant attention, and the federalization of so many aspects of Belgian political and social life promoted linguistic regionalism. Some even began to question whether Belgium can or should remain a single state.

At the same time, Belgium's immigrant population grew during the 1990s—bolstered by an influx of refugees, first from unrest in Bosnia and then from that in Kosovo. There was evidence of growing social tension related to this influx, and during the early 1990s anti-immigrant groups gained greater support—only to see that support fade somewhat by the end of the decade. Indeed, in 2000 the Belgian government offered an amnesty to illegal immigrants who had resided in Belgium for a minimum number of years. Moreover, in 2006 a large demonstration against racism in Antwerp, prompted by the murder in May of a Malian nanny and a Belgian toddler, revealed the dedication of many Belgians to a multicultural society.

Several laws passed in the early 21st century further reflected reformist attitudes. Gay marriage became legal; same-sex couples were permitted to adopt children; the private use of cannabis was decriminalized; and euthanasia was legalized.

The central role of Belgium (particularly Brussels) in the European unity project became more apparent, with massive urban renewal projects initiated in Brussels to make room for the expanding EU administrative corps. Brussels increasingly has assumed the role of administrative "Capital of Europe," giving that city a special role in international affairs and providing an antidote to the growing internal fragmentation of Belgium itself. In the process, Belgians tended to define their interests increasingly in international terms.

In 2007 the continued existence of a federalized Belgium was called into question after the Flemish Christian Democrats, victors in the June parliamentary elections, failed to form a governing coalition. After six months of political deadlock that threatened to end in the breakup of the country, King Albert II asked caretaker prime minister Guy Verhofstadt, head of the defeated Flemish Liberals and Democrats, to form an interim government. A new coalition government, made up of five French- and Flemish-speaking parties and led by the Flemish Christian Democrat Yves Leterme, finally took power in March 2008.

Leterme pledged to increase the governmental powers of the country's regions but was met with resistance from French-speaking parties, who saw the reforms as more beneficial to Flanders than to Wallonia. In July of that year Leterme offered to step down as prime minister, but the king rejected the resignation. Political turmoil—fueled by allegations of the government's questionable involvement in the bailout and sale of the Belgian portion of a financial firm—continued through the end of 2008.

In December Leterme resigned, and Herman Van Rompuy, a fellow Flemish Christian Democrat respected for his skills as a mediator, replaced him as prime minister. Van Rompuy's term was short-lived; in November 2009 he was named the first president of the EU's European Council. Compelled to fill the post of prime minister yet again, King Albert nominated Leterme, who began his second term—what some called a second chance—on November 25, 2009. Not five months later, on April 22, 2010, Leterme tendered his resignation once again, following the withdrawal of the Flemish Liberals and Democrats from the governing coalition.

In the election that followed in June 2010, the big winners were the separatist New Flemish Alliance, which finished first with 27 seats (a gain of 19 seats), and the French-speaking Socialists, who added 6 seats to reach a total of 26 seats. The various parties were unable to come to an agreement as coalition talks continued for more than a year while Leterme oversaw a caretaker administration. In the meantime, some Belgians wryly took solace in their country's capture of the modern world record for the number of days spent without a formal government. Despite having no formal government, in July 2011 Belgium became the second country in the EU to approve legislation that outlawed face coverings such as the Islamic veil.

After some 530 days without a government, Belgium was drawn into the debt crisis that had plagued other parts of Europe since 2009. In November 2011 the ratings agency Standard & Poor's downgraded Belgium's credit and confirmed a negative economic outlook for the country. Given the length of the political deadlock, lawmakers responded with surprising haste to that development. During a week of intense negotiations, a grand coalition of Christian Democrats, Liberals, and Socialists took shape, with Socialist Elio Di Rupo at its head. A career politician, Di Rupo had built a reputation as a talented negotiator. He was sworn in on December 6, 2011, becoming Belgium's first Socialist prime minister since 1974, its first Francophone prime minister in more than three decades, and the EU's first openly gay head of government. Later that month, the country was stunned when an ex-convict launched an attack on a crowded city square in Liège. Using grenades and an assault rifle, he killed at least three people and wounded dozens of others before taking his own life.

CHAPTER 11

LUXEMBOURG: THE LAND AND ITS PEOPLE

Luxembourg is one of the world's smallest countries. It is bordered by Belgium on the west and north, France on the south, and Germany on the northeast and east. Luxembourg has come under the control of many states and ruling houses in its long history, but it has been a separate, if not always autonomous, political unit since the 10th century. The ancient Saxon name of its capital city, Lucilinburhuc ("Little Fortress"), symbolized its strategic position as "the Gibraltar of the north," astride a major military route linking Germanic and Frankish territories.

Luxembourg is a point of contact between the Germanic- and Romance-language communities of Europe, and three languages are regularly employed in the grand duchy itself: Luxembourgish (the national language), German, and French. The peoples of Luxembourg and their languages reflect the grand duchy's common interests and close historical relations with its neighbours. In the 20th century, Luxembourg became a founding member of several international economic organizations. Perhaps most importantly, the grand duchy was an original member of the Benelux Economic Union (1944), which linked its economic life with that of the Netherlands and of Belgium and would subsequently form the core of the European Economic Community (EEC; ultimately succeeded by the European Union).

RELIEF AND SOILS

The northern third of Luxembourg, known as the Oesling (Ösling), comprises a corner of the Ardennes Mountains,

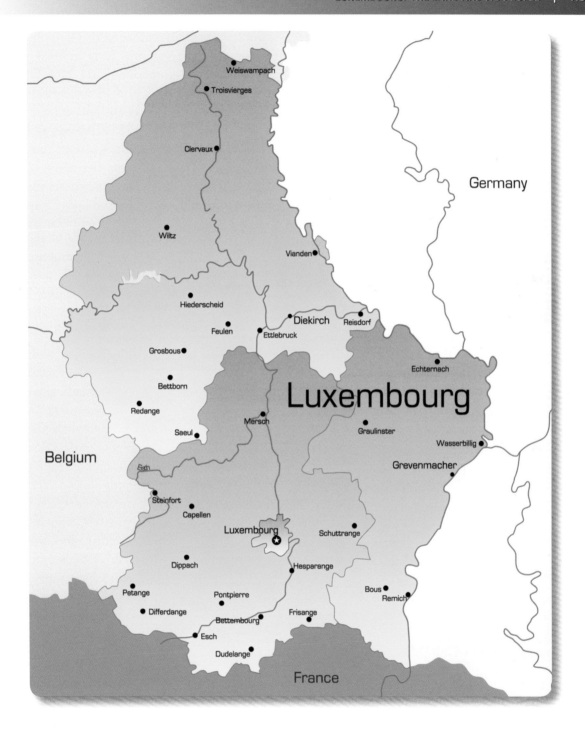

Luxembourg. Olinchuk/Shutterstock.com

which lie mainly in southern Belgium. It is a plateau that averages 1,500 feet (450 metres) in elevation and is composed of schists and sandstones. This forested highland region is incised by the deep valleys of a river network organized around the Sûre (or Sauer) River, which runs eastward through north-central Luxembourg before joining the Moselle (or Mosel) River on the border with Germany. The Oesling's forested hills and valleys support the ruins of numerous castles, which are a major attraction for the region's many tourists. The fertility of the relatively thin mountain soils of the region was greatly improved with the introduction in the 1890s of a basic-slag fertilizer, which is obtained as a by-product of the grand duchy's steel industry.

The southern two-thirds of Luxembourg is known as the Bon Pays, or Gutland (French and German: "Good Land"). This region has a more varied topography and an average elevation of 800 feet. The Bon Pays is much more densely populated than the Oesling and contains the capital city, Luxembourg, as well as smaller industrial cities such as Esch-sur-Alzette. In the centre of the Bon Pays, the valley of the northward-flowing Alzette River forms an axis around which the nation's economic life is organized. Luxembourg city lies along the Alzette, which joins the Sûre farther north.

In the east-central part of the Bon Pays lies a great beech forest, the Müllerthal, as well as a sandstone area featuring an attractive ruiniform topography. The country's eastern border with Germany is formed (successively from north to south) by the Our, Sûre, and Moselle rivers. The slopes of the Moselle River valley, carved up in chalk and calcareous clay, are covered with vineyards and receive a substantial amount of sunshine, which has earned the area the name of "Little Riviera." Besides vineyards, the fertile soils of the Moselle and lower Sûre valleys also support rich pasturelands. Luxembourg's former iron mines are located in the extreme southwest, along the duchy's border with France.

CLIMATE

Luxembourg has a mild climate with considerable precipitation. The north is slightly colder and more humid than the south. The mean temperatures in Luxembourg city range from the mid-30s °F (about 0.7 °C) in January to the low 60s °F (about 17 °C) in July, but in the Oesling both extremes are slightly lower. The Oesling receives more precipitation than the Bon Pays, but the greatest amount, about 40 inches (1,000 mm), and the least, about 27 inches (about 685 mm), fall in the southwest and southeast, respectively. The sheltered valley of the Moselle River benefits from a gentler and sunnier climate than does the rest of the duchy.

PEOPLE

Luxembourg has been one of the historic crossroads of Europe, and myriad peoples have left their bloodlines as well as their cultural imprints on the grand duchy. The Celts, the Belgic peoples known as the Treveri, the Ligurians and Romans from Italy, and especially the Franks were most influential. The language spoken by Luxembourg's native inhabitants is Luxembourgish, or Lëtzebuergesch, a Moselle-Franconian dialect of German that has been enriched by many French words and phrases. Luxembourgish is the national language; German and French are both languages of administration. There is a strong sense of national identity among Luxembourgers despite the prevalence of foreign influences. The great majority of Luxembourg's native citizens are Roman Catholic, with a small number of Protestants (mainly Lutherans), Jews, and Muslims.

Luxembourg has a high proportion of foreigners living within its borders. This is chiefly the result of an extremely low birth rate among native Luxembourgers, which has led to a chronic labour shortage. About two-fifths of the total population is of foreign birth and consists mainly of Portuguese, French, Italians, Belgians,

The town of Clervaux, in the Oesling, Luxembourg. E. Streichan/SuperStock

LUXEMBOURG CITY

Luxembourg's capital, Luxembourg (Letzeburg) City, is situated on a sandstone plateau into which the Alzette River and its tributary, the Petrusse, have cut deep winding ravines. Within a loop of the Alzette, a rocky promontory called the Bock (Bouc) forms a natural defensive position where the Romans and later the Franks built a fort, around which the medieval town developed. The purchase of this castle in 963 CE by Siegfried, count of Ardennes, marked the beginning of Luxembourg as an independent entity. The castle's old name, Lucilinburhuc ("Little Fortress"), is the origin of the name Luxembourg.

Luxembourg City's old town is a UNESCO World Heritage site. Encyclopædia Britannica

The old town consists of Luxembourg Castle's surviving fortifications, the Grand Ducal Palace, Notre-Dame Cathedral (the construction of which was begun by the Jesuits in 1613 and completed in 1621), and other historic buildings. The city eventually spread westward, and the suburbs of Grund, Clausen, and Pfaffenthal developed in lower-lying sections across the Alzette from the old town. These sections are linked by several bridges.

Over a 400-year period, Luxembourg Castle was repeatedly attacked and rebuilt—by the Spaniards, Austrians, French, and Dutch, successively—to become the strongest fortress in Europe after Gibraltar. One such reinforcement was undertaken by the French military engineer Sébastien Le Prestre de Vauban, who redesigned the city's defensive fortifications after having orchestrated its siege in 1684 in the service of Louis XIV.

From after the Congress of Vienna (1815) to 1866, the fortress was garrisoned by the Prussians as a bulwark of the German Confederation. With the Treaty of London, in 1867, Luxembourg was declared neutral, and the fortress, containing 15 miles (24 km) of casemates, three battlements with 24 forts, and an extensive (10-acre [4-hectare]) area of military barracks, was largely dismantled, an operation that took 16 years. Today visitors can tour the remaining 7 miles (11 km) of casemates or view the modern city below from the Chemin de la Corniche, a promontory built atop the old town wall.

The Grand Ducal Palace is home to the royal family, heirs of William I (1772–1843), king of the Netherlands and grand duke of Luxembourg (1815–40). The palace dates from 1572, and later additions were made in 1895. After renovations were completed in the 1990s, portions of the palace were opened to the public.

Notre-Dame Cathedral, a Gothic-style church, contains the tomb of John the Blind, king of Bohemia and count of Luxembourg from 1310 to 1346. Several members of the royal family and noted bishops are buried in the crypt.

The heart of the old town is the Fish Market (Marché-aux-Poissons), around which stand several 17th- and 18th-century buildings, including the mansion housing the Luxembourg National Museum (National Museum of History and Art). Um Bock, a 13th-century build-

Notre-Dame Cathedral and a portion of the fortress wall in Luxembourg City. S.E. Hedin—Ostman Agency

ing and the city's oldest, is also located at the Fish Market. Among the city's other cultural institutions are the Villa Vauban–Museum of the Art of the City of Luxembourg, MUDAM Luxembourg (Grand Duke Jean Museum of Modern Art), the Museum of the History of the City of Luxembourg, and the National Museum of Natural History. At the town of Hamm, 4 miles (6 km) to the east, is a World War II military cemetery with the graves of more than 5,000 U.S. soldiers, including those of Brig. Gen. Edward Betts and Gen. George S. Patton, Jr.

Luxembourg has long been a major road and railway hub. In the 20th century the city became a thriving financial centre, owing to banking laws that keep investors' identities confidential and allow the accounts of foreign nationals to earn interest tax-free. Luxembourg is the seat of the European Investment Bank, the European Court of Justice, and several other administrative offices of the European Union. In 1994 the old town was designated a UNESCO World Heritage site.

and Germans. Among the foreign workers are many in the iron and steel industry, and numerous others work in foreign firms and international organizations located in the capital.

SETTLEMENT PATTERNS

Northern Luxembourg is sparsely populated compared with the heavily urbanized and industrialized south. The north's rural population is clustered in villages of thick-set stone houses with slate roofs. The urban network in the south is dominated by the capital city, Luxembourg, which rises in tiers, with the upper (and older) section of the city separated from the lower-lying suburbs by the gorges of the Alzette and Petrusse rivers. A newer quarter housing many European organizations nestles in a picturesque site carved into the river valley's sandstone cliffs.

The second largest city in Luxembourg, Esch-sur-Alzette, lies in the extreme southwest and is a traditional iron- and steel-making centre. Its growth, like that of the neighbouring iron and steel centres of Pétange, Differdange, and Dudelange, has slowed since the shrinkage of those industries in western Europe in the late 20th century. The remainder of the country's population lives in towns and villages of relatively small size. Many of Luxembourg's villages date from ancient Celtic and Roman times or originated in Germanic and Frankish villages after about 400 CE. In addition, many medieval castle villages continue to thrive, centuries after the castles themselves fell into ruin.

DEMOGRAPHIC TRENDS

The 20th century witnessed a continual internal migration away from the countryside to urban areas, and the growth of Luxembourg's service sector at the expense of heavy industry has only accelerated this trend. Luxembourg city in particular continues to attract migrants from the rest of the country because of its vibrant banking and finance sector. The increasing concentration of the population in the southwest has led the government to try to locate some industries in rural areas. About three-fourths of Luxembourg's workforce is engaged in trade, government, and other service occupations, while about one-fifth of the workforce is employed in industry and construction, and the small remainder works in agriculture and other pursuits.

CHAPTER 12

THE LUXEMBOURGIAN ECONOMY

Luxembourg's economy is notable for its close connections with the rest of Europe, since Luxembourg itself is too small to create a self-sustaining internal market. Luxembourg's prosperity was originally based on the iron and steel industry, which in the 1960s represented as much as 80 percent of the total value of exports. By the late 20th century, however, the country's economic vigour stemmed chiefly from its involvement in international banking and financial services and in such noncommercial activities as hosting intra-European political activities. In the 21st century, information technology and electronic commerce also became important components of Luxembourg's economy. The result of the country's adaptability and cosmopolitanism is a very high standard of living; the Luxembourgers rank among the world's leaders in standard of living and per capita income.

AGRICULTURE

The agricultural resources of Luxembourg are quite modest. With the exception of livestock products, surpluses are scarce, and marginal soils in many parts of the country hinder abundant harvests. Most farming is mixed and includes both animal raising and gardening. Livestock and their by-products account for the bulk of agricultural production, cattle raising having gained in importance at the expense of pig and sheep raising. Wheat, barley, and other cereal grains are the next most important products, followed by root vegetables.

About one-half of the country's farms are smaller than 200 acres (50 hectares). The vineyards along the Moselle River produce some excellent wines.

RESOURCES AND POWER

Luxembourg's natural resources are far from abundant. In addition to its agriculture not being particularly prosperous, its once copious iron ore deposits had been exhausted by the 1980s. With the exception of water and timber, there are no energy resources. Indeed, Luxembourg has almost nothing that predisposes it to agricultural or industrial development. The roots of its economic growth lie in its use of capital and in the adaptability and ingenuity of its workforce rather than in natural resources.

MANUFACTURING AND TRADE

The production and export of iron and steel have long played major roles in

One of the plants of the steel and mining giant ArcelorMittal. © AP Images

ARCELORMITTAL

When the Arcelor and Mittal steel companies merged in 2006, they became the world's largest steelmaking company at the time, ArcelorMittal. Arcelor's roots were in the Luxembourgian company Aciéries Réunies de Burbach-Eich-Dudelange (ARBED SA), which was formed in 1911 through the merger of Les Forges d'Eich, Le Gallais, Metz et Cie. (established in 1838 under a different name); La Société Anonyme des Mines du Luxembourg et Forges de Sarrebruck (1856); and La Société Anonyme des Hauts Fourneaux et Forges de Dudelange (1882). Through its subsidiaries and affiliate companies, ARBED SA engaged in every step of steel production and processing, from the extraction of coal and iron ore (from its own mines) to the fabrication of highly specialized steel products, including the whole range of rolled-steel products and some finished products, especially wire. By the end of the 1970s ARBED SA was the sole remaining steelmaker in Luxembourg, with the government holding about one-third of its ownership. In 1980 it entered into a joint venture with Bethlehem Steel Corporation, an American steel company, to produce Galvalume, a sheet steel product patented by Bethlehem, for distribution to Europe and abroad. In the 1990s ARBED SA became increasingly involved in electronic commerce. In 2001 it merged with the Spanish company Aceralia and the French company Usinor to form Arcelor.

Mittal Steel was founded in Indonesia in 1976 by Lakshmi Mittal, an Indian whose father operated a steel mill in Calcutta in the 1960s. In 1989 Mittal purchased the troubled state-owned steelworks in Trinidad and Tobago, and a year later that facility had doubled its output and become profitable. He used a similar formula for success in numerous acquisitions around the world, purchasing failing (mostly state-run) outfits and sending in special management teams to reorganize the businesses.

In 2006 Mittal's attempts at a hostile takeover of Arcelor were initially blocked by the Luxembourgian government, which relented before year's end, allowing the merger of the two companies as ArcelorMittal. Although the government then divested itself of much of its ownership of the company, it maintained a small interest in ArcelorMittal, of which Lakshmi Mittal became chief executive officer.

Luxembourg's economy. Steel production was originally based on exploitation of the iron ore deposits extending from Lorraine into the southwestern corner of the grand duchy. This ore has a high phosphorus content, however, and it was not until the introduction of the basic Bessemer process in 1879 that the ore could be used for making steel. Thereafter, Luxembourg's metallurgical industries grew and flourished. During the 1970s, however, the worldwide demand for steel slumped, causing the steel industry's portion of Luxembourg's gross domestic product to fall. In response to this crisis, the government took measures aimed at helping the steel industry increase efficiency and maintain profitability. By the late 1970s ARBED (Aciéries Réunies de Burbach-Eich-Dudelange) SA was Luxembourg's only remaining steelmaker. In 2001 ARBED merged with the Spanish company Aceralia and the French company Usinor to form Arcelor, which subsequently joined Mittal to create ArcelorMittal, the world's largest steel company at the time of its formation in 2006.

Since the end of the 20th century, Luxembourg's economy has been increasingly dependent on foreign-owned factories and other multinational companies operating in the country. These factories primarily produce motor-vehicle tires, chemicals, and fabricated metals.

By the late 20th century Luxembourg had become an important international financial centre, and in the early 21st century it remained home to scores of banks, most of which were foreign-owned. Those banks operated in a climate of general secrecy permitted by the country's banking laws, which had come under criticism from some other countries. Luxembourg owes its prominent position in the world of finance to a number of other factors, perhaps chief of which is the government's own farsighted policies. In 1929 the government began to encourage the

EUROPEAN COURT OF JUSTICE

Headquartered in Luxembourg, the European Court of Justice (ECJ; also called Court of Justice of the European Communities) originated in the individual courts of justice established in the 1950s for the European Coal and Steel Community, the European Economic Community, and the European Atomic Energy Community. The function of these courts was to ensure the observance of law in those organizations' interpretation and application of their treaties. In 1958 a single, unified ECJ was created to serve all three of the European Communities (later succeeded by the European Union [EU]). In 1988 the Court of First Instance was established to reduce the court's workload; it began hearing cases the following year.

The ECJ reviews the legality of the acts of the Commission and the Council of Ministers of the EU, which are the executive bodies of that organization. The court typically hears cases involving disputes between member states over trade, antitrust, and environmental issues, as well as issues raised by private parties, compensations for damages, and so on. The court has the power to invalidate the laws of EU member states when those laws conflict with EU law. The ECJ serves as the final arbiter of the growing body of international law that has accompanied the economic and political integration of Europe. The court's full bench consists of 27 judges, who are appointed to renewable 6-year terms, and 8 advocates-general. Prior to 2004, the ECJ met as a full chamber for all cases, but it now may sit as a "grand chamber" of 13 judges or in "chambers" of 3 to 5 judges.

registering in Luxembourg of holding companies; those large corporations can control a number of subsidiary companies but are heavily taxed in many countries of the world. The liberal tax climate produced by the new policy led many industrial and financial corporations to maintain offices, often as their European headquarters, in Luxembourg City. Luxembourg formally joined the EU's Economic Monetary Union (EMU) in 1998, and in 2002 the country's longtime currency, the Luxembourgish franc, was replaced by euro.

Luxembourg City is also one of the capitals of the European Union (EU) and, as such, is home to the European Court of Justice; the European Investment Bank, which enjoys decision-making independence within the EU's institutional system; and several major EU administrative offices.

Most of the grand duchy's merchandise trade takes place with EU countries, especially with its three neighbours— Germany, Belgium, and France, which together receive about 60 percent of Luxembourg's exports and provide about 80 percent of its imports.

TRANSPORTATION AND COMMUNICATIONS

Luxembourg's internal road system is not extensive but is well maintained, and several highways link the country with its neighbours. A port at Mertert on the canalized Moselle River connects the grand duchy with the Rhine waterway system and provides it with an avenue for the international movement of goods. The government has operated the nation's railroads since World War II. They are modern, electrified, and mostly double-tracked. A major portion of international transportation to and from Luxembourg is by train, and the country is connected with its neighbours by a large number of lines. Findel Airport outside Luxembourg City has become a major European air terminal served by the lines of many countries. Luxair is the national airline.

Luxembourg's advanced telecommunications system provides it with close links both to EU countries and to other financial partners around the world, including Japan and the United States. The government operates the postal service in Luxembourg. RTL (Radio-Television-Luxembourg) Group SA, a privately owned broadcasting company that has radio and television outlets in a number of European countries, is also a satellite operator with a plethora of channels that reach as far as Great Britain and Scandinavia. RTL is arguably Europe's most important private radio and television broadcaster.

CHAPTER 13

LUXEMBOURGIAN GOVERNMENT AND SOCIETY

The grand duchy is a constitutional monarchy with hereditary succession. Executive power authority lies with the grand duke, who appoints the prime minister. The powers of the grand duke are primarily formal, however. Actual executive power lies with the prime minister and his ministerial council, or cabinet, who are responsible to the Chamber of Deputies. The members of this legislative assembly are elected by popular vote to five-year terms. Voting by all adult citizens, begun in 1919, is compulsory. Legislative elections have usually given rise to coalition governments formed alternatively by two of the three major parties: the Christian Social People's Party (Chrëschtlech Sozial Vollekspartei; CSV), the Socialist Workers' Party of Luxembourg (Lëtzebuergesch Sozialistesch Arbechterpartei; LSAP), and the Democratic Party (DP). In addition, a Council of State named by the grand duke functions as an advisory body. It is consulted on all draft legislation, advises the grand duke on administrative affairs, and serves as a supreme court in case of administrative disputes.

There are also three advisory bodies that are consulted before the passage of legislation affecting their particular area of the national life. The first of these consists of six confederations, three of which represent employers (commerce, guilds, and farmers) and three of which represent labour (workers, private employees, and civil servants). The second advisory group, the Social and Economic

Council, has become a major committee for the examination of all projects. The third, the Immigration Council, advises the government on problems involving housing and the political rights of immigrants.

Justice is in the hands of magistrates appointed for life by the grand duke, the final appeal lying with the Superior Court of Justice. In the criminal court of assizes, six magistrates sit as jury as well as judge.

Luxembourg is a member of the North Atlantic Treaty Organization (NATO) and has a small volunteer army. There is also a small paramilitary gendarmerie.

Luxembourg is divided administratively into three districts, each of which is headed by a commissioner appointed by the central government. Each district is in turn divided into cantons and subdivided into communes, or municipalities. Public works, health, and education are among the responsibilities of the communes, each of which is governed by an elected council and a mayor. These bodies also maintain liaison with the central government and act as its local agents.

HEALTH AND WELFARE

After World War I a broad system of social security and health services was introduced in Luxembourg to ensure maximum welfare protection to each citizen. Sickness benefits, in which patients pay only a small part of medical costs, as well as birth, family, and unemployment payments, are included in the plans. Housing conditions are generally comparable to those found in other western European countries. There has been some difficulty, however, in assimilating the many thousands of foreign workers and their families.

EDUCATION

Education is compulsory from age 6 to 15. The educational system offers a mix of primary and secondary schools run by state and local governments and by religious institutions. Considerable emphasis is laid on language studies. The principal language of instruction is Luxembourgish; however, German is introduced in the first year, and French is added in the second year. German remains the focus throughout primary school and in technical education, while in secondary classical education the emphasis is on French. Until the early 21st century there were no four-year universities in the grand duchy, so many young Luxembourgers have historically obtained their higher education abroad. In 2003 the University of Luxembourg was founded in Luxembourg City and now provides undergraduate and graduate degrees.

CHAPTER 14

LUXEMBOURGIAN CULTURAL LIFE

The major cultural institution of Luxembourg is the Grand Ducal Institute, which has sections devoted to history, science, medicine, languages and folklore, arts and literature, and moral and political sciences. It functions as an active promoter of the arts, humanities, and general culture rather than as a conservator. The Luxembourg National Museum (formally the National Museum of History and Art) surveys fine arts and industrial arts as well as the history of Luxembourg.

Other prominent museums include the Villa Vauban–Museum of the Art of the City of Luxembourg, MUDAM Luxembourg (Grand Duke Jean Museum of Modern Art), the Museum of the History of the City of Luxembourg, and the National Museum of Natural History. There is considerable public use of the National Library, the National Archives, and the Music Conservatory of the City of Luxembourg. The grand duchy also maintains cultural agreements with several European and other nations that provide it with the finest in the musical and theatrical arts. The Philharmonic Orchestra of Luxembourg (which was known as the Grand Orchestra of Radiotelevision Luxembourg before it came under government administration in 1996) is considered outstanding. There is an extensive market in Luxembourg city for works of painting and sculpture, both traditional and modern. The grand duchy's architectural heritage extends through practically the entire span of Europe's recorded history, from ancient

Grand Duke Jean Museum of Modern Art. Danita Delimont/Gallo Images/Getty Images

LUXEMBOURG NATIONAL MUSEUM

The Luxembourg National Museum (formally National Museum of History and Art) is located in the historic centre of Luxembourg City at the Fish Market (Marché-aux-Poissons). It is housed in an extensive late Gothic and Renaissance mansion. The museum has collections of Gallo-Roman art, coins, medieval sculpture, armour, and contemporary art, as well as a 25,000-volume library. There is also a special exhibit entitled "The Fortress of Luxembourg" with models.

In 1854 the Luxembourg Society of Natural Sciences established a museum that became the nucleus of the Luxembourg State Museums. The collections were moved to Fish Market square in 1922. From 1970 the earth sciences and astronomy exhibits were expanded, and in 1988 the State Museums were administratively divided into the National Museum of History and Art, which remained at the Fish Market, and the National Museum of Natural History, which completed its move to a separate location (on Münster Street) in 1996.

Gallo-Roman villas to medieval castles, Gothic and Baroque churches, and contemporary buildings.

A small publishing industry exists, printing literary works in French, German, and Luxembourgish. The grand duchy's newspapers express diverse political points of view—conservative, liberal, socialist, and communist. Luxembourg's influence is felt far beyond its borders through the medium of the RTL (Radio-Television-Luxembourg) Group. The group's early English-language radio service, Radio Luxembourg, played an important role in the history of rock music when it operated as Europe's premier broadcaster of rhythm and blues and early rock and roll from the United States in the 1950s.

CHAPTER 15

LUXEMBOURG: PAST AND PRESENT

The earliest human remains found in present-day Luxembourg date from about 5140 BCE, but little is known about the people who first populated the area. Two Belgic tribes, the Treveri and Mediomatrici, inhabited the country from about 450 BCE until the Roman conquest of 53 BCE. The occupation of the country by the Franks in the 5th century CE marked the beginning of the Middle Ages in the locality. St. Willibrord played a very important role in the area's Christianization in the late 7th century. He founded the Benedictine abbey of Echternach, which became an important cultural centre for the region.

MEDIEVAL PERIOD

The area successively formed part of the Frankish kingdom of Austrasia, of the Holy Roman Empire under Charlemagne and Louis I (the Pious), and then of the kingdom of Lotharingia. Luxembourg became an independent entity in 963, when Siegfried, Count de Ardennes, exchanged his lands for a small but strategically placed Roman castle lying along the Alzette River. This castle became the cradle of Luxembourg, whose name is itself derived from that of the castle, Lucilinburhuc ("Little Fortress"). Siegfried's successors enlarged their possessions by conquests, treaties, marriages, and inheritances. About 1060 Conrad, a descendant of Siegfried, became the first to take the title of count of Luxembourg. Conrad's great-granddaughter,

Countess Ermesinde, was a notable ruler whose great-grandson, Henry IV, became Holy Roman emperor as Henry VII in 1308. This Luxembourg dynasty was continued on the imperial throne in the persons of Charles IV, Wenceslas, and Sigismund. In 1354 the emperor Charles IV made the county a duchy. In 1443 Elizabeth of Görlitz, duchess of Luxembourg and niece of the Holy Roman emperor Sigismund, was forced to cede the duchy to Philip III (the Good), duke of Burgundy.

HABSBURG AND FRENCH DOMINATION

Along with the rest of the Burgundian inheritance, the duchy of Luxembourg passed to the Habsburgs in 1477. The division of the Habsburg territories in 1555–56 following Emperor Charles V's abdication put the duchy in the possession of the Spanish Habsburgs. In the revolt of the Low Countries against Philip II of Spain, Luxembourg took no part; it was to remain with what is now Belgium as part of the Spanish Netherlands.

The duchy was able to remain aloof from the Thirty Years' War (1618–48) for a time, but in 1635, when France became involved, a period of disaster began in Luxembourg, which was wracked by war, famine, and epidemics. Moreover, the war did not end for Luxembourg with the Peace of Westphalia in 1648, but only with the Treaty of the Pyrenees

in 1659. In 1679 France under Louis XIV began to conquer parts of the duchy, and in 1684 the conquest was completed with the capture of Luxembourg City. France restored Luxembourg to Spain in 1697, however, under the terms of the Treaties of Rijswijk. At the conclusion of the War of the Spanish Succession, by the treaties of Utrecht and Rastatt (1713–14), Luxembourg (along with Belgium) passed from the Spanish to the Austrian Habsburgs.

In 1795, six years after the beginning of the French Revolution, Luxembourg came under the rule of the French again. The old duchy was divided among three départements, the constitution of the Directory was imposed, and a modern state bureaucracy was introduced. The Luxembourg peasantry was hostile toward the French government's anticlerical measures, however, and the introduction of compulsory military service in France in 1798 provoked a rebellion (the Klëppelkrieg) in Luxembourg that was brutally suppressed.

PERSONAL UNION WITH THE NETHERLANDS

French domination ended with the fall of Napoleon in 1814, and the Allied powers decided the future of Luxembourg at the Congress of Vienna in 1815. The Congress raised Luxembourg to the status of a grand duchy and gave it to William I, prince of Orange-Nassau and king of the Netherlands. William obtained a Luxembourg that was considerably diminished, since those of its districts lying east of the Our, Sûre, and Moselle rivers had been ceded to Prussia. The status of the grand duchy during this period was complex: Luxembourg had the legal position of an independent state and was united with the Netherlands only because it was a personal possession of William I. But Luxembourg was also included within the German Confederation, and a Prussian military garrison was housed in the capital city.

The standard of living of Luxembourg's citizens deteriorated during this period. Under Austrian rule, and especially from 1735 on, the duchy had experienced an economic expansion. From 1816–17 on, however, William I ignored the duchy's sovereignty, treating Luxembourg as a conquered country and subjecting it to heavy taxes. Consequently, it was not surprising that Luxembourg supported the Belgian revolution against William in 1830, and, in October of that year, the Belgian government announced that the grand duchy was a part of Belgium, while William still claimed the duchy as his own. In 1831 the Great Powers (France, Britain, Prussia, Russia, and Austria) decided that Luxembourg had to remain in William I's possession and form part of the German Confederation. Moreover, the Great Powers allotted the French-speaking part of the duchy to Belgium (in which it became a province called Luxembourg), while William I was allowed to retain the Luxembourgish-speaking part. Belgium accepted this arrangement, but William I rejected it, only to subsequently accede to the arrangement in 1839. From that year until 1867, the duchy was administered autonomously from the Netherlands.

INDEPENDENT LUXEMBOURG

William I negotiated a customs union for Luxembourg with Prussia, and his successor, William II, ratified this treaty in 1842. Against its own will, Luxembourg had thus entered into the Prussian-led Zollverein, or Customs Union, but the grand duchy soon realized the advantages of this economic union. Luxembourg subsequently developed from an agricultural country into an industrial one. Its road network was extended and improved, and two railway companies were begun that formed the basis for the national railway company founded in 1946.

The restricted constitution that William II enacted for Luxembourg in 1841 did not meet the political expectations of its citizens. The Revolution of 1848 in Paris had its influence on the grand duchy, and William II that year enacted a new and more liberal constitution, which was in turn replaced by another constitution in 1856. In 1866 the German Confederation was dissolved, and Luxembourg became

Marie Adelaide, 1912, the year of her ascension to the throne. Branger/Roger Viollet/Getty Images

an entirely sovereign nation, though the Prussian garrison remained in the capital. Napoleon III of France then tried to purchase the grand duchy from William III. The two rulers had already agreed on the sum of five million florins when William III backed out because the Prussian chancellor, Otto von Bismarck, disapproved of the sale. The Great Powers soon came to a compromise (London; May 11, 1867): Prussia had to withdraw its garrison from the capital, the fort would be dismantled, and Luxembourg would become an independent nation. The grand duchy's

perpetual neutrality was guaranteed by the Great Powers, and its sovereignty was vested in the house of Nassau.

On the death of William III of the Netherlands in 1890 without a male heir, the grand duchy passed to Adolf, duke of Nassau (died 1905), who was succeeded by his son William (died 1912). Neither Adolf nor William interfered much in Luxembourg's government, but William's daughter, the grand duchess Marie Adélaïde, was more assertive and eventually became highly unpopular with the people. In 1914 the neutrality of Luxembourg was violated by Germany, which occupied the grand duchy until the Armistice of 1918. During the war, Marie Adélaïde had tolerated the illegal German occupation, for which she was criticized by the Allied powers after the liberation. Marie Adélaïde was forced to abdicate in favour of her sister Charlotte in 1919. In a referendum a few months later, the public voted overwhelmingly against the establishment of a republic and in favour of retaining Charlotte as grand duchess.

In December 1918 the Allied powers had forced Luxembourg to put an end to its customs union with Germany. For the grand duchy this meant the loss of its best customer (for cast iron and steel) as well as its main supplier of coal. Luxembourg urgently needed a new economic partner, and, though the people preferred an economic union with France, the grand duchy was forced to negotiate with Belgium, since France

CHARLOTTE

The second daughter of Grand Duke William IV, Charlotte (born Charlotte Aldegonde Élise Marie Wilhelmine, January 23, 1896, Château de Berg, Luxembourg—died July 9, 1985, Château de Fischbach) became grand duchess of Luxembourg when her sister Marie-Adélaïde abdicated in January 1919 after acquiring a pro-German reputation during World War I. Charlotte immediately called for a referendum, and in September three-quarters of the voters preferred her continued reign to a republic. Six weeks later she married Prince Félix of Bourbon-Parma (died 1970). They had six children: Jean, Élisabeth, Marie-Adélaïde, Marie-Gabrielle, Charles, and Alix. When Nazi Germany overran Luxembourg in May 1940, Charlotte fled with the government, settling in Montreal for the duration of the war. Her frequent radio messages of encouragement were never forgotten by a grateful people. In April 1961 she granted Prince Jean all of her ducal responsibilities in preparation for abdicating in November 1964.

Charlotte's popular reign provided stability during a time of sweeping change. Luxembourg's constitution was twice rewritten (1919 and 1948), providing universal suffrage and abolishing the country's much-violated disarmed neutrality. Labour laws and social security schemes were passed, and through the Benelux Economic Union, NATO, and the EEC, Luxembourg was integrated into post-World War II western Europe. During this time Charlotte's steadfast patriotism and democratic sympathies made her a symbol of Luxembourg's sovereignty and prosperity.

declared itself uninterested in such a union. The Belgium-Luxembourg Economic Union (BLEU) was established in 1921 and provided for a customs and monetary union between the two countries. The economic climate in Luxembourg remained rather dreary during the interwar period though.

In May 1940 the German army invaded and occupied Luxembourg for the second time; however, this time the government refused to collaborate and, together with the grand duchess, went into exile. Luxembourg was placed under German rule, and the French language was banned.

After Luxembourg's liberation in September 1944, it took part in the new international organizations being formed by the victorious Allies, including the United Nations. Luxembourg also joined the new Benelux Economic Union (1944) formed between Belgium, the Netherlands, and itself.

By taking part in the Brussels Treaty of 1948 and in the formation of NATO in 1949, Luxembourg abandoned its perpetual neutrality. The country improved its economic situation by obtaining a sound position within the European Coal and Steel Community (1952) and within the European

BENELUX ECONOMIC UNION

The Benelux Economic Union of Belgium, the Netherlands, and Luxembourg was formed with the objective of bringing about total economic integration between the three countries by ensuring free circulation of persons, goods, capital, and services; by following a coordinated policy in the economic, financial, and social fields; and by pursuing a common policy with regard to foreign trade.

Belgium and Luxembourg had bilaterally formed an economic union in 1921; plans for a customs union of the three countries were made in the London Customs Convention in September 1944 and became operative in 1948. By 1956 nearly all of the internal trade of the union was tariff-free. On February 3, 1958, the Treaty of the Benelux Economic Union was signed; it became operative in 1960. Benelux became the first completely free international labour market; the movement of capital and services was also made free. Postal and transport rates were standardized, and welfare policies were coordinated. In 1970 border controls were abolished.

The day-to-day operations of Benelux are conducted by the Secretariat-General; the executive authority of the organization rests with the Committee of Ministers, which meets quarterly.

Benelux was once regarded as a promising experiment by which neighbouring countries would form customs unions that might then merge into wider economic unions. Following the ratification of the treaty establishing the European Coal and Steel Community in 1952, however, interest in such developments shifted to plans for the European Economic Community (EEC; later succeeded by the European Union), of which Belgium, the Netherlands, and Luxembourg are original members. For practical issues of economic integration, Benelux served as a useful example for the EEC.

Economic Community (1957; later succeeded by the European Union). Prince Jean, Charlotte's son, was installed as lieutenant-représentant of Charlotte in 1961, and he inherited the throne in 1964 upon his mother's abdication.

When the European Union (EU) was created in 1993, Luxembourg assumed an active role. EU administrative offices were sited in the country, and Luxembourgers such as Prime Ministers Jacques Santer and Jean-Claude Juncker played especially prominent roles in the EU. In 1995, when Santer, who had served as prime minister since 1984, stepped down from that office to become the president of the European Commission, he was replaced by Juncker. As a result of the legislative elections of 1999, Juncker remained as prime minster, heading a coalition government made up of his Christian Social People's Party (Chrëschtlech Sozial Vollekspartei; CSV) and the Democratic Party that brought to an end 15 years of coalition rule by the CSV and the Socialist Workers' Party of Luxembourg (Lëtzebuergesch Sozialistesch Arbechterpartei; LSAP). Government by a CSV-LSAP coalition returned following elections in 2004 and was retained in 2009 elections, with Juncker remaining as prime minister throughout.

In 2000, at age 79, Grand Duke Jean formally abdicated as chief of state and was replaced by his son, Crown Prince Henri, who in 2001 became the first member of the Luxembourgian royal family to open a session of parliament since 1877.

At the time the EU was formed, non-citizens made up more than half of the workforce of Luxembourg. By the end of the 20th century, the country had gained a reputation as a centre for private banking and financial services (particularly mutual fund investments), media and satellite broadcasting, and electronic commerce. The economy remained robust into the 21st century, and for a period Luxembourg claimed the world's highest standard of living (highest gross domestic product per capita). Indeed, Luxembourg survived the world financial downturn that began in 2008 and the subsequent euro-zone debt crisis much better than many of its European neighbours.

CHAPTER 16

THE NETHERLANDS: THE LAND AND ITS PEOPLE

"Netherlands," which means low-lying country, is the official name of the nation that many people also know as Holland (from Houtland, or "Wooded Land"). That name was originally given to one of the medieval cores of what later became the modern state and is still used for 2 of its 12 provinces (Noord-Holland and Zuid-Holland). Today, many people throughout the world continue to use the name Holland to refer to the country as a whole. But whether it is called the Netherlands or Holland, its people are known as the Dutch. Their language is also called Dutch, though it, too, is known to some by another name, Netherlandic.

A parliamentary democracy under a constitutional monarch, the Netherlands includes its former colonies in the Lesser Antilles: Aruba, Bonaire, Curaçao, Saba, Sint Eustatius, and Sint Maarten. The capital is Amsterdam and the seat of government The Hague.

The Netherlands is bounded by the North Sea to the north and west, Germany to the east, and Belgium to the south. The country is indeed low-lying and remarkably flat, with large expanses of lakes, rivers, and canals. Some 2,500 square miles (6,500 square km) of the Netherlands consist of reclaimed land, the result of a process of careful water management dating back to medieval times. Along the coasts, land was reclaimed from the sea, and, in the interior, lakes and marshes were drained, especially alongside the many rivers. All this new land was turned into polders, usually surrounded by dikes.

Netherlands. Olinchuk/Shutterstock.com

The Netherlands is today one of the world's most densely populated countries. Although the population as a whole is "graying" rapidly, with a high percentage over age 65, Amsterdam has remained one of the liveliest centres of international youth culture. There, perhaps more than anywhere else in the country, the Dutch tradition of social tolerance is readily encountered. Prostitution, "soft-drug" (marijuana and hashish) use, and euthanasia are all legal but carefully regulated in the Netherlands, which was also the first country to legalize same-sex marriage. The Dutch reputation for tolerance has been tested in the late 20th and early 21st centuries, however, as an increase in immigration from non-European Union countries and a populist turn in politics has resulted in growing nationalism and even xenophobia.

Notwithstanding these developments, the Netherlands' relative independence of outlook was evident as early as the 16th and 17th centuries, when the Dutch rejected monarchical controls and took a relatively enlightened view of other cultures, especially when they brought wealth and capital to the country's trading centres. In that period Dutch merchant ships sailed the world and helped lay the foundations of a great trading country characterized by a vigorous spirit of enterprise. In later centuries, the Netherlands continued to have one of the most advanced economies in the world, despite the country's modest size. Today the Dutch economy is still thriving, open, and generally internationalist in outlook.

RELIEF

If the Netherlands were to lose the protection of its dunes and dikes, the most densely populated part of the country would be inundated (largely by the sea but also in part by the rivers). This highly developed part of the Netherlands, which generally does not lie higher than about 3 feet (1 metre) above sea level, covers more than half the total area of the country. About half of this area (more than one-fourth of the total area of the country) actually lies below sea level.

The lower area consists mainly of polders, where the landscape not only lies at a very low elevation but is also very flat in appearance. On such land, building is possible only on "rafts," or after concrete piles, sometimes as long as 65 feet (20 metres), have been driven into the silt layer.

In the other, higher area, the layers of sand and gravel in the eastern part of the country were pushed sideways and upward in some places by ice tongues of the Saale Glacial Stage, forming elongated ridges that may reach a height of more than 330 feet (100 metres) and are the principal feature of the Hoge Park Veluwe National Park. The only part of the country where elevations exceed 350 feet (105 metres) is the border zone of the Ardennes. The Netherlands' highest point, the Vaalserberg, in the extreme southeastern corner, rises to 1,053 feet (321 metres).

POLDER

Polders are tracts of lowland that are reclaimed from a body of water, often the sea, by the construction of dikes roughly parallel to the shoreline, followed by drainage of the area between the dikes and the natural coastline. Where the land surface is above low-tide level, the water may be drained off through tide gates, which discharge water into the sea at low tide and automatically close to prevent re-entry of seawater at high tide. To reclaim lands that are below low-tide level, the water must be pumped over the dikes. If a sediment-laden stream can be diverted into the polder area, the sediment may serve to build up the polder bottom to a higher level, thus facilitating drainage.

Soil in areas newly reclaimed from the sea contains so much salt that most plants will not grow. Procedures for ridding the soil of salt, therefore, must be used along with diking and draining to develop agriculturally productive land.

DRAINAGE AND DIKES

The Zuiderzee was originally an estuary of the Rhine River. By natural action it then became a shallow inland sea, biting deep into the land, and eventually it was hollowed into an almost circular shape by the action of winds and tides. In 1920 work was begun on the Zuiderzee Project, of which the IJsselmeer Dam (Afsluitdijk), begun in 1927, was a part. This 19-mile- (30-km-) long dam was completed in 1932 to finally seal off the Zuiderzee from the Waddenzee and the North Sea. In the IJsselmeer, or IJssel Lake, formed from the southern part of the Zuiderzee, four large polders, the IJsselmeer Polders, with a total area of about 650 square miles (1,700 square km), were constructed around a freshwater basin fed by the IJssel and other rivers and linked with the sea by sluices and locks in the barrier dam.

The first two polders created there—Wieringermeer and North East (Noordoost) Polder, drained before and during World War II—are used mostly for agriculture. The two polders reclaimed in the 1950s and '60s—South Flevoland Polder (Zuidelijk) and East Flevoland Polder (Oostelijk)—are used for residential, industrial, and recreational purposes. Among the cities that have developed there are Lelystad and Almere.

In the southwest, the disastrous gales and spring tide of February 1, 1953, which flooded some 400,000 acres (162,000 hectares) of land and killed 1,800 people, accelerated the implementation of the Delta Project, which aimed to close off most of the sea inlets of the southwestern delta.

These delta works were designed to shorten the coastline by 450 miles (725 km), combat the salination of the soil, and allow the development of the area through roads that were constructed over

ZUIDERZEE FLOODS

On December 14, 1287, a heavy storm over the North Sea generated surging waves that collapsed a thin land barrier, flooding the Zuiderzee inlet. A significant percentage of the country's population perished in the disaster (which caused 50,000 casualties), and it has been rated as one of the most destructive floods in recorded history. Called the St. Lucia flood, this event also created direct sea access for the village of Amsterdam, allowing its development into a major port city.

On November 18, 1421, the region was hit by another massive storm surge. Named St. Elizabeth's flood for the saint's November 19 feast day, this inundation engulfed Zeeland and southern Holland, flooding several villages and transforming a segment of reclaimed land called Grote Waard into an inland sea. As many as 10,000 people died as a result of the incident. Some areas that were flooded in this storm remain under water today.

Some one-fourth of the Netherlands lies below sea level; without human intervention, much of this area would be uninhabitable. The region has a long history of devastating floods that continually reshape the land. For more than 1,000 years the residents of this region have devised ways to reclaim land from encroachment by the sea. Medieval residents constructed canals to direct the flow of surplus water, while windmill-powered pumps became the predominate water removal system during the Renaissance. In the 18th century pumping stations and dikes were built, and in the 20th century the government spent vast sums to establish one of the world's premier flood-protection systems.

10 dams and 2 bridges built between 1960 and 1987. The largest of these dams, crossing the 5-mile- (8-km-) wide Eastern Schelde (Oosterschelde) estuary, has been built in the form of a storm-surge barrier incorporating dozens of openings that can be closed in the event of flood. The barrier is normally open, allowing salt water to enter the estuary and about three-fourths of the tidal movement to be maintained, limiting damage to the natural environment in the Eastern Schelde. In the interest of the commerce of the ports of Rotterdam and Antwerp, no dams were constructed in the New Waterway, which links Rotterdam to the North Sea, or the West Schelde, an approach to Antwerp, Belgium. The dikes along these waterways consequently had to be strengthened.

A region with a very specific character has been formed by the great rivers—Rhine, Lek, Waal, and Maas (Meuse)—that flow from east to west through the central part of the country. The landscape in this area is characterized by high dikes along wide rivers, orchards along the levees formed by the rivers, and numerous large bridges over which pass the roads and railways that connect the central Netherlands with the southern provinces.

SOILS

In the late Pleistocene Epoch (from about 126,000 to 11,700 years ago), the Scandinavian ice sheet covered the northern half of the Netherlands. After this period, a large area in the north of what is now the Netherlands was left covered by moraine (glacial accumulation of earth and rock debris). In the centre and south, the Rhine and Maas rivers unloaded thick layers of silt and gravel transported from the European mountain chains. Later, during the Holocene Epoch (i.e., the past 11,700 years), clay was deposited in the sheltered lagoons behind the coastal dunes, and peat soil often subsequently developed in these areas. If the peat soil was washed away by the sea or dug away by humans (for the production of fuel and salt), lakes were created. Many of these were reclaimed in later centuries (as mentioned above), while others now form highly valued outdoor recreational areas.

CLIMATE

The climate of the Netherlands is temperate, with gentle winters, cool summers, and rainfall in every season. Southerly and westerly winds predominate, and the sea moderates the climate through onshore winds and the effect of the Gulf Stream.

The position of the country—between the area of high-pressure air masses centred on the Azores and the low-pressure region centred on Iceland—makes the Netherlands an area of collision between warm and polar air masses, thus creating unsettled weather. Winds meet with little resistance over the flat country, though the hills in the south significantly diminish the velocity of the potent wind that prevails along the coast. On average, frost occurs 60 days per year. July temperatures average in the low mid-60s °F (about 17 °C), and those of January average in the mid-30s °F (about 2 °C). Annual rainfall averages about 31 inches (790 mm), with only about 25 clear days per year. The average rainfall is highest in summer (August) and autumn and lowest in springtime. The country is known—not least through the magnificent landscapes of Dutch painters—for its heavy clouds,

"View over a Flat Landscape," *oil on canvas by Philips Koninck, 1664; in the Museum Boymans-van Beuningen, Rotterdam.* Courtesy of the Museum Boymans-van Beuningen, Rotterdam, The Netherlands

and on an average day three-fifths of the sky is clouded.

PLANT AND ANIMAL LIFE

Most wild Dutch plant species are of the Atlantic district within the Euro-Siberian phytogeographic region. Gradients of salt and winter temperature variations cause relatively minor zonal differences in both wild and garden plants from the coast to more continental regions. The effects of elevation are negligible. Vegetation from coastal sand dunes, muddy coastal areas, slightly brackish lakes, and river deltas is especially scarce in the surrounding countries. Lakes, marshes, peatland, woods, heaths, and agricultural areas determine the general floral species. Clay, peat, and sand are important soil factors for the inland vegetation regions.

Animal life is relegated by region according to vegetation. Seabirds and other sea life, such as mollusks, are found especially in the muddy Waddenzee area and in the extreme southwest. Migrating birds pass in huge numbers through the Netherlands or remain for a summer or winter stay. Species of waterbirds and marsh and pasture birds are numerous. Larger mammals, such as roe deer, red deer, foxes, and badgers, are mostly restricted to nature reserves. Some species, such as boars, beavers, fallow deer, mouflons, and muskrats, have been introduced locally or reintroduced. Some reptiles and amphibians are endangered. Numerous species of river fish and river lobsters have become scarce because of water pollution. There is a diversity of brackish and freshwater animals inhabiting the many lakes, canals, and drainage ditches, but the vulnerable species of the nutritionally deficient waters have become rare.

Nature reserves have been formed by governmental and private organizations. Well-known reserves include the Naardermeer of Amsterdam, the Hoge Veluwe National Park, and the Oostvaardersplassen in the centre of the country. Some endangered species are protected by law.

ETHNIC GROUPS

Popular belief holds that the Dutch are a mixture of Frisians, Saxons, and Franks. In fact, research has made plausible the contention that the autochthonous inhabitants of the region were a mixture of pre-Germanic and Germanic population groups who in the course of time had converged on the main deltaic region of western Europe. There emerged from these groups in the 7th and 8th centuries some major polities based on certain ethnic and cultural unities that then came to be identified as Frisians, Saxons, and Franks.

The Dutch Republic originated from medieval statelets, and its legal successor, the Kingdom of the Netherlands, has attracted countless immigrants through the centuries. A strong impetus was the principle of freedom of thought, which engendered the relative tolerance that developed in the 16th and 17th centuries. These sentiments were—and are—most manifest in the prosperous commercial and industrial centres in the western provinces, which attracted many members of persecuted religious or political minorities. Among these were southern lowlanders, French Huguenots, and Portuguese Jews, along with many people who sought to improve their economic situation, such as Germans and non-Iberian Jews. In the 20th century, immigrants from the former Dutch overseas colonies added to the influx; they included Indonesians and peoples from the Moluccas and from Suriname on the northeast coast of South America. In recent decades, however, as Muslims from Turkey and Morocco arrived in large numbers, Dutch embracement of diversity has been more tenuous. At the beginning of the 21st century, not only did a virulent anti-immigrant movement emerge, but also the government required that immigrants pass a test in their country of origin relating to Dutch language and culture before they were allowed to enter the Netherlands.

LANGUAGES

The language in the whole of the country is Dutch, sometimes referred to as Netherlandic, a Germanic language that is also spoken by the inhabitants of northern Belgium (where it is called Flemish). Afrikaans, an official language of South Africa, is a variant of the Dutch spoken by 17th-century emigrants from the Holland and Zeeland regions. Apart from Dutch, the inhabitants of the northern province of Friesland also speak their own language (called Frisian in English), which is closer to English than to either Dutch or German.

In the major cities especially, many people are fluent in several languages, reflecting the country's geographic position, its history of occupation, and its attraction for tourists. English, French, and German are among the languages commonly heard.

THE HERITAGE OF DUTCH HUMANISM

The considerable hospitality exhibited by the Dutch is perhaps to some extent rooted in the spirit of humanism that was typical of the Dutch Republic of the 16th to the 18th century. Figures such as Desiderius Erasmus in the 16th century and Hugo Grotius in the 17th century epitomize that spirit. It resulted in a rather pragmatic mode of thinking that has dominated Dutch bourgeois culture since the 16th century, coexisting with growing commercial acumen. Evolving Dutch society came to encompass a diversity of religious traditions, from rigid Calvinism and more-tolerant forms of Protestantism to conformist Roman Catholicism. Calvinism was always the religion of the national elite, while Roman Catholicism could be practiced only behind closed doors before 1798 (when all religions were pronounced equal before the law), and at various times certain sects were persecuted. In comparison with some of

FRISIAN LANGUAGE

The Frisian language was formerly spoken from what is now the province of Noord-Holland (North Holland) in the Netherlands along the North Sea coastal area to modern German Schleswig, including the offshore islands in this area. Today, modern Frisian is spoken in only three small remaining areas, each with its own dialect. These dialects are West Frisian, which is spoken in the province of Friesland in the Netherlands, including the islands of Schiermonnikoog and Terschelling; East Frisian, which is spoken in the Saterland west of Oldenburg, Germany; and North Frisian, which is spoken along the west coast of Schleswig in Germany and on the offshore islands of Sylt, Föhr, Amrum, the Halligen Islands, and Helgoland.

Written records date from the end of the 13th century and are in Old Frisian, a stage of the language that lasted until the late 16th century. Old Frisian shows all the features that distinguish English and Frisian from the other Germanic languages.

Although Frisian was little used as a written language for about 300 years after the end of the Old Frisian period, there has been a revival in modern times in the West Frisian area. The language is now used in the schools and courts in the province of Friesland. There is also a Frisian Academy. East and North Frisian are being gradually supplanted by German.

its neighbours, the Netherlands historically has shown a remarkable degree of religious tolerance.

In terms of formal allegiance, the present Dutch population can be divided into three almost equal groups relative to religion: Roman Catholics (the southern provinces of Limburg and Noord-Brabant are traditionally almost monolithically Catholic, but in terms of absolute numbers more Catholics live north of the great rivers than in Noord-Brabant and Limburg), Protestants (particularly the adherents to the Netherlands Reformed Church), and the nonreligious. The adherents of Islam have developed a wide range of institutions in the Netherlands and constituted about 6 percent of the population at the turn of the 21st century.

Secularization has made its mark in the Netherlands; the Christian Democrat parties of the centre, whose political platform included planks such as public funding for religious education, had attracted more than 50 percent of the vote up to the 1960s, but in the 1990s they were ejected from government for the first time in the 20th century. Nonetheless, the educational institutions and political parties that evolved in the late 19th and early 20th centuries along denominational lines remain as potent as the more or less secularized parties and institutions that sprang from socialist and liberal movements. The "pillarization" of Dutch society—that is, the founding of separate institutions such as hospitals, schools, and periodicals by various groups—commands much less religiosity and devotion now, but these organizations are still central to education, political life, and public service.

These more or less converging societal groupings have not completely obliterated a range of age-old regional cultural distinctions. They are sometimes vividly preserved, as in the case of the northern province of Friesland, which proudly conserves the ancient Frisian culture. With more-recent immigration, new cultural groups are becoming significant.

SETTLEMENT PATTERNS

Modern urbanization in the Netherlands took place mainly in the 20th century. In 1900 more than half the population was still living in villages or towns of fewer than 10,000 inhabitants. A century later this proportion had decreased to about one-tenth. There has, nevertheless, been a decrease in the city-proper populations of the large metropolitan centres. These inner cities are now becoming economic and cultural centres, their populations having spread outward in search of newer housing and greater living space in suburbs, new residential quarters of rural settlements, and new towns. In the 1960s and '70s the authorities stimulated this development by subsidizing house building in a number of so-called growth nuclei and by moving several groupings of public offices from the western core area of the country to more-rural areas in the north, east, and south. More recently, however, government planning policy has aimed at again concentrating the

Old Church by a canal in the old inner town of Delft, Netherlands. J. Allan Cash Photolibrary/EB Inc.

population in and around the existing cities, especially in the western portion of the country.

In this part of the Netherlands, the bulk of the population is concentrated in the horseshoe-shaped urban core known as the Randstad ("Rim City," or "City on the Edge"), comprising such cities as Rotterdam, The Hague, Leiden, Haarlem, Amsterdam, Hilversum, and Utrecht. Extensions of the Randstad stretch toward the east (Arnhem, Nijmegen) and the south (Breda, Tilburg, Eindhoven), thus forming the so-called Central Netherlands Urban Ring. Other urban centres are Groningen in the northeast, Enschede and Hengelo in the east, and Maastricht and Heerlen in the southeast. It is government policy to keep traditional towns and cities separated by strips of agricultural or recreational land.

DEMOGRAPHIC TRENDS

Exceptionally high fertility rates until the 1960s contributed to the Netherlands' being one of the world's most densely populated countries. Since then, trends have shifted, owing mainly to wider use of birth control pills (a consequence of growing secularization) and to the increased participation of women in higher education and the workforce. At the beginning of the 21st century, Dutch birth and death rates were both among the world's lowest, resulting in a somewhat older society, with most population growth arising from immigration.

Emigrants exceeded immigrants by an average of almost 20,000 each year from 1947 to 1954. Thereafter the economy and labour potential of the more industrialized European countries attracted an increasing number of labour migrants from southern Europe, Turkey, and Morocco, so that the balance of in-migration and out-migration remained more or less static. From 1970 there was a continuous immigrant surplus, and in the early 21st century, one-fifth of the Netherlands' population was made up of residents born abroad or with at least one foreign-born parent. In the late 1990s, with most other doors to immigration closed by government policy and the possibility of entry for family reunification largely expended, the numbers of applications for asylum were high. There was also an increase in the immigration of Dutch nationals from the Netherlands Antilles. Following legislation in 2001 that further tightened immigration restrictions, the annual number of asylum seekers fell, but the issue of immigration remained on the political forefront.

For many years prior to 1970, internal migration showed a constant flow from the more rural provinces in the north, east, and south toward the more strongly urbanized western part of the country. After 1970, however, the trend toward migration to the west was reversed. Subsequent emigration was mainly from Zuid-Holland and Noord-Holland (the most heavily populated provinces) toward Utrecht and the less densely populated provinces, where government regional policy stimulated industrial growth—Groningen, Friesland, Drenthe, Gelderland, and Zeeland.

CHAPTER 17

THE DUTCH ECONOMY

Since World War II, the Netherlands has been a highly industrialized country occupying a central position in the economic life of western Europe. Although agriculture accounts for a small percentage of the national income and labour force, it remains a highly specialized contributor to Dutch exports. Because of the scarcity of mineral resources—with the important exception of natural gas—the country is dependent on large imports of basic materials.

The Netherlands has a market economy (meaning that the exchange of goods and services is governed by the market and not by government planning), but the state traditionally has been a significant participant in such fields as transportation, resource extraction, and heavy industry. The government also employs a substantial percentage of the total labour force and effects investment policy. Nonetheless, during the 1980s, when the ideological climate favoured market economics, considerable privatization was initiated, government economic intervention was reduced, and the welfare state was restructured. State-owned companies such as DSM (Dutch State Mines) and KLM (Royal Dutch Airlines) were among those privatized. Nonetheless, the Netherlands has, relatively speaking, a highly regulated mixed economy.

Since World War II, economic development has been consciously stimulated by government policy, and state subsidies have been granted to attract industry and services toward the relatively underdeveloped north and certain other pockets of economic stagnation. Despite these subsidies, the

Flower cultivation in the polders of South Holland near the border with North Holland in the Netherlands. Russ Kinne/Comstock

western part of the country remains the centre of new activity, especially in the service sector.

AGRICULTURE

The country's agricultural land is divided into grassland, arable farmland, and horticultural land. Dutch dairy farming is highly developed; the milk yield per acre of grassland and the yield per cow are among the highest in the world. A good percentage of the total milk production is exported after being processed into such dairy products as butter, cheese, and condensed milk. Meat and eggs are produced in intensively farmed livestock holdings, where enormous numbers of pigs, calves, and poultry are kept in large sheds and fed mainly on imported fodder. Most cereals for human consumption as well as fodder are imported.

Horticulture carried on under glass is of special importance. The export of hothouse tomatoes, cucumbers, bell peppers, cut flowers, and houseplants has greatly increased, and the Netherlands now contains a substantial share of the total European horticultural area under glass. Open-air horticulture also produces fruit, vegetables, cut flowers, and bulbs, the latter from the world-famous colourful bulb fields.

Only one-tenth of the land in the Netherlands is forested. The Dutch fishing industry, while not large, is nevertheless significant. At the beginning of the 21st century, three-fourths of the fish consumed in the Netherlands was foreign-caught, yet about four-fifths of the total catch was exported. As a result, the country is unusual in exporting more fish than it imports.

RESOURCES AND POWER

With the increasing use of oil and especially natural gas, coal mining (concentrated in the southeast) was discontinued in 1974 because of the rising cost of production. The Netherlands imports several million tons of coal annually to meet domestic and industrial needs, including those of such industrial installations as the steel works of IJmuiden at the mouth of the North Sea Canal.

The production of crude oil, of which there are minimal deposits, covers only a small part of Dutch requirements. The wells are located near Schoonebeek, in the northeast, and in the southwest. Large amounts of crude oil are imported for

Float in the Bloemencorso, an annual flower festival held in September in Aalsmeer, Netherlands. The J. Allan Cash Photolibrary

refining in the Netherlands, and much of the refined petroleum is exported.

The discovery of natural gas in 1959 had a tremendous influence on the development of the Dutch economy. The gas fields are in the northeastern Netherlands—with the largest field at Slochteren—and beneath the Dutch sector of the North Sea. Under the Geneva Convention of 1958, the Netherlands was allocated a 22,000-square-mile (57,000-square-km) block of the continental shelf of the North Sea, an area larger than the country itself. Technological advances led to an increase in offshore production in the last decades of the 20th century. One-third of the natural gas produced is exported, primarily to countries of the European Union (EU), helping to improve the balance of payments in the economic sector—in which

TULIP MANIA

Tulips were introduced into Europe from Turkey shortly after 1550, and the vividly coloured flowers became a popular if costly item. The demand for differently coloured varieties of tulips soon exceeded the supply, and prices for individual bulbs of rare types began to rise to unwarranted heights in northern Europe. By about 1610 a single bulb of a new variety was acceptable as dowry for a bride, and a flourishing brewery in France was exchanged for one bulb of the variety Tulipe Brasserie. The craze reached its height in Holland during 1633–37. Before 1633 Holland's tulip trade had been restricted to professional growers and experts, but the steadily rising prices tempted many ordinary middle-class and poor families to speculate in the tulip market. Homes, estates, and industries were mortgaged so that bulbs could be bought for resale at higher prices. Sales and resales were made many times over without the bulbs ever leaving the ground, and rare varieties of bulbs sold for the equivalent of hundreds of dollars each. The crash came early in 1637, when doubts arose as to whether prices would continue to increase. Almost overnight the price structure for tulips collapsed, sweeping away fortunes and leaving behind financial ruin for many ordinary Dutch families.

the Netherlands has usually had its largest deficit. The natural gas discoveries began a trend in Dutch industries toward greater use of domestically produced fuel.

One of the results of the reliance on gas is that nuclear power is very limited in the Netherlands. On the other hand, the flat maritime landscape is well suited to the use of wind turbines, which are increasingly employed in agricultural areas. Among the country's other resources are zinc, extracted at Budel, sodium at Delfzijl, and magnesium at Veendam.

MANUFACTURING

Modern Dutch industrial development began relatively late, about 1870, and production rose even during the Great Depression of the 1930s. Further development became a priority after World War II, when ascending population figures and growing farm-labour surpluses necessitated the creation of tens of thousands of jobs each year. Manufacturing industries accounted for about one-fifth of the labour force in the early 21st century but only about one-eighth of production value. Important components of the manufacturing sector include food and beverages, metal, chemical, petroleum products, and electrical and electronics industries. Textile manufacturing, shipbuilding, and aircraft construction were important historically, but employment in those sectors has greatly declined. The government has encouraged new industrial development in the fields of microelectronics, biotechnology, and the so-called digital economy.

FINANCE, TRADE, AND SERVICES

Commercial banking in the Netherlands is in the hands of a few large concerns, and there has been a trend toward mergers of banks and insurance companies over several decades. The state-owned Netherlands Central Bank supervises the banking system. The Amsterdam Stock Exchange, one of the oldest in the world, was founded in the early 1600s. In 1998 the Netherlands formally joined the EU's Economic and Monetary Union (EMU), and in 2002 the euro replaced the guilder as the Netherlands' sole currency.

Trade is conducted mainly with Europe and North America. The member states of the EU are the Netherlands' dominant trading partners, receiving three-fourths of Dutch exports and providing one-half of the country's imports.

Amsterdam Stock Exchange. © AP Images

In 1958 (just as the Common Market was established) some 40 percent of Dutch exports went to West Germany (now Germany), Belgium, Luxembourg, France, and Italy. By the beginning of the 21st century, the main trading partners were Germany, Belgium, the United Kingdom, France, Italy, the United States, Russia, and China. In the same period, the service industry accounted for about seven-tenths of the labour force and about two-thirds of gross domestic product (GDP), with tourism playing a vital role. The most frequent foreign visitors are Germans, Britons, Americans, and Belgians.

LABOUR AND TAXATION

Dutch employers are organized mainly in separate but closely cooperating organizations: one Roman Catholic and Protestant and one nondenominational. The labour force had a tripartite organization before the Socialist and Roman Catholic unions merged as Netherlands Trade Union Federation (Federatie Nederlandse Vakbeweging; FNV), leaving the Protestant union, the National Federation of Christian Trade Unions (Christelijk Nationaal Vakverbond; CNV), and a few small independent organizations far behind in membership. Employer organizations and labour unions are represented on the Joint Industrial Labour Council, established in 1945 for collective bargaining, and on the Social and Economic Council, which serves mainly to advise the government. These corporatist arrangements were substantially deregulated in the 1980s as neoliberal, market-oriented policies were carried out. Socioeconomic planning remains extremely important, however, and the Central Planning Bureau's economic models are integral to all forms of economic policy.

The Dutch government uses both direct and indirect taxation to finance its extensive welfare programs. In 1969 it began imposing a value-added tax (VAT; a levy on the amount that a business firm adds to the price of a commodity during production and distribution of a good). In addition to a graduated personal income tax, there is also a property tax, a motor vehicle tax, an excise tax on certain products, an energy tax, and a tax on legal transactions.

TRANSPORTATION AND TELECOMMUNICATIONS

In the Netherlands transportation is of special importance because the country functions as a gateway for the traffic of goods between western Europe and the rest of the world. (Amsterdam, for example, has been the centre of diamond exchange for centuries.) Trade flows through Dutch harbours, continuing its passage by riverboat, train, truck, and pipeline. Maritime traffic accounts for more than half the total amount of goods loaded and unloaded in the Netherlands, and, indeed, the whole southern part of the

KLM

KLM (Koninklijke Luchtvaartmaatschappij NV: "Royal Air Transportation Company") was founded on October 7, 1919, by a group of banking and business interests led by a former Dutch pilot, Albert Plesman (1889–1953), who headed the company until his death. KLM's first route, between Amsterdam and London, went into service on May 17, 1920, and was followed the same year by a route to Copenhagen, via Hamburg. In 1923 a route to Brussels was introduced. As early as 1921 KLM (which was also known in English as Royal Dutch Airlines) had opened the world's first airline reservations and ticket office, in Amsterdam.

In 1928 Plesman also founded Koninklijke Nederlandsch–Indische Luchtvaart Maatschappij (KNILM), the Royal Netherlands–East Indies Airlines, which in 1930 inaugurated regular flights from the Netherlands to Batavia (now Jakarta) in the Dutch East Indies, a trip of 8,700 miles (14,000 km), until 1940 the world's longest scheduled air route. KNILM merged with KLM in 1945.

In the 1920s and '30s KLM's routes spread throughout the Netherlands and Europe. During World War II, however, KLM lay largely dormant except in the West Indies, where its service, begun in 1941, grew rapidly, expanding to nine Caribbean and Latin American countries by 1945.

In 1945 KLM resumed its European service. On May 21, 1946, it became the first European airline to introduce scheduled service across the North Atlantic, to New York. The same year, it established trunk lines across the South Atlantic, to Curaçao and South America.

In 2004 KLM joined SkyTeam, an international airline alliance. The same year, the airline was acquired by Air France to create Air France–KLM, one of the world's largest air carriers. Under the terms of the deal, however, the two airlines continued to operate as separate companies, retaining their own hubs, flights, and logos. Until that merger, KLM was the world's oldest continuously operating airline.

North Sea may be likened to an immense traffic square, fed by the Thames, Rhine, Maas, and Schelde rivers, with links into the hinterland of the continent that make it one of the greatest commercial arteries of the world. Rotterdam has the country's best-equipped modern harbour, the largest on the continent. Europoort, the region between Rotterdam and the North Sea, can easily be reached by the biggest oceangoing ships; it serves as an approach via the New Waterway Canal to Rotterdam harbour. For some 40 years, until it was eclipsed by busier Asian ports in the early 21st century, Rotterdam handled more tonnage than any other harbour in the world. In petroleum processing, too, Rotterdam is one of the world's leading centres, with facilities to receive the largest supertankers. The number of rivercraft is probably unsurpassed by any other country.

Other important ports, though dwarfed by Rotterdam-Europoort, are Amsterdam and, on the Western Schelde, Flushing and Terneuzen. KLM initiated scheduled service between Amsterdam and London in 1920 and became one of the world's leading airlines, merging with Air France in 2004 to form Air France-KLM.

Amsterdam Airport (Schiphol)—on the site of the former Haarlem Lake at about 13 feet (4 metres) below sea level—is among Europe's largest airports. Smaller airports of international importance are Rotterdam (Zestienhoven), Eindhoven, and Maastricht.

In terms of internal traffic, motor vehicles, accommodated by a comprehensive road network, dominate both passenger and goods transport, despite the fact that there is a dense modern railway network. Dutch road haulage companies are market leaders and constitute a large slice of such business in the EU. Moreover, Dutch shipping companies handle about two-fifths of the EU's freight transport by water. The Netherlands' network of inland waterways, made up of some 3,000 miles (4,800 km) of rivers and canals, is linked with Belgian, French, and German systems. Besides such natural waterways as the Rhine, Lek, Waal, and Maas rivers, many artificial waterways—the Juliana Canal, the Amsterdam-Rhine River Canal (between Amsterdam and Tiel), the Maas-Waal Canal (west of Nijmegen), and others—connect the major ports on the coast with the hinterland.

The telecommunications system in the Netherlands is highly advanced, with extensive fibre-optic and mobile networks. Per capita cell phone usage in the Netherlands is comparable to that of most western European countries (though considerably less pervasive than in Scandinavia); per capita personal computer use is high by western European standards.

CHAPTER 18

DUTCH GOVERNMENT AND SOCIETY

The Kingdom of the Netherlands is a constitutional monarchy. The monarchy is hereditary in both the male and female lines. The constitution, which dates from 1814, declares that the head of state, the monarch, is inviolable and thereby embodies the concept of ministerial responsibility. It further provides that no government may remain in power against the will of the parliament. The States General (Staten-Generaal), as the parliament is officially known, consists of two houses: the First Chamber (Eerste Kamer), or Senate, whose members are elected by the members of the councils of the 12 provinces; and the directly elected Second Chamber (Tweede Kamer), or House of Representatives. Both houses share legislative power with the government, officially known as the Crown (Kroon), defined as the head of state acting in conjunction with the ministers. The two houses control government policy. The First Chamber can only approve or reject legislation but does not have the power to propose or amend it.

Every four years, after elections to the Second Chamber have been held, the government resigns, and a process of bargaining starts between elected party leaders aspiring to form a government that will be assured of the support of a parliamentary majority. It usually takes a few months of maneuvering before a formateur, as the main architect of such a coalition is known, is ready to accept a royal invitation to form a government. The head of state then formally appoints the ministers. In the event of political crises resulting in the

The floor of the First Chamber (Eerste Kamer), the Senate of the Netherlands. AFP/Getty Images

fall of the government before the end of a four-year period, the same process of bargaining takes place. The monarch, acting on the advice of the ministries, has the right to dissolve one or both chambers, at which time new elections are held.

LOCAL GOVERNMENT

In local government, the most important institutions are the municipalities (gemeenten). Since World War II the number of municipalities—which once totaled more than 1,000—has been dramatically reduced as a result of redivisions. Each municipality is run by a directly elected council that is presided over by a burgemeester (mayor), who is appointed by the national government and serves as chairman of the executive, the members of which are elected by and from the council; in the early 21st century, there was active discussion of directly electing mayors. In those areas to which

INTERNATIONAL CRIMINAL COURT

Established by the Rome Statute of the International Criminal Court (1998) to prosecute individuals accused of genocide, war crimes, and crimes against humanity, the International Criminal Court (ICC) commenced operations on July 1, 2002, after the requisite number of countries (60) ratified the statute (some 140 countries signed the agreement). The ICC was established as a court of last resort to prosecute the most heinous offenses in cases where national courts fail to act. It is headquartered in The Hague. By 2002 China, Russia, and the U.S. had declined to participate in the ICC, and the U.S. had campaigned actively to have its citizens exempted from the court's jurisdiction.

the councils' own ordinances are applicable, the municipalities are autonomous. In many instances, national legislation or provincial ordinances provide for the cooperation of municipal authorities.

The country is divided into 12 provinces: Groningen, Friesland, Drenthe, Overijssel, Flevoland, Gelderland, Utrecht, Noord-Holland, Zuid-Holland, Zeeland, Noord-Brabant, and Limburg. Their administrative system has the same structure as the municipal government: directly elected councils (staten), which elect the members of the executive, except for the chairman, who is appointed by the national government. The main functions of the provinces include oversight of the municipalities within their borders and of district water-control boards (waterschappen).

JUSTICE

In the Netherlands the ordinary administration of justice is entrusted exclusively to judges appointed for life; there is no jury system. There are cantonal courts (kantongerechten), which exercise jurisdiction in a whole range of minor civil and criminal cases. More important cases are handled by one of the district courts (rechtbanken), which also can hear appeals from cantonal court decisions. Appeals against decisions from the district courts are heard by one of five courts of appeal (gerechtshoven). The Supreme Court (Hoge Raad) ensures a uniform application of the law, but it cannot determine constitutionality. In the legislative process itself, the government and the parliament together pass judgment on the constitutionality of a bill under consideration. Laws that are at variance with the country's international agreements cannot be enforced by the courts.

The Netherlands also plays an important role in international law. The Hague is the seat of the International Criminal Court, the International Court of Justice, and Europol.

INTERNATIONAL COURT OF JUSTICE

The International Court of Justice (ICJ) was the successor to the Permanent Court of International Justice, the judicial body of the League of Nations. Its first session was held in 1946. Its jurisdiction is limited to disputes between states willing to accept its authority on matters of international law. Its decisions are binding, but it has no enforcement power; appeals must be made to the UN Security Council. Its 15-member body of judges, each of whom serves a nine-year term, is elected by countries party to the court's founding statute. No two judges may come from the same country.

POLITICAL PROCESS

The Second Chamber, the provincial councils, and the municipal councils are elected according to a system of proportional representation. In general elections for the Second Chamber, it can take as little as 0.66 percent of the overall vote to get one of the seats in the chamber. As a result, a large number of parties and political movements are represented in the parliament. The principal Dutch political parties in the early 21st century included the Christian Democratic Appeal (CDA), formed in the 1970s from a coalition of the leading Christian parties; the Labour Party (Partij van de Arbeid; PvdA); the liberal People's Party for Freedom and Democracy (Volkspartij voor Vrijheid en Democratie; VVD); the Socialist Party; Democrats 66 (D66); and the Party for Freedom (Partij voor de Vrijheid; PVV), led by Geert Wilders, an anti-Islam populist, who draws on support for the now defunct List Pim Fortuyn (LPF), named for its founder, Wilhelmus Fortuyn, an anti-immigration populist who was assassinated in 2002. There is also a comparatively high proportion of women representatives in the States General (more than one-third in the early 21st century). The franchise is extended to all Dutch citizens who have reached age 18, except for a few special groups, such as the mentally impaired. About three-fourths of the citizenry are registered voters.

SECURITY

The Dutch armed forces consist of an army, a navy, and an air force; there is also a small unit of military police. Until the 1990s, all male citizens were liable for military service at age 18; however, the end of the Cold War, the reunification of Germany, and the disbandment of the Warsaw Pact rapidly changed Dutch defense needs. The military is now an all-volunteer force open to males and females who are at least age 20. With fewer personnel than before, it concentrates on crisis control and higher mobility.

HEALTH AND WELFARE

Following World War II, the Netherlands developed an elaborate system of social security, providing all its citizens with universal health care and old age and unemployment benefits. All citizens are entitled to four national insurance schemes: the General Old Age Pensions Act, the General Widows and Orphans Act, the Exceptional Medical Expenses Act, and General Disability Benefits. There also are four employee insurance schemes: the Sickness Benefits Act, the Disability Insurance Act, the Compulsory Health Insurance Act, and the Unemployment Insurance Act. The system is supplemented by a number of social services, the most important being the General Family Allowance Act, which provides for family allowances for children up to age 17 and under certain circumstances for older children (including those not entitled to student grants), and the National Assistance Act, under which benefits are paid to claimants who have little or no income.

The system is one of the most generous in the world, but since the 1980s its costs have become increasingly prohibitive. As with the systems employed by many other Western democracies,

there were major revisions to the Dutch scheme, such as cost-sharing provisions and restrictions involving temporary workers, the self-employed, and non-Dutch nationals. The government pension is used in combination with pensions from employers and from private insurance plans.

HOUSING

A severe housing shortage began developing after the mid-20th century and became a source of political controversy. By the 1970s, in the face of continually growing demand, even an unprecedented boom in housing construction proved inadequate. Demographic changes led to a rapid increase in the number of households, and rising standards of living fueled the consumption of space per person. This crisis abated by the mid-1970s, only to be replaced by a financial one.

Rent controls, as well as alternative investment opportunities and the introduction of the social security of the welfare state, reduced the private rental sector from more than 60 percent in 1947 to less than 15 percent by the late 1980s. The expansion of the postwar housing stock was made possible only by massive investment in subsidized rental housing, run by not-for-profit housing associations. Concurrently, the generously subsidized homeowner sector expanded. Today, just over half of Dutch homes are owned by their occupants (still a low figure by EU standards). Since the early 1990s the government has stepped back from its central role in controlling and subsidizing rents and has concentrated available public resources more on lower income groups. By 2001, a century after the Housing Act of 1901, the Netherlands officially declared an end to the housing shortage.

EDUCATION

All primary, secondary, and higher education is provided by either governmental (municipal or state) or private institutions. The latter are, with a few exceptions, run by Protestant and Roman Catholic organizations. All private schools are, when they conform to legally fixed standards, financed from governmental funds on an equal footing with their public (openbare) counterparts. Dutch secondary education is not a comprehensive system (that is, the same for all pupils) but one consisting of several tracks. Among these are the five-year Higher General Education track, the mandatory preparation for institutions of higher education other than the university; and the six-year Preparatory Scientific Secondary Education track, which is mandatory for university admittance.

The system of higher education is a binary one. There are dozens of institutions for Higher Professional Education, and they cover many professional fields complementary to those served by the country's principal universities. The latter are all publicly financed. A number of the major universities cover a general range of disciplines, including the four state universities—of Leiden (founded 1575), Groningen (1614), Utrecht (1636), and Limburg at Maastricht (1976)—and the (former municipal) University of Amsterdam (1632), the Erasmus University at Rotterdam (1973), the (originally Calvinist) Free University at Amsterdam (1880), the (originally Roman Catholic) Radboud University of Nijmegen (1923), and the University of Tilburg (1927). Other governmental universities are more specialized: the universities of technology at Delft (1842), Eindhoven (1956), and Enschede (Twente University; 1961) and the Agricultural University at Wageningen (1918). In addition, the Open University, established in 1984, provides for both university and vocational education through correspondence courses.

ENVIRONMENTAL CONTROL

In the Netherlands, as in all industrialized countries, the increasing pollution of both the natural and man-made environments is a major problem. Pollution in the Netherlands has certain specific aspects that are closely linked to the country's geography. For example, the maritime situation, together with the low-lying character of the coastlands, gives rise to a serious salination problem. The great European rivers—the

Rhine, Maas, and Schelde—have historically transported many waste products to the Netherlands and into the adjoining North Sea. High population density and its associated intensive land use also increase the concentration of all forms of pollution.

Dutch policy regarding the environment is among the toughest and most ambitious in the world. The government sets stiff targets for reducing pollution and other environmental damage, which firms are then invited to meet by their own measures. Since the late 1980s national environmental policy plans have increasingly addressed the causes of pollution. Thus, commuters are encouraged to travel by public transport; farmers are induced to reduce the use of pesticides and artificial fertilizers; and industries are regulated to promote cleaner production processes and to reduce emissions of pollutants into the air, water, and soil.

CHAPTER 19

DUTCH CULTURAL LIFE

The cultural life of the Netherlands is varied and lively. Dutch painting and crafts are world renowned, and Dutch painters are among the greatest the world has ever known. The Dutch themselves take great pride in their cultural heritage, and the government is heavily involved in subsidizing the arts, while abjuring direct artistic control of cultural enterprises. Indeed, the long-enduring tradition of Dutch freedom of expression has undoubtedly played a significant role in the flowering of Dutch culture through the ages.

DAILY LIFE AND SOCIAL CUSTOMS

The symbols of Dutchness—wooden shoes, lace caps, tulips, and windmills—are known throughout the world, but they tell only a small part of the story of contemporary life in the Netherlands. Except in places such as Vollendam and Marken and on occasions of national celebration, traditional dress long ago gave way to a style of dress in line with that of the rest of northern Europe. Flowering bulbs and tubers, including tulips, remain an important export commodity, and various festivals celebrate them. They are also displayed in the annual spring flower exhibition at Keukenhof Gardens and in venues such as the Aalsmeer flower market.

Dutch cuisine is notable for many individual dishes, including filled pancakes (pannekoeken); pastries such as banket (an almond paste-filled treat), oliebollen (a deep-fried pastry dusted with powdered sugar), and speculaas

GOUDA

Gouda, a semisoft cow's-milk cheese named for the Dutch town of its origin, is traditionally made in flat wheels of 10 to 12 pounds (4.5 to 5.4 kilograms), each with a thin natural rind coated in yellow paraffin. So-called baby Goudas are produced in smaller wheels of 10 to 20 ounces (310–620 grams). Gouda has a smooth-textured interior of pale ivory colour. Flavours are bland and creamy, except for aged Gouda, which is darker gold in colour, stronger and saltier in flavour, and harder in texture. Low-fat Goudas are also produced.

Gouda is one of the oldest of European cheeses, probably dating to the 12th century, and is widely imitated in other cheese-producing countries. True Gouda has "Holland" stamped on the rind; farm-made Gouda, more pronounced in character than factory-made versions, bears an imprint of the word "Boerenkaas," which means "farmer's cheese."

(spice cookies); and a great variety of hard cheeses, including Edam and Gouda, the world-renowned varieties that originated in the towns for which they are named.

Jenever, the Dutch ancestor of gin, is a malted barley-based spirit produced in two basic types, jonge ("young") and oude ("old," which contains a higher percentage of malt wine and thus is stronger and often yellowish as a result of the aging of the malt wine). Both types contain a variety of botanicals, notably juniper (genever), for flavouring. The Dutch also take pride in their beer and brewing tradition, especially that established by the world-famous Heineken brewery. Dutch licorice, which is exceptionally salty, is a popular candy. Indonesian rijsttafel ("rice table")—which developed as a method by which Dutch plantation owners could sample many Indonesian foods in the colonies—was imported

to the Netherlands and has become a staple cuisine in larger Dutch cities. In addition to the holidays of Christian tradition (Easter, Christmas, Pentecost, and Ascension), the Dutch celebrate Queen's Day (April 30), Remembrance Day (May 4), and Liberation Day (May 5), though the last is commemorated only at five-year intervals.

PAINTING AND SCULPTURE

The history of Dutch painting offers such a deep, rich lode of names that only a few can be touched on here. Certainly among the most revered are those of Rembrandt van Rijn and Vincent van Gogh. Rembrandt, painting in the 17th century, became a master of light and shadow, a technique reflected in his landscapes as well as such portraits as his monumental group portrait now known as *Night Watch*. Van Gogh, born in the

Museum-goers view Rembrandt's Night Watch *in Amsterdam's Rijksmuseum.* AFP/Getty Images

19th century, was a powerful influence in the development of modern art.

Among other great painters of the Low Countries are Jan van Eyck, the founder of the Flemish school; allegorist Hiëronymus Bosch; portraitist Frans Hals; landscapists Albert Cuyp and Jacob van Ruisdael; still-life artists such as Johannes Vermeer, Willem Heda, and Willem Kalf; and the geometrically inclined Piet Mondrian. Highlights of Dutch architecture range from the Dutch Baroque works of Pieter Post to 21st-century practitioners such as Rem Koolhaas. The Schroeder House (1924), in Utrecht, designed by De Stijl architect Gerrit Thomas Rietveld, was designated a UNESCO World Heritage site in 2000.

LITERATURE AND THE PERFORMING ARTS

Dutch literature and theatre have always been handicapped by the smallness of the proportion of the human race that speaks Dutch. Perhaps the

VINCENT VAN GOGH

At age 16 Vincent (Willem) van Gogh (born March 30, 1853, Zundert, Netherlands—died July 29, 1890, Auvers-sur-Oise, near Paris, France) was apprenticed to art dealers in The Hague, and he worked in their London and Paris branches (1873–76). After brief attempts at missionary work and theology, he studied drawing at the Brussels Academy; late in 1881 he settled at The Hague to work with a Dutch landscape painter, Anton Mauve. During his early years he painted three types of subjects—still life, landscape, and figure—all interrelated by their reference to the daily life of peasants (e.g., *The Potato Eaters*, 1885). After briefly studying at the Antwerp Academy, in 1886 he left to join his brother Theo, an art dealer, in Paris. There he met Henri de Toulouse-Lautrec, Paul Gauguin, and others involved in Impressionism and Post-Impressionism. By the summer of 1887 he was painting in pure colours and using broken brushwork that was at times pointillistic, and by the beginning of 1888 his Post-Impressionist style had crystallized. He left Paris in February 1888 for Arles, in southeastern France. The pictures he created over the following 12 months—depicting blossoming fruit trees, views of the town and surroundings, self-portraits, portraits of Roulin the postman and other friends, interiors and exteriors of the house, sunflowers, and landscapes—marked his first great period. Gauguin arrived in October 1888, and for two months he and van Gogh worked together; but, while each influenced the other to some extent, their relations rapidly deteriorated. On Christmas Eve 1888, disaster struck: physically and emotionally exhausted, van Gogh argued with Gauguin and then, reportedly, cut off the lower half of his own left ear (although some scholars have suggested that Gauguin was responsible). At the end of April 1889, van Gogh entered an asylum but continued to paint; during his 12-month stay he completed 150 paintings and drawings. A move to Auvers-sur-Oise in 1890 was followed by another burst of activity, but he soon suffered a relapse and died that July of a self-inflicted gunshot wound. His 10-year artistic career produced more than 800 paintings and 700 drawings, of which he sold only one in his lifetime. He is considered the greatest Dutch painter since Rembrandt.

greatest name of Dutch letters was that of the Renaissance humanist Erasmus. Contemporary Dutch writers who are internationally known include Harry Mulisch and Cees Nooteboom. The country's performing arts are widely encouraged and supported. The National Ballet at Amsterdam and the Netherlands Dance Theatre at The Hague are internationally renowned. Theatre companies are all private foundations, though the state and the municipalities provide financial assistance. The Dutch film industry is small. Among the most noteworthy recent directors are Johan van der Keuken, Marleen Gorris, and Paul Verhoeven. The International Film Festival Rotterdam is the country's

RIJKSMUSEUM

The Amsterdam galleries of the Rijksmuseum ("State Museum"), which today house the national art collection of the Netherlands, originated with a royal museum erected in 1808 by Napoleon I's brother Louis Bonaparte, then king of Holland. The first collection consisted of paintings that had not been sent to France from the Nationale Kunst-Galerij, an art museum established in 1800. After the Bonapartes were ousted, the collection was installed in the Trippenhuis and was opened to the public in 1815 as the Rijksmuseum te Amsterdam. A new building was designed by P.J.H. Cuypers in the Gothic Revival style and was opened in 1885.

Though particularly strong in 17th-century Dutch art, the Rijksmuseum also has major collections of other schools of western European painting and sculpture, Oriental art, and the decorative arts. Associated with the museum is the Rijksprentenkabinet, which has one of Europe's finest collections of prints and drawings, as well as of illuminated manuscripts.

leading film festival, and the Nederlands Filmmuseum in Amsterdam is the national motion picture archive.

MUSIC

The Netherlands has not produced composers of the stature of some of its neighbouring countries, although it has built a fine reputation for performance. The Amsterdam Concertgebouw Orchestra is world famous, and the Residentie Orchestra at The Hague and the Rotterdam Philharmonic Orchestra also have fine reputations. Various other towns have orchestras and choral groups, and there is a Dutch National Opera Company. Noted musical events include the World Music Festival at Kerkrade and the North Sea Jazz Festival at Rotterdam.

CULTURAL INSTITUTIONS

The Netherlands has a rich range of state-supported museums. The most famous is the Rijksmuseum at Amsterdam, noted for its collection of works by the great 17th-century Dutch masters (especially Rembrandt).

Other major museums endowed by the state include the Mauritshuis in The Hague, Het Loo (the former royal palace) in Apeldoorn, and the Stedelijk Museum in Amsterdam, recognized for its collection of contemporary paintings. Two museums, the Rijksmuseum Vincent van Gogh in Amsterdam and the Rijksmuseum Kröller-Müller in Otterlo (Veluwe), are renowned for their collections of paintings by van Gogh. Often overlooked are a number of exceptional smaller museums such as the

Huis Lambert van Meerten (Lambert van Meerten House) in Delft and the Nederlands Tegelmuseum (Netherlands Tile Museum) in Otterlo, both of which specialize in tiles. The most popular folk museums are the Openluchtmuseum (Open Air Museum) at Arnhem and the Zuiderzeemuseum at Enkhuizen. Another notable museum is the Anne Frank House in Amsterdam, where a German Jewish family hid from Nazis for more than two years during World War II.

SPORTS AND RECREATION

Favourite regions for open-air recreation are the seacoasts with their wide sandy beaches and the many interior lakes in the western and northern parts of the country. They are frequented by both Dutch and foreign visitors. The Dutch also are attracted to hilly areas, such as the Veluwe, while foreign visitors go in droves to the old cities in the western part of the country,

AMSTERDAM 1928 OLYMPIC GAMES

The eighth occurrence of the modern Olympic Games was held in Amsterdam from May 17 to August 12, 1928. Track-and-field and gymnastics events were added to the women's slate at the 1928 Olympics. There was much criticism of the decision, led by the baron de Coubertin and the Vatican. Women athletes, however, had formed their own track organizations and had held an Olympic-style women's competition in 1922 and 1926. Their performances at these events convinced the International Amateur Athletic Federation (IAAF; later International Association of Athletics Federations) that women were capable of a high level of athletic competition and deserved a place at the Olympics.

Germany returned to Olympic competition at the 1928 Games, which featured the debut of the Olympic flame. Approximately 3,000 athletes (including nearly 300 women), representing 46 countries, participated in the Olympics. The men's athletics competition was noteworthy for two reasons. It was the last Olympic Games for the great Paavo Nurmi and Ville Ritola of Finland. It was also the poorest performance to date for the U.S. team, which won only three of a possible 12 gold medals in running events. Percy Williams of Canada won both the 100- and 200-metre runs. Controversy arose in the women's 800-metre run when several women collapsed from exhaustion at the end of the race; Olympic officials concluded that the distance was too long for women, and it was not until the 1960 Games in Rome that women were allowed to compete in a race of more than 200 metres.

The Japanese team won the most medals in the swimming competition. Johnny Weissmuller of the United States concluded his Olympic career with gold medals in the 100-metre freestyle swim and the 800-metre freestyle relay. The Hungarian sabre team won the first of seven consecutive gold medals.

with Amsterdam ranking as the most popular destination. Favourite foreign vacation spots for the Dutch are the Mediterranean coasts during the summer holidays and the Alps during winter holidays.

Cycling is a popular activity—for commuting, recreation, and sport—involving at least half the population. Other favourite sports include tennis, field hockey, and ice skating. The Elfstedentocht is a popular ice-skating race that passes through 11 cities in the province of Friesland; it is held only during winters with heavy ice. The Dutch are also avid players and fans of football (soccer), and club teams such as the storied Ajax of Amsterdam and the Dutch national team have experienced much international success, not least in the 1970s, when the national team, led by Johan Cruyff, Johan Neeskens, and Ruud Krol pioneered the concept of "total football," a style of play developed by Dutch coach Rinus Michels that emphasized all-around skill, versatility, and creativity to perform both defensive and attacking duties. In the 1974 World Cup tournament the Dutch team put on a memorable display of total football that earned them the nickname "Clockwork Orange" (a name borrowed from the novel by Anthony Burgess but inspired by the team's orange jerseys). Although the Netherlands lost to West Germany in the championship match, Cruyff's individual brilliance won him the tournament's Golden Ball (Most Valuable Player) award.

The Netherlands made its Olympic debut in the 1900 Games in Paris, and the Summer Games were held in Amsterdam in 1928.

Dutch Olympic athletes have won medals in cycling, speed skating, and swimming.

MEDIA AND PUBLISHING

The constitution guarantees freedom of the press but does not allow journalists to protect their sources. The Dutch press has a long-standing reputation for high-quality reporting, newspapers having been printed in Amsterdam as early as 1618. One of the oldest newspapers in Europe is the *Oprechte Haerlemse Courant*, now called the *Haarlems Dagblad*, which was founded in 1656. By far the greatest circulation is enjoyed by the right-of-centre *De Telegraaf*, from Amsterdam. The most widely read newspapers in political and intellectual circles are the liberal *NRC Handelsblad* in Rotterdam and the left-leaning *De Volkskrant* in Amsterdam. Several free tabloids and Internet-based dailies have taken over some market share.

The majority of radio and broadcast television transmissions are produced by a small number of associations, all under private initiative. They were originally very much part of the pillarization system, and each represented a political or religious point of view, such as Roman Catholicism, various forms of

Protestantism, Socialism, Humanism, and others. Most of these associations, however, have long since lost their ideological distinctiveness and illustrate how the shell of the pillarized system has remained in existence long after its contents have ebbed away. Nevertheless, religious organizations, political parties, and small factional groups are still guaranteed access to the airwaves by Netherlands Broadcasting Corporation, which is responsible for news and the programming of unreserved airtime. The government itself exerts no influence on the programming, and advertising is restricted and is controlled by a separate foundation. All public broadcasting is financed by a licensing fee and by the yield from television and radio advertising. Commercial broadcasting was introduced in the early 1990s, and there are now a host of terrestrial and satellite channels that can be received in most parts of the country, thanks to the extremely dense Dutch cable television network.

CHAPTER 20

THE NETHERLANDS: PAST AND PRESENT

On January 23, 1579, the agreement at Utrecht was concluded, forming a "closer union" within the larger union of the Low Countries led by the States General sitting in Brussels. Included in the Union of Utrecht were the provinces and cities committed to carrying on resistance to Spanish rule: Holland, Zeeland, Utrecht, Gelderland (Guelders), and Zutphen (a part of Overijssel) as the first signatories, followed in the next year by the whole of Overijssel, most of Friesland, and Groningen, all in the north, and in the south by the cities of Antwerp and Breda in Brabant and Ghent, Brugge (Bruges), and Ypres (Ieper) in Flanders. Designed to establish a league for conduct of the war of independence and ultimately to strengthen the central government in Brussels, the Union of Utrecht became in fact the foundation of a separate state and a distinct country in the northern Netherlands. The new state was named the United Provinces of the Netherlands, or, more briefly, the Dutch Republic, and its government was known in the international community as the States General.

THE UNITED PROVINCES

The people of the northern Netherlands began to be distinguished from the inhabitants of the south (to whom the name Flemings continued to cling) by the appellation Hollanders (French: Hollandais; Italian: Olandese; German: Holländer; and so forth), after their principal province. The

English, however, came to apply exclusively to the Hollanders the term Dutch, which previously they had applied to all German speakers (from German Deutsch, Dutch Duits). The name Netherlanders, which remained in use in the Low Countries for the inhabitants of the United Provinces specifically and for all those, north or south, who spoke Dutch (Netherlandic), passed out of currency in most foreign countries or came to be restricted to the northerners. The transformation had a price: the erosion of the bond of historical identity between northerners and southerners—or Dutch and Belgians, as they would be called beginning in the 19th century.

The treaty that formed the basis of the new northern union established a military league to resist the Spaniards on a "perpetual" basis, and it provided for closer political arrangements between the provinces than those of "allies" in the ordinary sense. The provinces united "for all time as if they were a single province"; each remained sovereign in its internal affairs, but all acted as a body in foreign policy. Decisions on war and peace and on federal taxation could be made only unanimously. The union did not throw off the formal sovereignty of the king of Spain, but it confirmed the effective powers of the provincial stadtholders (formally the "lieutenants," or governors, of the king) as their political leaders (there was no "stadtholder of the United Provinces," as foreigners often assumed, although several of the provincial stadtholderates were often united in the same person). The union moved away from the religious settlement embodied in the Pacification of Ghent of two years before and toward a predominance of the Calvinists and their monopoly of public practice of religion in the key provinces of Holland and Zeeland.

The immediate political significance of the union was that it complemented the Union of Arras, concluded earlier in January, which began the reconciliation of the southerners with King Philip II of Spain. The two "unions," parallel but opposite, thus undermined the policy of William I (Prince William of Orange) of collaboration between Roman Catholics and Calvinists throughout the Low Countries in resistance to the Spanish domination, which required mutual toleration between the religions. But it took some time before the "general union," with its base in the States General at Brussels, fell apart irrevocably. For another half decade the prince struggled to keep intact the broader union and at the same time to ensure its military and political support from abroad. Although Archduke Matthias of Habsburg, named governor-general by the States General in 1577 after the deposition of Don Juan, remained the formal head of state until 1581, the prince continued to exercise his leadership. That the prince was the head and heart of the rebellion was recognized by Philip II in 1580, when he put him under the ban of outlawry. William's

Apology in defense of his conduct was followed in 1581 by the Act of Abjuration (Akte van Afzwering), by which the States General declared that Philip had forfeited his sovereignty over the provinces by his persistent tyranny. This was a declaration of independence for the whole of the Low Countries, but the military and political events of the next decade limited its permanent effect to the northern provinces under the "closer union" of Utrecht.

FOREIGN INTERVENTION

Yet independence did not become William's objective even after the proclamation of the Act of Abjuration. Archduke Matthias returned home in 1581 after William turned to François, duke of Anjou, who agreed to take over the "lordship" of the Low Countries in 1580. The prince hoped for assistance from the duke's brother, King Henry III of France, and considered the lordship of Anjou as only a kind of limited, constitutional sovereignty like that which the rebels had hoped to impose on Philip II at the beginning of their rising. Anjou, however, saw the lordship as a means to total dominion over the Netherlands. Irritated by restraints upon his authority, he even attempted the seizure of power by military force, which resulted in the so-called French Fury of January 17, 1583, when his troops tried to capture Antwerp. The coup misfired, but William managed to keep Anjou (who returned to France) in his post despite the outraged feelings of the Netherlanders.

Holland and Zeeland were on the verge of offering the title of count to William when he was assassinated on July 10, 1584, at Delft, by Balthasar Gérard, a fanatical young Roman Catholic from Franche-Comté, spurred by the promises of the ban of Philip II. William's death did not end the rebellion, as Philip had hoped, but it did result in the almost unnoticed disappearance of the central government in Brussels. The States General, which now met at The Hague in Holland, represented only the provinces in the Union of Utrecht.

With the Spaniards steadily overrunning Flanders and Brabant, the Dutch in their plight did not immediately abandon William's policy of seeking foreign assistance. But after Henry III of France and Elizabeth I of England both refused sovereignty over the country, the States General in 1586 named as governor-general Robert Dudley, earl of Leicester, whom Elizabeth had sent to command Dutch and English auxiliary forces against the Spaniards after the fall of Antwerp. Leicester, like Anjou before him, endeavoured to make himself absolute master of the country, relying on the support of popular Calvinism and of the outlying provinces that were jealous of Holland to create a strong centralized government under his authority. Holland thwarted Leicester's efforts, which culminated in an attempted invasion of Holland from

Utrecht in 1587. With Leicester's departure, the United Provinces put aside all efforts to obtain a foreign protectorate and stood forth as an independent state.

THE FORMATION OF A NEW GOVERNMENT

Although derived from historical institutions, the government of the United Provinces was in practice largely a new set of institutions, not created but confirmed by the Union of Utrecht. Their primary force lay in the provinces, seven in number (Holland, Zeeland, Utrecht, Gelderland, Overijssel, Friesland, and Groningen), which were ruled by assemblies of provincial States representing the towns and the landed nobility. Although the stadtholders (who after a few years came to be drawn exclusively from the house of Orange) were elected by the States of the provinces, they at the same time possessed important prerogatives

HOUSE OF ORANGE

The Dutch royal family, the house of Orange, derives its name from the medieval principality of Orange, in old Provence in southern France. The counts of Orange became independent upon the disintegration of the feudal kingdom of Arles. They were vassals of the Holy Roman emperors from the 12th century, and they early began to style themselves princes. When Philibert de Chalon, prince of Orange, died in 1530, he was succeeded by his sister Claudia's son René of Nassau, who in 1538 succeeded his father, Henry III of Nassau-Dillenburg-Breda, not only in his German patrimony but also in scattered possessions in the Netherlands. Dying in 1544, René bequeathed his titles to his young cousin, William I of Nassau-Orange.

Known as William I the Silent, the prince of Orange led the Netherlands' revolt against Spain from 1568 to his death in 1584 and held the office of stadtholder in four of the rebelling provinces. This was the start of a tradition in the Dutch Republic whereby the stadtholderships were for long periods monopolized by the princes of Orange and counts of Nassau, supported by an enduring Orange "party" composed of nobles, orthodox Calvinist leaders, artisans, and peasants against the rivalry of the patriciate of Holland. The gifted 16th- and 17th-century stadtholders were followed by less effective Orange leaders in the 18th century. The last stadtholder fled to England in 1795 as the republic collapsed.

His son, the next titular prince of Orange, became sovereign prince of the Netherlands in 1814 and king in 1815, as William I. He and his successors, William II and William III, were also grand dukes of Luxembourg; and the title prince of Orange was borne by heirs apparent to the Dutch throne. With King William III the male line died out in 1890; but the Dutch queen Wilhelmina decreed in 1908 that her descendants should be styled princes and princesses of Orange-Nassau.

in the selection of members of the town governments from which the provincial assemblies ultimately derived their authority, and they were the acknowledged military leaders of the republic. Central government passed from the Council of State to the States General, which was more explicitly subordinated to provincial authority. Although it conducted the military and diplomatic work of the republic, the States General failed to obtain effective rights of direct taxation (except for import and export duties assigned to the admiralties), and its major decisions were taken under the rule of unanimity.

In practice the province of Holland, by far the wealthiest province in the union and the contributor of more than half the revenues of the central government, became the preponderant political force in the country, along with the stadtholders of the house of Orange. The relationship between Holland and the house of Orange governed the republic's politics for the two centuries of its existence. As collaborators, Holland and the princes of Orange could make the clumsy governmental system work with surprising effectiveness; as rivals, they imperiled its potency as a state, at least until one or the other emerged a temporary victor, but neither force was able to rule permanently without the other.

The decades immediately after 1587 were marked by close collaboration between Johan van Oldenbarnevelt, "advocate" of Holland (the legal and executive secretary of the provincial States), and Maurice of Nassau, William I's second son (the first, Philip William, became prince of Orange and remained loyal to Spain), who was named stadtholder of Holland and Zeeland and became the commander of the republic's armies. The result was a series of military triumphs over the Spanish forces under Alessandro Farnese, duke di Parma e Piacenza. Maurice recaptured the Dutch territories north of the great rivers and extended them southward into much of Brabant and enough of Flanders to cut off Antwerp from the sea. These victories are recorded in the historical memory of the Dutch as "the closing of the garden," the territory that became the republic of the United Provinces and then (with a few additions) the modern Kingdom of the Netherlands. These victories were accompanied by England's and France's diplomatic recognition of the States General as the government of an independent state.

ASCENDANCY OF THE DUTCH ECONOMY

The military prowess of the fledgling republic rested upon the wealth of Holland—which managed in wartime to maintain and extend its trade to all Europe and, after the turn of the century, even to East Asia. Amsterdam replaced Antwerp, the great port on the Schelde River, as the principal warehouse and trading centre for all Europe, even while

Holland maintained the leadership in shipping it had already garnered during the 16th century. The foundation of Dutch economic prosperity lay in the fishing and shipping industries. Even during the period of Antwerp's ascendancy, ships from Holland and Zeeland had carried a large portion of the goods that passed through the Schelde, and now that Amsterdam had taken over from Antwerp, Dutch shipping only expanded its predominance. Dutch fishermen had harvested the North Sea for centuries, and the salted cargoes were sold widely throughout western and central Europe.

Dutch trade benefited, as had that of Flanders, from the location of the country at the nexuses of the great north-south and east-west trade routes of Europe. To these was added the route to the East Indies early in the 17th century. Amsterdam and the lesser ports of Holland and Zeeland became the principal European suppliers of grain and naval stores from the Baltic, to which they shipped manufactured goods and wines from the south. Germany's principal exports were now shipped down the Rhine, as Dutch ports replaced the Hanseatic towns of northern Germany. The bulk of French exports were carried in Dutch ships, and even Spain and Portugal depended on the Dutch for grain and naval stores (thereby enabling the Dutch to finance their war of independence). During the 17th century the Dutch assumed a major role in supplying grain and other northern commodities to the countries of the Mediterranean and also became the principal importer of spices and other luxury goods from the East. England, too, relied to a great extent upon Dutch shipping. The Dutch advantages lay not only in their situation but also in the efficient design of their bulky flyboats (fluiten), manned by small crews at less cost than any of their competitors.

Modern banking institutions developed to meet the needs of the vastly expanding trade. Amsterdam's "exchange bank" was instituted in 1609 to provide monetary exchange at established rates, but it soon became a deposit bank for the safe settling of accounts. Unlike the Bank of England, established almost a century later, it neither managed the national currency nor acted as a lending institution (except to the government in emergencies). Private bankers met the need for credit, as well as acting as brokers in financial transactions. The need for commercial exports, as well as a growing population at home, spurred industry in many towns. Although the shipbuilders on the Zaan, northwest of Amsterdam, and the sugar refiners in particular developed large-scale operations, sometimes including machinery, Dutch industry generally remained small in scale, as indeed nearly all manufacturing was in the 17th century.

Dutch industry was heavily dependent on trade, and major manufactures grew up in the western towns connected with international commerce. In processing and finishing textiles, Dutch manufacturers were often capable of undercutting competition abroad. Agricultural products were also traded. Grain was produced on Dutch farms, especially in the inland provinces, but rather than compete with the massive grain imports from the Baltic, coastal agriculture focused on cash crops for use in industry (flax, hemp, dyes, etc.), dairy and livestock farming, and market gardening. This kind of market-oriented agriculture was more profitable than the traditional production of basic foodstuffs.

THE TWELVE YEARS' TRUCE

The Twelve Years' Truce, which began in 1609, arose out of political controversies that were to dominate the republic for the next two centuries. The collaboration between the house of Orange and the leaders of the province of Holland, which had thwarted Spain in its reconquest of the Netherlands north of the great rivers, was replaced by an intermittent, but often fierce, rivalry between them, in which the other tensions of Dutch political life were reflected and incorporated: the jealousy among the lesser provinces of a Holland that they considered too wealthy, too mighty, and too arrogant but that they knew they needed for their own defense; the misunderstanding between maritime and landward provinces; the annoyance of landed nobles that they were dependent upon the

goodwill of burghers in Holland (they preferred the prince of Orange, whom they saw as one of themselves); the resentment of the popular classes, men of small property and of none, toward the town regents (members of government) from whom they looked to the princes of Orange to protect them; and the antipathy of the Reformed clergy toward the regents, who obstructed their desire to make the state serve the church. The debate over whether to conclude a peace with Spain mingled these various interests with that of the house of Orange, partly because Maurice opposed peace, partly because it involved making some compromise with Spain, and partly because it would mean a reduction of his influence in the state; but the province of Holland in particular, under Oldenbarnevelt's leadership, felt that the independence and security of the United Provinces had been sufficiently assured to permit a reduction of the immense expenditures for the war. When Spain reduced its immediate proposal to a truce rather than permanent peace, agreed to treat the United Provinces as independent and sovereign, which was just short of outright recognition, and put aside efforts to win guarantees for Dutch Catholics, the pressure for conclusion of a truce could not be withstood.

The Twelve Years' Truce did not, however, end controversy within the republic. If anything, it only sharpened Maurice of Nassau's opposition to Holland and Oldenbarnevelt. The staunch Calvinists endeavoured to hold the Reformed Church to the strict orthodoxy expounded by Franciscus Gomarus, a Leiden professor of theology, against the broader, less rigorous tenets upheld by his colleague Jacobus Arminius. The Gomarists demanded that the government uphold their principles because the Reformed Church was the only true church, but they reserved for themselves the right to declare what the correct doctrines were; and they vigorously asserted that other religious groups, Catholic, Protestant, and Jewish alike, should be suppressed or at least penalized and restricted. On the other hand, the Arminians had the support of the leaders of Holland and a majority of its towns, who felt that what was in effect the state church had to be under the authority of the government. Both out of principle and out of a desire not to hamper trade with men of all religions, they favoured a broadly inclusive Reformed Church and toleration for those outside its ranks.

The efforts of Gomarists to seize churches for their own use in defiance of town authorities led to incipient civil war. Maurice broke openly with the dominant party in Holland when it attempted to set up little provincial armies in Holland and Utrecht. In 1618 he acted under the authority of the States General—in which the majority of provinces favoured the Gomarists (now called the Contra-Remonstrants because they had opposed an Arminian petition) over the Remonstrants (Arminians)—to crush the resistance of Oldenbarnevelt's party. Oldenbarnevelt, two of his chief supporters in Holland (including the great jurist Hugo Grotius), and an ally in Utrecht were arrested and tried for treason by a special court instituted by the States General. The defendants affirmed that they were subject only to the authority of the sovereign province that they served. The sentence, which to foes of the house of Orange over the centuries became an act of judicial murder, sent Oldenbarnevelt, then aged 71, with almost four decades of service as Holland's leader, to his death by beheading in May 1619. Grotius and another defendant (the third had committed suicide) were sentenced to life imprisonment, although Grotius escaped, sensationally, a few years later.

During those fateful months, the Reformed Church held a national synod at Dordrecht. Dominated by the Contra-Remonstrants, the synod expelled the Remonstrants, reaffirmed the doctrines of the church along Gomarian lines, and ordered the preparation of a new translation of the Bible (the famous States Bible, which consolidated the Dutch language much as the contemporary King James Version consolidated English). The triumph of Maurice and the Contra-Remonstrants meant that war with Spain would be a virtual certainty upon the expiration of the Twelve Years' Truce in 1621—all the more because the Spanish authorities in the southern Netherlands insisted upon including rights for Dutch Catholics in a permanent treaty and even sought an acknowledgment by the States General of the nominal overlordship of the king of Spain. Maurice did not use his new uncontested power to reform the complicated incoherence of the Dutch constitution; the structure of government and the distribution of formal power remained the same. Maurice was not a politically minded ruler and was satisfied as long as he had his way in military matters. The United Provinces remained essentially republican in character.

WAR WITH SPAIN (1621–48)

The war resumed in 1621 under Maurice's leadership. But his victory touch was gone, and the republic appeared to be in danger when the great fortress of Breda, on the southern frontier, fell to the Spaniards in 1625. Only a few weeks before, Maurice had died. The danger was all the greater because the Austrian Habsburgs, in alliance with their Spanish cousins, were waging a successful struggle against their Protestant foes in Germany in the first stages of the Thirty Years' War. But Maurice's half brother, Frederick Henry, who succeeded him as prince of Orange, stadtholder, and commander in chief, resumed the course of victory. He completed the recapture of the towns recently gained by the Spaniards and extended the territory under the States General to the key fortress of Maastricht on the Maas (Meuse), well to the south. At the same time, the Dutch navy won a series of victories over the Spaniards, including Piet Heyn's celebrated capture of their silver fleet off the coast of Cuba (1628) and the destruction of a Spanish fleet in the Downs, off the English coast, by Maarten Tromp in 1639.

Frederick Henry turned out to be a more subtle and purposeful politician than Maurice. On the one hand, he ended the suppression of the Remonstrants, with whose religious views he sympathized, without exasperating the Contra-Remonstrants beyond repair. On the other hand, he established a firm grip over the policies of the republic, notably by establishing a close alliance with France aimed at the joint conquest of the Spanish Netherlands. Frederick Henry's political predominance within the republic was based upon his control of the lesser provinces, which had a majority in the States General and which could outweigh the influence of Holland.

Gradually Holland turned against him, especially after he arranged the marriage of his young son William (later William II) to Princess Mary Stuart, daughter of Charles I of England, on the eve of the English Civil War (1642–51). This fateful dynastic bond tied the interests of the house of Orange to the royal families of England, first to the Stuarts and later to the Hanoverians. The position of the house of Orange, however, was elevated by the connection; the French monarchy granted Frederick Henry the honorary address of "His Highness," normally restricted to royalty; and the debate over the function of the princes of Orange in Dutch politics began to be conducted as a controversy over monarchy. A quasi-royal court rose up around Frederick Henry, and this in turn only clarified and strengthened the republicanism of his opponents, especially in Holland, who feared that the political leadership of the princes of Orange would be turned into an explicit monarchy.

During the 1640s, however, Frederick Henry lost his physical and intellectual powers (the prematurely aged victim of stress) and was unable to prevent Holland from reasserting its predominance over the republic's policies. The States General entered into peace negotiations with Spain at Münster in Westphalia. Frederick Henry died in 1647 before the conclusion of the talks, and his son, William II, could not prevent the signing and ratification of the treaty in January 1648. Spain now formally acknowledged the independence of the Dutch and indeed even urged its friendship upon the United Provinces, warning of the threat to both the Dutch and the Spanish from the rising power of France.

Prince William was not ready to accept a permanent peace, and he negotiated secretly with the French for a resumption of the war, not only against Spain but also against republican England, which had executed his father-in-law, King Charles I, in January 1649. Needing a powerful army to wage the anticipated war, William bitterly fought the efforts of Holland to reduce the standing army and thereby to permit more rapid payment of the huge debt accumulated over the 80 years' struggle for independence. Efforts at compromise broke down during the spring of 1650 as the Hollanders and William each sought to compel the other to concede political inferiority.

William decided to make use of his preponderance in the States General, and he led a delegation from that body to the towns of Holland to seek a change of their vote in the States of Holland; such a delegation was a direct violation of what Holland saw as its provincial sovereignty. Rebuffed by a number of town governments, most importantly by those of Amsterdam and Dordrecht, William decided to cut through the resistance by force. At The Hague, on July 30, 1650, he arrested six of the States' deputies from the recalcitrant towns and sent them to the castle of Loevestein (where Grotius had been imprisoned) on charges of having resisted lawful orders of the States General. At the same time, he sent an army to seize Amsterdam, but it was thwarted by delays on its march and by the determined resistance of the municipal authorities, supported by the common people. Amsterdam, however, faced a siege that might gravely imperil its trade, while the besiegers themselves ran the danger of being drowned should Amsterdam open the dikes. A compromise was soon worked out whereby William's opponents were released but were required to withdraw from government. William had cleared the way for his policies but at the price of arousing deep fears among the Dutch people—most of all in the powerful province of Holland—of military dictatorship, monarchical rule, and renewed involvement of the country in war. But before he could carry out his plans, William II died of smallpox in early November. A posthumous son, William III, was born a week later.

THE FIRST STADTHOLDERLESS PERIOD

Fate thus intervened to give Holland's leaders, now intensely distrustful of Orangist influence, a chance to take over the country from the leaderless party of their antagonists. They governed the country for a little more than two decades, during what is known as the "first stadtholderless period" (1650–72) because the five leading provinces did not appoint a successor to William II. (It should be noted, however, that William II's cousin, William Frederick, of the junior branch of Orange-Nassau, continued to govern Friesland as well as Groningen, which also elected him stadtholder.) During the early months of 1651,

a Great Assembly of the States General, with expanded delegations from all the provinces, met at The Hague to consider the new situation. Holland was satisfied to consolidate the leadership it had so unexpectedly regained and conciliated the lesser provinces by leaving undisturbed the religious settlement of 1619 and by granting amnesty to those who had supported William II in 1650. But Holland's fears of the increased powers of the central government had been so stiffened that it depended upon its own preponderance, rather than upon constitutional reforms, to achieve effective government.

Yet efficiency of rule, so difficult to obtain when the powers to make and apply policy were so widely scattered, became all the more necessary when the republic became embroiled in war with the English Commonwealth in 1652. Nonetheless, the system was surprisingly efficient. The conflict with England arose out of a medley of causes: first, the English republicans, after their successes against the royalists, took up the cause of defending English commercial interests against the Dutch and passed the Navigation Act of 1651, forbidding Dutch shippers from acting as middlemen in English trade both in Europe and overseas; second, the English sought to bring the Dutch into a political union directed primarily against the Stuarts and their cousins of the house of Orange. But the Dutch, whatever resentment the Hollanders bore against the

Orange dynasty, were unwilling either to court civil war or to abandon their dearly won independence in a union that would make them junior partners to the English. An accidental clash between the Dutch and English fleets led to full-scale war in which a greatly improved English navy won the upper hand. By 1654 the Dutch were compelled to accept peace on English terms, including a secret promise by Holland ("Act of Seclusion") to exclude forever the prince of Orange from the stadtholderate and the supreme command.

The decision to accept a humiliating peace as the only way to terminate a disastrous war had been taken at the insistence of the young Johan de Witt, who had taken office in 1653 as councillor pensionary of Holland (the same office once held by Oldenbarnevelt). With the return of peace, de Witt became the brilliant leader of the republic's foreign and domestic policy. He rebuilt the Dutch navy, reduced indebtedness, improved the financial condition of both the States General and the States of Holland, and restored the republic's prestige in Europe. Carefully averting any renewal of strife with England, he was able not only to compel France to back down in a naval dispute but also to send a powerful Dutch fleet to save Denmark from Swedish conquest in the First Northern War (1657–60).

When the exiled English king, Charles II, was restored to his throne in 1660, de Witt continued his policy of staying on good terms with England no matter who ruled there; this policy, however, foundered on the same two issues—commercial rivalry and the status of the house of Orange—that had brought about the war of 1652–54. Charles not only accepted the renewal of the Navigation Act of 1651 but intensified the rivalry with the Dutch by demanding forcefully that they acknowledge his sovereignty over the adjacent seas, pay tribute for the right to fish in the North Sea, and open the Dutch East Indies to English traders. When naval warfare resumed in 1664 off Africa, followed by war in Europe the next year, Charles took up the cause of the young prince of Orange. By persuading the Orangists that his price for peace was restoration of William III to the offices of his forefathers, the English monarch built up a friendly party in the United Provinces that urged acceptance of his terms and even fostered a conspiracy to overthrow the government of de Witt and his friends. But de Witt managed to meet the new threat. An Orangist plot in Holland was uncovered and put down in 1666.

When Charles had demanded too high a price for Dutch friendship in 1660–62, de Witt had negotiated an alliance with the French, who feared that the restoration of the prince of Orange would create a hostile Anglo-Dutch coalition. Furthermore, success in the fighting at sea increasingly went to the newly rebuilt Dutch navy. In 1667 the Dutch fleet sailed up the Thames and the Medway

TREATY OF BREDA

Agreed to on July 31, 1667, by England, the Dutch Republic, France, and Denmark, the Treaty of Breda brought to an inconclusive end the second Anglo-Dutch War (1665–67), in which France and Denmark had supported the Dutch. The Dutch had the military advantage during the war (fought mostly at sea) but were compelled to make peace quickly to deal with Louis XIV's invasion of the Spanish Netherlands. The English Navigation Acts were changed in favour of the Dutch to permit Dutch ships to carry to England goods that had come down the Rhine River. Several Dutch trading principles were accepted, including confining the definition of "contraband" to implements of war. The Dutch position in world trade had not been shaken, and England had failed to take over a part of the spice trade. England, however, received New Netherland (New York, New Jersey) and some outposts in Africa from the Dutch, and recovered Antigua, Montserrat, and St. Kitts, in the West Indies, from France. The Dutch retained Surinam and, in the East Indies, Pulo Run. France retained French Guiana and recovered Acadia from England.

to Chatham, destroying the English shipyards and burning the fleet at its moorings. In that same year, however, the French, under Louis XIV, who had only belatedly sent naval and land forces to aid the Dutch, began an invasion of the Spanish (southern) Netherlands (present-day Belgium) in the War of Devolution. As French conquest of the southern Low Countries constituted a threat to both the Dutch Republic and Britain, those states came to terms in the standoff Treaty of Breda (July 31, 1667), followed in January by an Anglo-Dutch alliance compelling France to make peace with Spain.

This Triple Alliance (so called because Sweden became a third partner) proved to be de Witt's undoing, although he had no effective diplomatic strategy to put in its place. Louis XIV, balked in his aim of conquest, considered that the

Dutch had betrayed their alliance and turned to Charles II with proposals for a joint war against the United Provinces. Charles, bitterly resentful over his humiliating defeat at Chatham, accepted the French offer of a richly subsidized alliance. Even as the threat from France emerged more clearly, the Orangists imagined that the Dutch could still win over Charles by the restoration of William III, but they were able to obtain only the prince's appointment as commander in chief early in 1672. Charles joined the French in open war in the spring of 1672, counting upon William to accept rule of a rump Dutch Republic after France and Britain had taken away important territories for themselves. But William, who was given full power, including the stadtholdership, during a storm of riots and near rebellion that swept the country in June and July after the French invasion penetrated to its heart, took over the leadership of the Dutch defense from de Witt, who was lynched by a mob in The Hague in August. With William's support, the States General rejected the Anglo-French terms.

WILLIAM III

The tide of war now turned against the aggressors. The Dutch navy under Adm. Michiel Adriaanszoon de Ruyter repeatedly defeated the allied fleets off the coast of the republic, while the Dutch armies held on behind the flooded polders of the "water line." When other powers—Spain, at first as an auxiliary and then as a full participant, the German emperor, and Brandenburg—joined the Dutch side, the French armies withdrew from the republic. During six years of bitter war, William III was able to bring about the withdrawal of England (1674) and the defeat of all French war aims against the Dutch; yet his Grand Alliance was unable to bring Louis XIV to his knees, although Spain paid the price of a peace negotiated at Nijmegen in 1678. But during these years in which his political control of the republic, while strong, was not absolute, William was no more interested in constitutional reform than de Witt, his predecessor in the leadership of the country, had been. He was satisfied to expel adversaries from office and dominate the decisions taken by men who represented the same groups and the same social principles as those whom they replaced; but Holland, whose wealth ultimately was the basis for all Dutch power, political and military, slipped from under his thumb and asserted its autonomy of judgment and decision. The transformation of the republic, which had been from its origins an aristocracy dominated by mercantile wealth, into an oligarchy of inherited power, continued unimpeded by William; he had used the violence of the urban citizenry during the crisis of 1672 to unseat his opponents, including de Witt, but he was no more sympathetic than they had been to the vague democratic aspirations that were expressed here and there.

During the decade after the conclusion of the Peace of Nijmegen, the tension between William and Holland (particularly Amsterdam) worsened, because the prince was fixed upon a policy of renewed resistance to Louis XIV, while the Hollanders preferred peace at any reasonable price. But the upsurge of the threat from France in the late 1680s—the French incursions into western Germany and the threat of French domination of England under James II, a stalwart Roman Catholic and a pensioner of Louis XIV—brought William and Holland into agreement upon the need to support the prince's expedition to England in 1688, which resulted in his acceptance of the English throne, jointly with his wife, Mary Stuart, early the next year. William, as king-stadtholder, had to give primacy to English interests because England was the more powerful partner in the alliance. He therefore approved the arrangement whereby England concentrated its efforts against France on the sea, while the Dutch did so on land; the result was neglect of the Dutch navy. Ironically, the final triumph of the English over the Dutch in their commercial rivalry was a consequence of their alliance, not their enmity.

The war begun in 1689 ended with a stalemate peace in 1697, followed by two treaties between the maritime powers and France for partition of the Spanish monarchy. In 1700, however, Louis XIV accepted the bequest of the Spanish throne for his grandson, Philippe d'Anjou (Philip V of Spain), and war was resumed the next year.

William died, childless, in 1702. When Holland again took the initiative for government without a stadtholder, it was followed by the other provinces with much greater alacrity than had been the case in 1650–51. Resentment had built up against William, who had been preoccupied with foreign affairs and did little to improve domestic politics, and the absence of an adult heir meant that there was no effective opposition to the new course. Leadership of the Dutch state for the next 45 years came from the councillor pensionaries of Holland, who were often able men but either unwilling or unable to do more than conduct current business without attempting the delicate and explosive task of restructuring the government. On the contrary, constitutional rigidity became the credo not only of Dutch republicans but also of the Orangist party, with the only point in contention between them being whether the prince of Orange-Nassau, who was stadtholder of Friesland, should be elected to the same office in the other provinces. William IV, who followed his father in Friesland in 1711, was chosen stadtholder in Groningen in 1718 and in Gelderland (and the district of Drenthe) in 1722. Even without a stadtholder in the principal provinces, Dutch subordination to English interests remained intact during the War of the Spanish Succession (1701–13) and the succeeding years of peace.

DUTCH CIVILIZATION IN THE GOLDEN AGE (1609–1713)

The century from the conclusion of the Twelve Years' Truce in 1609 until either the death of Prince William III in 1702 or the conclusion of the Peace of Utrecht in 1713 is known in Dutch history as the "Golden Age." It was a unique era of political, economic, and cultural greatness during which the little nation on the North Sea ranked among the most powerful and influential in Europe and the world.

THE ECONOMY

It was a grandeur that rested upon the economic expansion that continued with scarcely an interruption until 1648, at the end of the Thirty Years' War. The half century that followed was marked

Painting of a Dutch East India Company fleet returning to Amsterdam. The Bridgeman Art Library/ Getty Images

by consolidation rather than continued expansion, under the impact of the revived competition from the other nations, notably England and France, whose policies of mercantilism were to a large degree directed against the near monopoly of the Dutch over the trade and shipping of Europe. Although the Dutch tenaciously resisted the new competition, the long-distance trading system of Europe was transformed from one largely conducted through the Netherlands, with the Dutch as universal buyer-seller and shipper, to one of multiple routes and fierce competitiveness. Nonetheless, the wealth earned during a long century of prosperity made the United Provinces a land of great riches, with more capital by far than could find outlet in domestic investment. Yet the economic burden of repeated wars caused the Dutch to become one of the most heavily taxed peoples in Europe. Taxes were imposed on the transit trade in and out of the country. But as mercantile competition became stiffer, the rate of such taxation

DUTCH EAST INDIA COMPANY

In 1602 the Dutch government granted a trade monopoly to the Dutch East India Company (formally United East India Company) in the waters between the Cape of Good Hope and the Straits of Magellan with the right to conclude treaties with native princes, to build forts and maintain armed forces, and to carry on administrative functions through officials who were required to take an oath of loyalty to the Dutch government. Under the administration of forceful governors-general, most notably Jan Pieterszoon Coen (1618–23) and Anthony van Diemen (1636–45), the company was able to defeat the British fleet and largely displace the Portuguese in the East Indies.

In 1619 the company renamed Jacatra Batavia (now Jakarta) and used it as a base to conquer Java and the outer islands. By the late 17th century the company had declined as a trading and sea power and had become more and more involved in the affairs of Java. By the 18th century the company had changed from a commercial-shipping enterprise to a loose territorial organization interested in the agricultural produce of the Indonesian archipelago. Toward the end of the 18th century the company became corrupt and seriously in debt. The Dutch government eventually revoked the company's charter and took over its debts and possessions in 1799.

could not be safely increased, and the burden therefore fell increasingly on the consumer. Excise and other indirect taxes made the Dutch cost of living one of the highest in Europe, although there was considerable variance between the different areas of the republic.

Dutch prosperity was built not only upon the "mother trades"—to the Baltic and to France and the Iberian lands—but also upon the overseas trades with Africa, Asia, and America. The attempt of the Spanish monarchs (who also ruled Portugal and its possessions from 1580 to 1640) to exclude Dutch merchants and shippers from the lucrative colonial commerce with East Asia led the Dutch to trade directly with the East Indies. Individual companies were organized for each venture, but the companies were united by command of the States General in 1602 in order to reduce the costs and increase the security of such perilous and complex undertakings; the resulting Dutch East India Company established bases throughout the Indian Ocean, notably in Ceylon (Sri Lanka), mainland India, and the Indonesian archipelago.

The Dutch East India Company, like its rival English counterpart, was a trading company granted quasi-sovereign powers in the lands under its dominion. Although the East India fleets that returned annually with cargoes of spices and other valuables provided huge profits for the shareholders, the East India trade of the 17th and 18th centuries never provided more than a modest fraction of Dutch earnings from European trade.

The West India Company, established in 1621, was built upon shakier economic foundations; trade in commodities was less important than the trade in slaves, in which the Dutch were preeminent in the 17th century, and privateering, which operated primarily out of Zeeland ports and preyed upon Spanish (and other) shipping. The West India Company had to be reorganized several times during its precarious existence, while the East India Company survived until the end of the 18th century.

SOCIETY

The social structure that evolved with the economic transformation of Dutch life was complex and was marked by the predominance of the business classes that later centuries called the bourgeoisie, although with some significant differences. The social "betters" of Dutch aristocracy were only to a limited extent landed nobles, most of whom lived in the economically less advanced inland provinces. Most of the Dutch elite were wealthy townsmen whose fortunes were made as merchants and financiers, but they frequently shifted their activities to government, becoming what the Dutch called regents,

members of the ruling bodies of town and province, and drawing most of their incomes from these posts and from investments in government bonds and real estate.

The common people comprised both a numerous class of artisans and small businessmen, whose prosperity provided the base for the generally high Dutch standard of living, and a very large class of sailors, shipbuilders, fishermen, and other workers. Dutch workers were in general well paid, but they were also burdened by unusually high taxes. The farmers, producing chiefly cash crops, prospered in a country that needed large amounts of food and raw materials for its urban (and seagoing) population. The quality of life was marked by less disparity between classes than prevailed elsewhere, although the difference between a great merchant's home on the Herengracht in Amsterdam and a dockworker's hovel was all too obvious. What was striking was the comparative simplicity even of the wealthy classes and the sense of status and dignity among the ordinary people, although the exuberance that had earlier marked the society was toned down or even eliminated by the strict Calvinist morality preached and to some extent enforced by the official church. There was, too, a good deal of mingling between the burgher regents who possessed great wealth and political power and the landed gentry and lesser nobility who formed the traditional elite.

RELIGION

One of the characteristic aspects of modern Dutch society began to evolve in this period—the vertical separation of society into "pillars" (zuilen) identified with the different Dutch religions. Calvinist Protestantism became the officially recognized religion of the country, politically favoured and economically supported by government. But the Reformed preachers were thwarted in their efforts to oppress or drive out other religions, to which a far-reaching toleration was extended. Mass conversion to Calvinism had been confined mainly to the earlier decades of the Eighty Years' War, when Roman Catholics still frequently bore the burden of their preference for the rule of the Catholic monarchs in the southern Netherlands. Sizable islands of Roman Catholicism remained in most of the United Provinces, while Gelderland and the northern parts of Brabant and Flanders conquered by the States General were overwhelmingly Roman Catholic, as they remain today.

Although public practice of Catholicism was forbidden, interference with private worship was rare, even if Catholics sometimes bought their security with bribes to local Protestant authorities. Catholics lost the traditional form of church government by bishops, whose place was taken by a papal vicar directly dependent upon Rome and supervising what was in effect a mission; the political authorities were generally tolerant of secular priests but not of Jesuits, who were vigorous proselytizers and were linked to Spanish interests. Protestants included, along with the predominant Calvinists of the Reformed Church, both Lutherans in small numbers and Mennonites (Anabaptists), who were politically passive but often prospered in business. In addition, the Remonstrants, who were driven out of the Reformed Church after the Synod of Dort (Dordrecht; 1618–19), continued as a small sect with considerable influence among the regents.

There were also other sects emphasizing mystical experiences or rationalist theologies, notably the Collegiants among the latter. Jews settled in the Netherlands to escape persecution; the Sephardic Jews from Spain and Portugal were more influential in economic, social, and intellectual life, while the Ashkenazim from eastern Europe formed a stratum of impoverished workers, especially in Amsterdam. Despite unusually open contacts with the Christian society around them, Dutch Jews continued to live in their own communities under their own laws and rabbinic leadership. Successful though some Jews were in business, they were by no means the central force in the rise and expansion of Dutch capitalism. Indeed, no clear pattern can be detected of religious affiliation affecting the growth of the Dutch business community; if anything, it was the official Dutch Reformed Church that fulminated most angrily against capitalist attitudes and practices, while the merely tolerated

BENEDICT DE SPINOZA

When asked about the value of his life's work, the Dutch-Jewish philosopher Benedict de Spinoza (born Baruch de Spinoza, November 24, 1632, Amsterdam—died February 21, 1677, The Hague) replied, "I do not presume that I have found the best philosophy, I know that I understand the true philosophy." Spinoza's parents had fled from the Inquisition in Portugal to Amsterdam, where they could openly practice their Jewish faith. In his youth Spinoza was skeptical about such religious doctrines as the authorship of the Pentateuch (the first five books of the Bible) and the existence of God. His early interest in new scientific and philosophical ideas led to his expulsion from the synagogue in 1656, and thereafter he earned his living grinding lenses for eyeglasses and microscopes. In 1660 he moved to Rijnsburg, a small village on the Rhine River, to practice his trade and read. Three years later he settled in Voorburg, near The Hague, where he worked on his *Tractatus Theologico-Politicus* (1670).

His philosophy represents a development of and reaction to the thought of René Descartes; many of his most striking doctrines are solutions to difficulties created by Cartesianism. He found three unsatisfactory features in Cartesian metaphysics: the transcendence of God, mind-body dualism, and the ascription of free will both to God and to human beings. To Spinoza, those doctrines made the world unintelligible, since it was impossible to explain the relation between God and the world or between mind and body or to account for events occasioned by free will. In his masterpiece, *Ethics* (1677), he constructed a monistic system of metaphysics and presented it in a deductive manner on the model of the *Elements* of Euclid. He was offered the chair of philosophy at the University of Heidelberg but declined it, seeking to preserve his independence. His other major works include the unfinished *Tractatus Politicus*.

faiths often saw their adherents, to whom economic but not political careers were open, prospering and even amassing fortunes.

CULTURE

The economic prosperity of the Dutch Republic in this "golden century" was matched by an extraordinary flowering of cultural achievement, which drew from the country's prosperity not only the direct resources of financial nourishment but also a driving and sustaining sense of purpose and vigour. This was reflected in the first instance by a notable series of historical works: the contemporary chronicles of the revolt by Pieter Bor and Emanuel van Meteren; the highly polished account by Pieter Corneliszoon Hooft, a masterpiece of narration and judgment in the spirit of Tacitus; the heavily factual chronicle of Lieuwe van Aitzema, with its interspersed commentary of skeptical wisdom; Abraham de Wicquefort's history of the Republic (principally under the first stadtholderless administration); and the histories and biographies by Geeraert Brandt. These were works in which a proud new nation took account of its birth pangs and its growth to greatness. Only in the latter part of the century did Dutch historians begin to express a sense that political grandeur might be transient.

Political theorists shared the same concerns, although the effort to fit new experience and ideas into the traditional categories derived from Aristotle and Roman law created an air of unreality about their work, perhaps even more than was true of political thinkers elsewhere in Europe. Theorists such as the Gouda official Vrancken in the days of the foundation of the republic and Grotius in the early 17th century portrayed the republic as essentially unchanged since the early Middle Ages or even since antiquity—a country where sovereignty resided in provincial and town assemblies, which had partly lost their control to counts and kings before regaining it in the revolt against Philip II. The next surge of political debate came after mid-century, when for a little more than two decades the country was governed without a prince of Orange as stadtholder.

The controversy over whether the young Prince William had any right by birth to the offices of his forefathers probed the fundamental character of the republic, for even a quasi-hereditary stadtholdership created an incipient monarchy within the traditional structure of aristocratic republicanism. The debate involved the issue not so much of centralization versus provincialism as where the leadership of the republic properly lay, whether in the house of Orange or in the province of Holland and notably its greatest city, Amsterdam. Only the celebrated philosopher Benedict de Spinoza, an outsider by origin and character (a Jew by birth and upbringing), elevated these political questions to the level of universality.

Another great philosopher of the 17th century who resided in the Dutch Republic was the Frenchman René Descartes. Though an outsider, Descartes found in the Netherlands a freedom from intellectual inquisitions and personal involvements. He lived there for two decades while engaged in studies that would help transform modern thought.

Scientific activity in the United Provinces also reached a high level. The physicist Christiaan Huygens approached Isaac Newton himself in power of mind and importance of scientific contribution. The engineer and mathematician Simon Stevin and the microscopists Antonie van Leeuwenhoek and Jan Swammerdam rank in the front of their fields.

Dutch literature, which knew great creativity during the Golden Age, remained the possession of the relatively small number of those who spoke and read Dutch. Figures such

REMBRANDT VAN RIJN

As a young man, Rembrandt van Rijn (born July 15, 1606, Leiden, Netherlands—died October 4, 1669, Amsterdam) was apprenticed to masters in Leiden and in Amsterdam. His early paintings show his interest in the "spotlight effects" of light and shadow that were to dominate his later paintings. Early in his career he began the studies of his own face and the more-formal self-portraits that make up almost a tenth of his painted and etched work. After moving to Amsterdam about 1631, he quickly became the city's most fashionable portrait painter and a popular teacher. In 1632 he produced the celebrated *Anatomy Lesson of Dr. Nicolaes Tulp*. Yearning for recognition as a biblical and mythological painter, in 1635 he produced *The Sacrifice of Isaac* and in 1636 *Danaë*. In 1634 he married Saskia van Uylenburgh (d. 1642), a woman of property. That same year he completed his largest painting, the extraordinary but controversial *The Militia Company of Captain Frans Banning Cocq* (known as *The Night Watch*), which was a watershed in his life and art. For unknown reasons, his portrait commissions thereafter declined, and he began to focus his attention on etching, a medium in which he was self-taught. In 1656, after transferring most of his property to his son, he applied for bankruptcy. In his last decade he treated biblical subjects like portraits and also continued to paint self-portraits. These late works exhibit a lively brushwork and a new treatment of light. In addition to being an innovator, he was an acute observer of life and a sensitive renderer of those observations in his drawings, etchings, and paintings. The human figure, Rembrandt's central subject, contributes to the sense of a shared dialogue between viewer and artist, the foundation of Rembrandt's greatness and of his popularity today.

as the historian P.C. Hooft or the poets Constantijn Huygens and Joost van den Vondel (the last of whom was also a distinguished playwright) wrote with a power and a purity worthy of the best that France and England produced at that time. Music was hampered by the Calvinists' antipathy to what they saw as frivolity. Organ music was barred from services in Reformed churches, although town authorities frequently continued its performance at other times. The great organist-composer J.P. Sweelinck was more influential in encouraging the creative wave in Germany than among his own countrymen.

The art whose achievements rank at the very top was painting, which rested upon the broad patronage of a prosperous population. Group portraits of regents and other influential citizens adorned town halls and charitable establishments, while still lifes and anecdotal paintings of popular life hung in profusion in private homes. Some of the greatest work, from the brushes of such painters as Frans Hals,

Jan Steen, and Johannes Vermeer, were painted for these markets, but the greatest of Dutch painters, Rembrandt van Rijn, broke through the boundaries of the group portrait to create works with his own extraordinary mood and inward meaning.

Landscape painters, notably Jacob van Ruisdael, captured the distinctive Dutch flatland, broad skies with massed clouds, and muted light. Architecture remained at a lesser level, merging with some success the native traditions of brick buildings and gable roofs and fashionable Renaissance styles. Sculpture remained a largely foreign art.

THE 18TH CENTURY

Once the Dutch fleet had declined, Dutch mercantile interests became largely dependent on English goodwill, yet the rulers were more concerned with reducing the monumental debt that weighed heavily upon the country. During the 18th century, Dutch trade and shipping were able to maintain the level of activity reached at the end of the 17th century, but they did not match the dramatic expansion of French and especially English competitors. The Dutch near monopoly was now only a memory. Holland remained rich in accumulated capital, although much of it could find no outlet for investment in business. Some went into the purchase of country houses, but a great deal was used to buy bonds of foreign governments;

the bankers of Amsterdam were among the most important in Europe, rivaling those of London and Geneva.

ECONOMIC AND POLITICAL STAGNATION

Dutch culture failed to hold its eminence; individuals such as medical scientist Hermann Boerhaave or jurist Cornelis van Bynkershoek were highly respected, but they were not the shapers and shakers of European thought. Dutch artists were no longer of the first order, and literature largely followed English or French models without matching their achievements. The quality of life changed; instead of the seething activity of the 17th century, the 18th century was one of calm and easeful pleasantness, at least for men of property. The middling classes in town and countryside also knew continuing prosperity; conditions for the labouring classes continued to be hard, although foreign visitors thought the workers lived better there than elsewhere. There was a residual class of unemployed who subsisted on the charity of town governments and private foundations. Religious life was more relaxed, particularly among Protestants. Roman Catholics, still without political rights but facing milder restrictions, fell into a quarrel between adherents of Jansenism, which followed Augustinian theology, especially in the matter of predestination, and supporters of Rome, in particular the

Jesuits; the former split off to form the Old Catholic Church, a small denomination that still exists. The educated classes widely accepted the principles and attitudes of the Enlightenment, although without the sharp hostility to religion that characterized the French philosophes.

During the second stadtholderless period of Dutch government (1702–47), the republican system became an immobile oligarchy. The "liberty" defended by the regents as soundly republican was in practice the rule of hereditary patricians, responsible to neither the citizenry below nor a stadtholder above. Although William IV yearned for restoration to the offices held by the princes of Orange before him in the provinces to the south, he accepted, with no less admiration and commitment than the regents, the perfection and immutability of the Dutch constitutional system, with the single difference that he envisioned it including the stadtholderate for all the provinces.

It was not until the War of the Austrian Succession (1740–48) that the power of the regents began to crumble. As in 1672, disaster on the battlefield proved the Achilles' heel of a regime that had not built up a broad popular political base. The regents had not been able to overcome the traditional commitment of the people to the house of Orange as their natural leader and saviour. French and Prussian armies swarmed over the Austrian (formerly Spanish) Netherlands and were poised for invasion of the United Provinces, which were linked by alliance with England, although they had remained formally neutral. When the French forces crossed into Dutch territory, rioting reminiscent of 1672, although less widespread and violent, led to the fall of the second purely republican government and the election of William IV as hereditary stadtholder of all the provinces. Otherwise there was little change; some regents were compelled to step down from their posts, and leadership in the hands of the prince of Orange was uncontested. William rebuffed the efforts of burghers in Amsterdam and other towns who had supported his restoration in order to achieve democratic reforms, in which participation in government would be extended to men of modest property (although not to wage workers or to paupers).

THE PATRIOT MOVEMENT

During the next decades, in the face of the rigid conservatism of the princes of Orange (William V succeeded his father in 1751 and assumed personal government in 1759) and under the influence of the French Enlightenment, an essentially new political force began to take shape. Known as the Patriot movement after an old party term used by both republicans and Orangists, it applied fundamental criticism to the established government. Although the

Patriot movement was representative of the new democratic and Enlightenment ideals, it had strong roots in native Dutch traditions. From the beginning, the United Provinces had rejected specifically democratic institutions in favour of frankly aristocratic government (in the Aristotelian sense), but the notion that the regents had a duty to serve not their own private interests but those of the country and the people had persisted in theory and in mood. When the aristocracy ceased to recruit new members from below and thus became an enclosed caste, the discrepancy between its claim of service to the general welfare and the reality of its practice became evident.

The Patriot movement took in a wide range of supporters: discontented noblemen such as the Gelderland baron Joan van der Capellen tot den Pol; wealthy bankers and businessmen without a voice in government; artisans and shopkeepers, traditionally Orangist in sympathy, who were dismayed to find their claims to an effective role in the politics of their towns rebuffed by the princes; and intellectuals committed to the new Enlightenment rejection of arbitrary power. The Patriots included in their ranks many Protestant dissenters and Roman Catholics, but Jews continued to look to the prince of Orange as their protector. Some regents, holding firm to the republicanism of their ancestors and resenting the return of the stadtholderate, found

a new base for their ideas in the Patriot movement. Most regents, however, saw more peril in the new movement for broader popular government than in the stolid conservatism of the princes of Orange; a reconciliation between the camps of the patrician republicans and the Orangists began to take shape under the impact of a common threat from below.

Again the events of war imperiled the established regime. Although the diplomacy of William V was firmly based upon the alliance with England, London became exasperated with the Dutch during the American Revolution (1775–83), when they attempted to continue to expand their profitable trade with the new American country as well as with France. Dutch flirtations with the Russian-sponsored League of Armed Neutrality, resistance to British searches of neutral vessels, and indications of Dutch negotiations for an alliance with the Americans only worsened relations. Finally, open hostilities erupted in the fourth Anglo-Dutch War (1780–84). The Dutch navy, sorely neglected for more than a half century, was utterly unprepared to battle the powerful British fleet, and the Dutch fleet's attempts to convoy their merchantmen brought only disaster.

The onus of defeat fell upon the stadtholder. He was unable to stand firm against the increased agitation of the Patriots, who forced their way into governments of town after town in

Holland and other provinces. Holland began organizing its own army, distinct from that under the prince's command, and civil war seemed in the offing. William V fled to Gelderland with his wife, Wilhelmina, the sister of Prussian King Frederick II. Holland declared him deposed.

It was the strong-willed Wilhelmina, rather than her hesitant and rather docile husband, who took the lead in the restoration of the stadtholderate. Dutch politics had now become a concern of the great powers. France sided with the Patriots, not out of sympathy with their principles but because they opposed the stadtholder, who had fallen back into dependence upon English and Prussian support. As long as Frederick II ruled in Prussia, Wilhelmina's pleas for armed intervention fell on deaf ears, but when the throne passed to his nephew Frederick William II in 1786, the way opened for action. The Patriots counted on the support of the French, but the government at Versailles, then entering the final financial and political crisis of the monarchy that erupted in the Revolution of 1789, could give no more than verbal encouragement. Wilhelmina, working closely with the English ambassador, arranged to create a crisis by seeking to return to Holland; her detention at the provincial border was taken by Prussia as justification to send an army into the United Provinces. The Prussians quickly swept away the makeshift militias of Holland and Utrecht and restored the stadtholder, William V, to his offices. A period of repression of Patriots followed; many went into exile, first in the Austrian Netherlands and then in France.

The outbreak of the French Revolution in 1789 gave new hope to the exiles and their friends at home. They looked now for more effective French assistance and at the same time found in the French revolutionary experience practical ideas for the reorganization of the government at home, notably the principle of a single, indivisible republic. The Patriots' hopes rose when the armies of the French Revolution swept over the Austrian Netherlands (which had had a brief interlude of independence in 1789–90) in 1792, but the French forces retreated the next year. It was not until 1794 that they returned to Belgium (as it now became customary to call the southern Netherlands), driving up to and then across the frontier of the United Provinces. The moment for which the Dutch Patriots had long been waiting was at hand: French power would more than outweigh the English and Prussian strength upon which the stadtholder relied (Prussia made a separate peace with France in 1795), and a democratic revolution, thwarted in 1787, would be possible. The freezing of the great rivers during the winter permitted the French forces to cross into the Dutch heartland, but, even before they arrived, the Patriots seized the reins of state from helpless William V, who abandoned office and fled to England.

THE PERIOD OF FRENCH DOMINANCE (1795–1813)

The old republic was replaced by the Batavian Republic, and the political modernization of the Netherlands began—a process that would take more than half a century and pass through many vicissitudes, yet it was one marked by an extraordinary lack of violence. For all its flaws and inconsistencies, the old regime of the United Provinces had enjoyed many of the institutions and practices that other countries had to create in the fire of revolution: the sovereignty of parliamentary assemblies, wide-ranging political and religious toleration, equality of all citizens before the law, and an unusually broad distribution of the benefits of economic prosperity, however far the social system was from equality. Even the sense of nationhood had put down deep roots, although the awareness of differences of religion remained powerful. In a word, the Dutch had already achieved a large measure of the "liberty, equality, and fraternity" that had become the slogan of the French Revolution. The task that confronted the Batavian and the successor regimes was to adapt old institutions and create new ones that could meet the needs of a new era. But the Dutch statesmen had to operate within the confines of a small power shorn of most of its military and naval strength and yet more dependent than most other countries upon its trading and shipping.

THE BATAVIAN REPUBLIC (1795–1806)

The Batavian Republic lasted 11 years, during which it proclaimed the sovereignty of the people but was in many respects a protectorate of France. The organization of government had to be approved not only by the Dutch people but also by whatever government happened to be in control in France. The constitutions therefore reflected not only Dutch conditions and ideas but also the arrangements in effect in Paris; nonetheless, they did create a new type of political system, a new regime, in the Netherlands. After much debate, the ancient historic provinces—so unequal in wealth, population, and influence—were replaced by a unitary republic divided into departments and electoral constituencies that were roughly equal in population, if not in wealth. The representatives elected to the National Assembly (which replaced the historic States General) were not delegates of provincial assemblies by whose decisions they were bound but deputies with full independence of judgment. The ancient system of government, with its medley of assemblies and boards with imperfectly differentiated functions, was replaced by a modern system of separate and explicitly defined legislative, executive, and judicial branches; functionally organized ministries directed the work of foreign affairs, internal affairs, war, and navy. The full

RUTGER JAN SCHIMMELPENNINCK

A lawyer in Amsterdam from 1784, Rutger Jan Schimmelpenninck (born October 31, 1761, Deventer, Netherlands—died February 15, 1825, Amsterdam) became active in the Patriot Party's committee of revolution in 1794 and headed the committee when it deposed the Dutch Republic's hereditary stadtholder, Prince William V of Orange, in January 1795. President of the city government in 1796, Schimmelpenninck also sat as an elected delegate to the first and second National Assemblies (1796–98) of the Batavian (formerly the Dutch) Republic. He led a group of moderate delegates who wrote a compromise constitution aimed at satisfying both unitarian (those favouring a unitary government) and federalist (those favouring a federal government) delegates.

After the two extremist factions rejected the constitution, a coup d'état (June 1798) established a unitary government, and Schimmelpenninck was appointed ambassador to France (1798–1802), where he gained the confidence of Napoleon. He then served as ambassador to Great Britain until the outbreak of war between Britain and France in 1803, when his efforts to maintain the republic's neutrality failed. As a man esteemed by Napoleon, he was sent back to France as ambassador the same year. When Napoleon imposed a change of government on the republic (1805) and it became the Batavian Commonwealth, he appointed Schimmelpenninck head of government as councillor pensionary (*raadpensionaris*). In one year Schimmelpenninck reformed the tax system, as well as the educational system, by granting recognition and aid to all parochial schools (Catholic, Protestant, and Jewish). In 1806, however, Napoleon removed him from office and transformed the Commonwealth into the Kingdom of Holland with his brother, Louis Bonaparte, as king. Schimmelpenninck retired from government (1806) but returned to public life when Napoleon made him a baron of the French Empire and appointed him to the French Senate (1811). After returning home in 1813, he served in the Dutch First Chamber (senate) from 1815 to 1821.

legal equality of all citizens in all parts of the country was proclaimed; the residents of North Brabant, Zeeland-Flanders, Limburg, and Drenthe gained the same rights as all other citizens of the republic, just as their districts, once excluded from the States General, now participated in the national government equally with all others.

The Reformed Church lost its standing as the sole official, protected church, supported out of state revenues, and equal status was accorded to all religious denominations, including Roman Catholicism and Judaism. Yet full separation of church and state was not proclaimed, and their relationship was to continue as one of the central factors in Dutch politics for more than a century. The historic privileges of class and locality were abolished; the liberty of each and all under the law and before the courts replaced the diverse "liberties" of town and province, noble and regent. Where, before, town governments had co-opted their members, deputies to the National Assembly were now elected; but the franchise was limited to property holders, and these chose their representatives not directly but through electors named by primary assemblies. Most of these institutional changes were permanent, though the republican form of government was replaced by a kingdom in 1806 and never reestablished.

While these momentous changes were being debated and adopted, the ordinary work of state and nation had to continue amid conditions of almost unprecedented difficulty. England reacted to the French occupation of the Netherlands and the flight and overthrow of the stadtholder by a declaration of war and a blockade. Dutch overseas trade and fishing, the country's most essential occupations, were brought to a near standstill, while most of the Dutch colonies were seized by the English on behalf of William V. The French, however, remained relentless in their own exploitation of the occupied "fraternal republic." The Dutch government, which took over the whole accumulated burden of national and provincial indebtedness, had also to bear the costs of the French occupying forces and to pay immense sums in tribute to the Paris government; indeed, the forced circulation of vastly inflated French assignats (paper currency) at face value was a scarcely disguised and very effective form of French taxation directly upon the Dutch people. Nor did the successive French governments—republican, consular, or imperial—grant the Dutch any greater freedom of trade with France or other countries under its control in compensation for the lost overseas business.

As trade declined and industry languished, Dutch agriculture began to resume a primacy in the economy; it had always employed the majority of the workforce. The venturesome spirit for which Dutch businessmen had been so famed a century or two before seemed to be lost, replaced by what the Dutch themselves called a jansalie (stick-in-the-mud) attitude; once-bustling cities dwindled to mere market towns; even Amsterdam lost much of its population. As a result, it became difficult to consolidate the new government. A multiple executive modeled on the French Directory and lacking a firm base in established political institutions and practices reflected the intrigues of individuals rather than the programs of clearly delineated parties. The victors quarreled among themselves and looked to Paris to decide between them, or at least passively accepted its dictum, given by coups d'état organized or approved by the French army command.

In 1805 Napoleon I gave quasi-dictatorial powers to R.J. Schimmelpenninck. Schimmelpenninck, called councillor pensionary after the fashion of the old provincial leaders, was actually an uncrowned and nearly absolute monarch (although, ultimately, power continued in Napoleon's hands); he nonetheless carried into practice many of the modernizing reforms that had been proposed but not adopted.

Napoleon, however, decided the next year to incorporate the Dutch state directly into his "Grand Empire" of vassal states.

THE KINGDOM OF HOLLAND AND THE FRENCH EMPIRE (1806–13)

Renamed the Kingdom of Holland, the Netherlands received as its monarch Napoleon's younger brother Louis. The four years of his kingship constituted one of the strangest episodes in Dutch history. Louis Bonaparte was a stranger in the land, yet he took its interests to heart, evading his brother's commands and winning the respect, if not quite the affection, of his subjects. The reconciliation of former Orangists, republicans, and Patriots began under his rule, for, in the face of the apparent permanence of the Napoleonic empire, they entered his government and worked together. Nonetheless, the brute fact remained that, for Napoleon, Holland was the kingpin of the "continental system,"

which he hoped would bring England to its knees by cutting off its continental exports. French officials enforced the vigorous suppression of the smuggling of English and colonial goods to the Continent through Holland that had sprung up over the previous decade with London's connivance. King Louis's resistance to his brother's efforts and his refusal to put French interests ahead of those of the Dutch led to the emperor's decision to oust his brother from his throne in 1810 and to incorporate Holland into the French Empire.

Little changed, however; the same officials—some Dutch, some French—continued to do the work of government in the country, which remained outside the French tariff system. As long as the Napoleonic empire seemed firmly based and permanent, Dutchmen served the new sovereign as they had King Louis, all the more readily because the exiled prince of Orange gave permission for such collaboration. Dutch soldiers continued to fight in Napoleon's campaigns, suffering heavy losses in the Russian invasion of 1812. But as it became increasingly obvious, after the failure of the Russian and Spanish campaigns, that the Napoleonic empire was collapsing, influential Dutchmen began to prepare for the creation of a new and independent regime; it was taken for granted that its head would be the prince of Orange—the son of William V, who had died in 1806—and that it was desirable that it be established by the Dutch people rather than imposed by the eventual allied victors. The movement for restoration was led by a remarkable figure, Gijsbert Karel van Hogendorp, a man of firm political principle who had refused to serve any of the governments that ruled in Holland after 1795 yet accepted the necessity for a reestablished prince of Orange to govern the country as a limited constitutional sovereign.

During the autumn of 1813, van Hogendorp secretly planned a takeover of government from the French, which became possible without bloodshed during November as French troops withdrew to their homeland. On November 30, the hereditary stadtholder, at the invitation of van Hogendorp's provisional authority, returned from England to proclaim his reign as hereditary prince.

THE KINGDOM OF THE NETHERLANDS (1814–1918)

In 1814 Prince William granted a charter establishing a constitutional monarchy, with restricted powers for a Parliament elected by a narrow property suffrage. At the insistence of the victorious powers meeting at the Congress of Vienna, he took the title of king of the Netherlands and was also given sovereignty over the southern Netherlands, which included both present-day Belgium and Luxembourg. During the campaign against Napoleon after his return from Elba in 1815, Dutch troops played a role in his defeat at Waterloo.

KING WILLIAM I

The reign of King William I, as the restored prince of Orange was now called, was one of the most critical periods in the history of the Netherlands. During this quarter-century the adaptation of the country to the conditions and requirements of modernity moved in a complex and even contradictory way, guided by a monarch who in his economic policy was far more forward-looking than most of his fellow citizens but who in politics resisted the expansion of Parliament and the introduction of liberal principles. He was a 19th-century version of the "enlightened despot," a man intent upon power not so much for its own sake as in order to serve the welfare of his country as he saw it.

The role of the States General—which continued to represent a general electorate of tax-paying citizenry—was strictly limited to the enactment of laws proposed by the government and to approval of a long-term budget; it was in no sense the representative of a sovereign people. The ministers of state were the agents of the king and responsible to him, not to the States General. Yet the basic structure of modern government had been created in the Netherlands; constitutional debate would be concerned with redistributing powers and responsibilities among existing institutions.

William I was at his best in confronting the problem of reviving the economic life of the country after the shattering impact of the long French occupation. He put the support of both the government and his own private fortune behind encouragement of commerce and, to a lesser extent, of industry. He sponsored the formation of the Netherlands Trading Society, a nominally private firm that undertook the important but costly and risky enterprise of reorganizing Dutch long-distance trade and shipping, particularly to the Netherlands East Indies, which England returned to Dutch sovereignty as part of the peace settlement. With the reopening of trade between the European continent and the wider world, the advantages of the Dutch position at the mouth of the great rivers favoured the revival of the traditional branches of Dutch enterprise; but competition from the ports of other countries, notably from Hamburg and Bremen, as well as from Britain, remained strong. Only in the Netherlands East Indies did the Dutch have a clear advantage over their rivals.

The most difficult problem faced by the new regime in the Netherlands was the relations between Holland (which now became the everyday name for all the northern Netherlands, in Dutch as well as foreign usage) and Belgium. The king was passionately devoted to the preservation of a single state encompassing all the Low Countries, a unity lost in the revolt against Spain more than two centuries before and for the restoration of which he had paid by ceding most of the Dutch colonies (except the East Indies) to the United Kingdom. However, the sense of common nationhood, cultural and political, was quite weak among the people. The Belgians resented assuming a share of the burden of debt inherited by Holland; they were oriented toward industry, Hollanders toward trade. French was the language of the leading classes in the south, and the use of Dutch as the official language was bitterly opposed even by Flemings, who resented the Dutch version of the common Dutch-Flemish language. Most Flemings, as devout Roman Catholics, were hostile to the predominantly Protestant northern Dutch elite. William's efforts to assume the control that Napoleon had possessed over the Belgian Roman Catholic Church met fierce resistance.

At the same time, the authoritarian character of William's government, particularly the sharp censorship of the press in Belgium, aroused the antipathy of liberals to the regime. The result was the outbreak of the Belgian Revolution of 1830 and the proclamation of Belgian independence. William, supported by a majority of Dutchmen, who were angered by what they saw as Belgian ingratitude, was able to defeat the hastily organized Belgian army; but the

European powers intervened to secure Belgian independence, although it was not until 1839 that a final settlement was reached and the last Dutch troops withdrew from Belgian soil. William, deeply despondent, abdicated the next year, leaving to his son, King William II, the task of coming to terms with the new situation.

WILLIAM II AND WILLIAM III

The new king was not a man of clear ideas or strong will, but he was able to do what his father dared not even envisage—oversee the transformation of the Netherlands into a parliamentary, liberal state. When the crisis of the 1848 revolutions broke, first in France and then in central Europe, an alarmed William II turned to the leading liberal thinker, J.R. Thorbecke, to guide the change. A new constitution was written, largely modeled on the British (and Belgian) pattern, which gave effective supremacy to the States General and made the monarch a servant and not the master of government. The king died the next year, and the work of transformation continued under his son, William III (1849–90), who named Thorbecke prime minister. The constitutional monarchy was consolidated, even though Thorbecke stepped down in 1853 because of Protestant rioting against the reestablishment of a Roman Catholic hierarchy, with its archbishopric at Utrecht.

Gradually, over the next century, the scope of Dutch democracy was extended to include ever-broader sections of the Dutch population in the franchise; universal male suffrage was achieved during World War I, and suffrage was extended to women in 1919. During this period modern political parties took shape, organized along religious and ideological lines; the principal groups were formed by Calvinists (the Anti-Revolutionary Party), socialists, liberals, and Roman Catholics. Other smaller minority parties developed subsequently. The central issue of political controversy became the schoolstrijd ("school conflict"), which pitted the liberal (and later socialist) advocates of state schools against the combined Calvinist and Catholic parties, which demanded state support for private ("special") schools equivalent to that provided to state schools. For several decades, liberals remained generally in control and made few concessions on the school issue. But when the Protestant leader Abraham Kuyper formed a coalition with the Catholics in 1888, the religious parties were able to gain power and to favour the special schools over the public schools. Their policy was assailed by the secular parties, the traditional liberals, the progressives, and the socialists. The liberals, however, were at odds with the other secular parties on other issues, notably economic policies and the extension of the suffrage. The liberals

WILHELMINA

The daughter of King William III and his second wife, Emma of Waldeck-Pyrmont, Wilhelmina (born August 31, 1880, The Hague—died November 28, 1962, Het Loo, near Apeldoorn) became queen of the Netherlands on her father's death (November 23, 1890) under her mother's regency. She was inaugurated September 6, 1898, at Amsterdam's Nieuwe Kerk, and soon gained widespread popular approval. On February 7, 1901, she married Duke Henry of Mecklenburg-Schwerin and gave birth to a daughter, Princess Juliana, on April 30, 1909. During World War I, Wilhelmina was influential in maintaining the Netherlands' neutrality.

When Germany invaded the Netherlands on May 10, 1940, Wilhelmina issued a proclamation to her nation of "flaming protest" and a few days later left for England with her family and members of the Cabinet. Throughout the war, she exhorted her people over Radio Orange to maintain their spirit until the nation's liberation, and she was welcomed back with enthusiasm when the German occupation was ended in 1945. After abdicating the throne in favour of Juliana on September 4, 1948, because of poor health, Wilhelmina retired to her palace, Het Loo, near Apeldoorn. Her memoirs, *Eenzaam maar niet alleen* (1959; *Lonely but Not Alone*, 1960), reveal the deep religious feeling that dominated her life.

tended to be the most conservative party on economic issues and favoured a restricted electorate; the progressives were vigorously democratic in outlook, as were the socialists, who also favoured universal suffrage, protection of the right to strike, labour legislation, and other welfare measures.

These struggles between various ideologies—Catholic, Calvinist, socialist, and liberal—gradually resulted in the growth of the system of "pillars," by means of which the country was split into more or less self-contained worlds, in which each group could live a largely separate life within the Dutch state. This distinctive political culture, known as "the politics of accommodation,"

"pillarization," or verzuiling, was to characterize Dutch public life for much of the 20th century, up to at least the 1960s.

Another major issue of the latter half of the 19th century was the role of the Dutch East Indies. Until the 1860s, the Dutch operated a highly profitable monopoly regime there called the "Culture System," which had been introduced to force the production of certain crops for export. Its profits helped balance the Dutch domestic budget and allowed essential investment in transportation and public services. At the same time, private enterprise clamoured for a share of the profits. Finally, there were humanitarian objections to the harsh conditions in the distant archipelago. As a result, the colony was opened up and deregulated, yet it continued to provide a significant part of Dutch national income all the way up to the outbreak of World War II.

QUEEN WILHELMINA AND WORLD WAR I

During the first half of the reign of Queen Wilhelmina (1890–1948), the political situation remained fundamentally unchanged. The major parties came to recognize that the school struggle interfered with the solution of other problems. An agreement in principle was reached on the eve of World War I, by which the secular parties accepted state support for religious schools on a basis of equal funds in exchange for enactment of universal male suffrage. When war broke out in 1914, the Netherlands, which had declared its neutrality, put aside the proposed reforms in order to concentrate on the immediate problem of maintaining the country's livelihood in the face of blockades. The "Pacification," as the compromise was called, was adopted in 1917 and put into effect after the return of peace. The war years saw almost all political controversies set aside, while the government took unprecedented action in maintaining trade and guiding economic life. Although spared the horrors of combat, the Dutch had to maintain a large standing army, and mutinies broke out among the soldiers in 1918.

The century from the restoration of Dutch independence in 1813 until World War I saw fundamental transformations of Dutch life. The economic base was modernized; the role of agriculture diminished, with most Dutch farmers producing dairy, meat, and horticultural products for the market; and trade and shipping were revived in the face of fiercely competitive conditions. But most important was the rise of industry—first textiles in the eastern provinces, then coal in the southeast, and finally modern manufactures, notably the great Philips electrical products factories at Eindhoven. Rotterdam became one of the world's busiest ports and the centre of chemical and other industries. These changes were paralleled in society by the gradual extinction of pauperism, the domination of middle-class businessmen and professional men, and the gradual improvement of the conditions of working people and farmers, especially after the mid-19th century.

Although religious freedom in the Netherlands was generally as great as anywhere else in Europe, orthodox Calvinists faced major difficulties, especially during the first half of the 19th century, when they protested against the modernizing ideas of the mainstream Calvinist Reformed (Hervormde) Church; their efforts to create independent religious communities met with sharp resistance from the government. Some of the Gereformeerden (the older name for "Reformed" used by the

ANNE FRANK

Early in the Nazi regime of Adolf Hitler, Otto Frank (1889–1980), a German Jewish businessman, took his wife and two daughters to live in Amsterdam. In 1941, after German forces occupied the Netherlands, his daughter Anne (born June 12, 1929, Frankfurt am Main, Germany—died March 1945, Bergen-Belsen concentration camp, near Hannover) was compelled to transfer from a public to a Jewish school. Faced with deportation (supposedly to a forced-labour camp), the Franks went into hiding on July 9, 1942, with four other Jews in the back-room office and warehouse of Otto Frank's food-products business. With the aid of a few non-Jewish friends who smuggled in food and other supplies, they lived confined to their secret annex until August 4, 1944, when the Gestapo, acting on a tip from Dutch informers, discovered them.

The family was transported to Westerbork, a transit camp in the Netherlands, and from there to Auschwitz in German-occupied Poland on September 3, 1944, on the last transport to leave Westerbork for Auschwitz. Anne and her sister Margot were transferred to Bergen-Belsen the following month. Anne's mother died in early January, just before the evacuation of Auschwitz on January 18, 1945. Both Anne and Margot died in a typhus epidemic in March 1945, only weeks before the liberation of Bergen-Belsen. Otto Frank was found hospitalized at Auschwitz when it was liberated by Russian troops on January 27, 1945.

Friends who had searched the family's hiding place after their capture later gave Otto Frank the papers left behind by the Gestapo. Among them he found Anne's diary, which was published as *The Diary of a Young Girl* (originally in Dutch, 1947). Precocious in style and insight, it traces her emotional growth amid adversity. In it she wrote, "In spite of everything I still believe that people are really good at heart."

The diary has been translated into more than 65 languages and is the most widely read diary of the Holocaust, and Anne is probably the best-known of Holocaust victims. A new English translation, published in 1995, contained material edited out of the original version, making the new work nearly one-third longer. The Frank family's hiding place on the Prinsengracht—a canal in Amsterdam—has become a museum.

conservatives) emigrated, many of them to the United States; however, in the second half of the century, this group prospered at home and took its place at the heart of the pillarized Dutch system.

The cultural life of the Netherlands remained very largely confined within national boundaries; Dutch thinkers, writers, and artists responded strongly to influences from Germany, France, and England but themselves had little impact abroad. Dutch scientists maintained a respected position for their country; Hugo de Vries was one of the principal founders of the science of genetics, while the physicist Hendrik Antoon

Lorentz contributed greatly to Einstein's theories of relativity. Dutch artists were generally imitative; although The Hague school of Impressionists displayed great gifts, only Vincent van Gogh, who spent most of his active life in France, achieved world reputation. Dutch literature ran parallel to main currents abroad; the Réveil early in the century was a movement of intensely religious romanticism with strongly conservative ideas, while Eduard Douwes Dekker (pseudonym Multatuli) in mid-century expressed the moods of social criticism with great power; the movement of "Men of the 'Eighties" (Tachtigers) brought to the fore an emphasis on aesthetic values and spirituality; and early in the 20th century, a literature of social protest reemerged.

THE NETHERLANDS SINCE 1918

The movement of the Netherlands into modernity was accelerated after 1918. Although the country became a member of the League of Nations, it reaffirmed its neutrality, which seemed to have obtained the respect of the powers and which was symbolized by the presence of the International Court of Justice at The Hague. There was considerable harshness in relations with Belgium, which not only abandoned its neutrality for a close alliance with France but demanded territorial cessions from Holland. The Dutch government, although humiliated by a demand that it present its case before the peace conference at Versailles, successfully resisted any amputation of its territory. The Dutch, for their part, refrained from giving any official support to the Flemish nationalist movement in Belgium, although a Great Netherlands movement, principally among intellectuals, emphasized the underlying unity of the Dutch and Flemings. Domestic politics followed the same course, with the Protestant political parties continuing to provide leadership for generally conservative policies, especially after the onset of the Great Depression in the 1930s.

WORLD WAR II

At the outbreak of World War II in 1939, the Dutch sedulously maintained their neutrality, although their sympathies lay overwhelmingly with the Allied powers. Nonetheless, when Nazi Germany undertook the campaign against France in the spring of 1940, its forces struck not only against Belgium in order to outflank the French defenses but also against the Netherlands. The Dutch land armies were overwhelmed in less than a week, and the government, accompanied by Queen Wilhelmina and the royal family, withdrew to England, where they formed a government in exile.

Much of the work of public administration and civil government under German military occupation was continued by Dutch organs of state, which made some effort to buffer German political repression, deportation of Jews, and forced employment of Dutch labour in Germany. A resistance movement sprang up, which, with the exception of the Dutch Nazi collaborators, spanned all groups from the conservatives to the communists. The Germans retaliated by executing Dutch hostages for such measures of resistance as the strike of Amsterdam dockworkers against the seizure and deportation of Dutch Jews to extermination camps in Germany. Some Jews were able to "go underground" (into hiding) with the assistance of friends, but the large majority were taken away to their deaths.

In the final phases of the war, particularly after the Allied failure to capture bridgeheads across the rivers at Nijmegen and Arnhem, the Dutch suffered from severe food shortages, and, during the last months before liberation (May 1945), they were near famine (the so-called Hunger Winter).

THE LATE 20TH CENTURY

After the war many aspects of Dutch life changed dramatically. Wilhelmina and her government returned from exile to reestablish a regime more strongly democratic than ever before. Anticipating the characteristic difficulties of postwar reconstruction, the government, industry, and labour agreed upon a plan for industrial and commercial expansion, with avoidance of the rapid expansion of prices or wages that would bring a threat of inflation. The plan worked effectively for more than two decades, and the Dutch were able to avoid drastic inflation until the breakdown of such corporatist consensus in the 1960s.

Dutch industrialization moved forward with speed and depth, expanding to include the large-scale production of steel, electronics, and petrochemicals. Putting aside the policy of neutrality as a failure, the Netherlands entered vigorously into the postwar Western alliances, including the North Atlantic Treaty Organization (NATO) and the various organizations of European unity (the Common Market; later the European Community within the European Union); however, its influence was limited, even though it joined with Belgium and Luxembourg in a closer union (Benelux). Indonesia, where Dutch authority was reestablished after wartime occupation by Japanese forces, soon became the scene of a nationalist revolution. After some hesitation as well as bitterness, the Dutch were obliged to grant it full independence. In the Caribbean area, the Netherlands Antilles remained part of the Dutch kingdom, although no longer under the authority of the government at The Hague, and in 2010 it ceased to exist as a political entity as its constituent units achieved various degrees of independence within the Dutch kingdom; the island of Aruba gained an autonomous status within the Antilles in 1986. Surinam became independent in 1975 and was renamed the Republic of Suriname in 1978.

Dutch political alignments since the mid-20th century have evolved only gradually and until the 1990s were always dependent on the Christian Democrat parties of the centre. The first postwar governments were dominated by an alliance of the Labour and Catholic parties, which continued until the Labour Party went into opposition in 1958. Thereafter, with the exception of 1973–77, when the country had a left-led government, and 1981–82 and 1989–91, when it was ruled by a centre-left coalition, governments were formed by centre-right coalitions. After the early 1980s the government was faced not only with recurrent economic problems but also with the emotion-charged issue of siting U.S. nuclear cruise missiles (as part of the NATO defense strategy) in the country. It finally reached the decision in 1985, against widespread popular opposition, that 48 missiles would be sited by 1988. The issue was dissolved by the subsequent ending of the Cold War between the United States and the Soviet Union.

During the 1960s the generally peaceful mood of Dutch public life was broken by rioting of youth and labour groups, especially in Amsterdam. The most difficult crisis affected the royal family. The marriage (1966) of Princess Beatrix, the heiress to Queen Juliana (who had succeeded Wilhelmina on her abdication in 1948), to a German diplomat aroused acrimonious debate. The unsanctioned marriage of Princess Irene to a Spanish Carlist prince had already come as a shock even to Roman Catholics, but it was less difficult politically because she lost her right of succession. Juliana's husband and consort, Prince Bernhard, was involved in a bribery scandal and withdrew from public office. Juliana abdicated in 1980 and was succeeded as queen by Beatrix.

By the 1970s Dutch politics, like Dutch society in general, had largely ceased to practice what was strictly defined as pillarization. Pillarization had received official confirmation in the Pacification of 1917 and removed most of the tinder from Dutch politics, but it also kept ordinary Dutchmen ideologically separated from each other to a greater degree than in most other Western countries. Yet, because the leaders of the pillar organizations worked well with each other and the right of each pillar to exist and function was unquestioned, public life generally ran smoothly.

In the 1960s the system began to disintegrate. New radical political parties were formed, and, in the face of rapid secularization of the vote, the various Christian parties joined together in the Christian Democratic Appeal (CDA). However, the religious vote has continued to decline, and in the 1990s there were "purple" coalitions for the first time, between the (red) Labour Party and the (blue) Liberals (conservatives). The Communist Party, once influential

Mark Rutte, who became the Dutch prime minister in 2010. © AP Images

beyond its small numbers, disbanded in 1991. The far-left groups joined with environmentalists to form an electoral group called Green-Left, which garnered about 5 percent of the vote beginning in the late 1990s.

INTO THE 21ST CENTURY

In the 1990s, while the economy prospered, environmental concerns increased, not only because of the country's vulnerability to rising sea levels, river flooding, and the effects of pollution but also because Dutch industry and agriculture were themselves major sources of pollution. In 2006 the Dutch government spurred the European Union (EU) to take a larger role in combating the effects of climate change.

In the later 20th century, the Netherlands had gained a reputation for liberal social policies, such as the toleration of prostitution and of the limited use and sale of marijuana and hashish. Same-sex marriages and euthanasia were legalized, and penal sentences were relatively light. The Netherlands also was one of the most heavily planned and regulated Western societies, though there were efforts to reduce the role of the state in the 1980s and '90s.

Although the Dutch tradition of tolerance generally extended to its immigrant population, anti-immigrant politician Pim Fortuyn was able to tap into increasing Dutch uneasiness in 2002. Just nine days before that year's election, Fortuyn was assassinated—the country's first modern political killing. Nevertheless, his party gained enough support to become part of a centre-right governing coalition. Because of disputes within Fortuyn's party, however, the government resigned after only three months in office. In subsequent years, other anti-immigration parties rose in prestige, such as the Party for Freedom. Tension over immigration continued, with national debates on immigrant amnesty and assimilation, the clash of Christian and Islamic culture, and occasional acts of violence, notably the politically charged murder of filmmaker Theo van Gogh in 2004. By 2006 the government required all potential immigrants to pass a test on Dutch culture and language (taken in their home country) before they could enter the Netherlands.

In 2003 Prime Minister Jan Peter Balkenende, head of the Christian Democratic Appeal, formed a centrist coalition with the liberal Democrats '66 and the People's Party for Freedom and Democracy. In the parliamentary elections of 2006, the Socialist Party made large gains, though the CDA retained its majority with Balkenende at the helm in a governing coalition with the Labour Party and the Christian Union. But the political landscape has changed a great deal in the Netherlands since the 1990s, symbolized by the two dramatic political assassinations. In 2005, in the first national referendum held in two centuries, Dutch voters rejected the new constitution of the EU, a result almost inconceivable in a country that, before about 2000, was classically pro-Europe and, perhaps more importantly, had generally been happy to leave such matters to its Eurocentric political elite. Having taken its populist turn, the Netherlands is now perhaps a less unusual country. It remains prosperous, but its welfare state is less distinctively generous, and the famed liberal state has been reined in, while skepticism of European integration and anti-Islam sentiments are increasingly loudly voiced.

Following disagreements over the continued presence of Dutch soldiers in Afghanistan, the Labour Party withdrew from the Netherlands' governing coalition in February 2010. The Labour Party had demanded that the Dutch force return home by August 2010, as anticipated, while the CDA had backed an extended deployment. The collapse of the government triggered parliamentary elections in June, with results that reflected both a growing anxiety over the economy—because of concern in the euro zone about the expanding sovereign debt crisis—and a new surge of anti-immigrant sentiment. The prime beneficiary of the latter was the anti-Islam Party for Freedom (Partij voor de Vrijheid; PVV), led by Geert Wilders, which finished a strong third to the virtually deadlocked Liberal and Labour parties, with the CDA dropping about half its seats to finish fourth. As no party had secured an outright majority, it took months of negotiation before the Liberals and the CDA agreed, in October, to form a centre-right governing coalition, with Liberal leader Mark Rutte as prime minister. Although Wilders's party was excluded from the cabinet, its key role in policy making was assured, as the minority government required the PVV's parliamentary support in order to pass legislation.

Throughout 2011, Rutte's coalition government introduced a series of austerity measures designed to reduce the country's deficit. Protests erupted as voters voiced their opposition to cuts to popular social welfare programs, and Wilders began to distance himself from the coalition. When Rutte in April 2012 presented a budget designed to bring the Netherlands into line with the EU's recently adopted deficit cap, Wilders responded by withdrawing his support for the coalition. The government collapsed, and Rutte remained in office as the head of a caretaker administration while early elections were scheduled.

CONCLUSION

In looking at a map of the world, it would be easy to undervalue the role of the Low Countries to the history of civilization. Tucked on the edge of northwestern continental Europe, these three countries simply do not take up much of the globe's surface, yet their contributions to art, culture, politics, philosophy, engineering, and commerce belie their size.

Traversing the world's oceans, Dutch navigators were among the first Europeans to set their eyes on exotic lands in Asia and Oceania, and Dutch merchant ships long dominated ocean-going commerce. Dutch engineers tamed the sea with dikes and reclaimed lowlands with technology that ranged from horsepower and windmills to steam, diesel, and electric pumps. Luxembourg became one the world's most productive blast furnaces, and steel made in Luxembourg remains internationally renowned. Dutch Patriots heroically won independence from the 17th century's reigning imperial colossus, Spain, and, later, Belgium, too, would gain its sovereignty, establishing important democratic institutions in the process. Yet even as they forged their independent identities, economies, and cultures, Belgium, Luxembourg, and the Netherlands were pioneers in international financial, economic, and political cooperation. Their Benelux Economic Union became not just the core but in many ways the model for the cooperative experiments in democratic transnational government that would become the European Union.

How much less magical the landscape of Europe would be without the grand architecture of the picturesque canal cities of Amsterdam and Brugge; how diminished the collective world of the mind would be without the insights of Erasmus and Spinoza; how much poorer the world of art would be without the gifts bestowed by the technical brilliance of Flemish painting and the Dutch masters. Even a partial list of only the most famous of these artists is overwhelming. The names Bruegel, Rubens, Bosch, Rembrandt, Vermeer, Hals, Steen, van Gogh, and Magritte conjure images of some the most memorable art ever created. Indeed, the Low Countries' contributions to world culture have been no little things.

AGRARIAN Of or relating to fields or lands or their ownership ; characteristic of farmers or their way of lie.

CAROLINGIAN Of or relating to a Frankish dynasty dating from about 613 and including among its members the rulers of France from 751 to 987, of Germany from 752 to 911, and of Italy from 774 to 961.

CASTELLAN A governor or warden of a castle or fort.

CHARTER A written instrument or contract (as a deed) executed in due form.

COMMUNE The smallest administrative district of many countries, especially in Europe.

EUTHANASIA The act or practice of killing or permitting the death of hopelessly sick or injured individuals (as persons or domestic animals) in a relatively painless way for reasons of mercy.

FEUDALISM The system of political organization prevailing in Europe from the 9th to about the 15th centuries having as its basis the relation of lord to vassal with all land held in fee and as its chief characteristics homage, the service of tenants under arms and in court, wardship, and forfeiture.

FIEF A feudal estate.

HUMANISM The revival of classical letters, individualistic and critical spirit, and emphasis on secular concerns characteristic of the Renaissance.

MEGALITH A very large, usually rough stone used in prehistoric cultures as a monument or building block.

MESOLITHIC Of, relating to, or being a transitional period of the Stone Age between the Paleolithic and the Neolithic.

MYSTICISM The belief that direct knowledge of God, spiritual truth, or ultimate reality can be attained through subjective experience (as intuition or insight).

NEOLITHIC Of or relating to the latest period of the Stone Age; characterized by polished stone implements.

PATRICIATE The position or dignity of a patrician, a member of one of the original citizen families of ancient Rome.

PODSOLIZATION A process of soil formation, especially in humid regions, involving principally leaching of the upper layers with accumulation of material in lower layers and development of characteristic horizons.

POLDER A tract of low land (as in the Netherlands) reclaimed from a body of water (as the sea).

PRINCIPALITY The territory or jurisdiction of a prince; the country that gives title to a prince.

SEIGNEURY The territory under the government of a feudal lord.

SOCIALISM Any of various economic and political theories advocating collective or governmental ownership and administration of the means of production and distribution of goods.

SUFFRAGE The right of voting.

VASSAL A person under the protection of a feudal lord to whom he or she has vowed homage and fealty.

VILLA A country estate.

BIBLIOGRAPHY

HISTORY OF THE LOW COUNTRIES

Paul Arblaster, *A History of the Low Countries*, 2nd ed. (2012), is a readable, informative survey. J.C.H. Bloom and E. Lamberts (eds.), *History of the Low Countries*, new ed. (2006), trans. by James C. Kennedy, is comprehensive. Petrus Johannes Blok, *History of the People of the Netherlands*, 5 vol. (1898–1912, reprinted 1970; originally published in Dutch, 8 vol., 1892–1908), is a classic history of the northern territories, although now outdated, particularly so on the history of the Middle Ages. Ivo Schöffer, *A Short History of the Netherlands*, 2nd rev. ed. (1973), provides a useful history of the northern Netherlands.

Henry Stephen Lucas, *The Low Countries and the Hundred Years' War, 1326–1347* (1929, reprinted 1976), is a reliable and richly documented account of political events. A series of books by Richard Vaughan, *Philip the Bold: The Formation of the Burgundian State*, new ed. (2002), *John the Fearless: The Growth of Burgundian Power*, new ed. (2002), *Philip the Good: The Apogee of Burgundy*, new ed. (2002), and *Charles the Bold: The Last Valois Duke of Burgundy*, new ed. (2002), are well-documented studies of the Burgundian dukes and the growth of their political power. *J. Huizinga, The Waning of the Middle Ages: A Study of the Forms of Life, Thought, and Art in France and the Netherlands in the XIVth and XVth Centuries* (1924, reprinted 1985; originally published in Dutch, 1919), is a classic work. Walter Prevenier and Wim Blockmans, *The Burgundian Netherlands* (1986; originally published in Dutch, 1983), is a magnificently illustrated scholarly general synthesis concerning the period 1380–1530. Geoffrey Parker, *The Dutch Revolt*, rev. ed. (2002), analyzes the period 1565–1659; and Johnathan Israel, *The Dutch Republic: Its Rise, Greatness, and Fall 1477–1806* (1995), covers the same ground and more.

BELGIUM

Overviews of all aspects of the country are contained in Marina Boudart, Michel Boudart, and René Bryssinck (eds.), *Modern Belgium* (1990). Frank E. Huggett, *Modern Belgium* (1969), is thorough and discerning. R.C. Riley (compiler), *Belgium* (1989), is a bibliography. Important aspects of the impact of the European Union on Brussels are highlighted in A.G. Papadopoulos, *Urban Regimes and Strategies: Building Europe's Central Executive District in Brussels* (1996). The country's history is considered in Bernard Cook, *Belgium:*

A History (2002); and Benno Barnard et al., *How Can One Not Be Interested in Belgian History: War, Language and Consensus in Belgium Since 1830* (2005), an outgrowth of a symposium held at Trinity College, Dublin.

LUXEMBOURG

An introduction to the country is provided by P. Margue et al., *Luxembourg* (1984), in French, a well-illustrated work covering history, politics, ethnography, language and literature, natural history, and the economy. Christophe Sohn (ed.), *Luxembourg: An Emerging Cross-border Metropolitan Region* (2012), is a study of the geography and economy of Luxembourg. Works focusing on Luxembourg's history include James Newcomer, *The Grand Duchy of Luxembourg: The Evolution of Nationhood, 963 A.D. to 1983* (1984); and Pit Péporté et al., *Inventing Luxembourg* (2010).

NETHERLANDS

Colin White and Laurie Boucke, *The UnDutchables: An Observation of the Netherlands, Its Culture and Its Inhabitants*, 6th ed. (2010), is a humourous and insightful overview of Dutch culture. Frits van Oostrom, *The Netherlands in a Nutshell: Highlights from Dutch History and Culture* (2008), is an illustrated examination of key topics. Further resources (mainly in English) may be found in Peter King and Michael Wintle (compilers), *The Netherlands* (1988), an annotated bibliography. Michael Wintle *An Economic and Social History of the Netherlands, 1800–1920: Demographic, Economic and Social Transition* (2000), has a narrower focus.

INDEX